Be Your Own Dating Service

Be Your Own Dating Service

A Step-by-Step Guide to
Finding and Maintaining Healthy Relationships

❤ ❤ ❤

Nina Atwood

AN OWL BOOK
Henry Holt and Company
New York

*This book is dedicated
to the memory of my mother, Jean Alden,
with gratitude for her example of
unconditional love.*

Henry Holt and Company, LLC
Publishers since 1866
115 West 18th Street
New York, New York 10011

Henry Holt® is a registered trademark
of Henry Holt and Company, LLC.

Copyright © 1996 by Nina Atwood
All rights reserved.
Published in Canada by Fitzhenry & Whiteside Ltd.,
195 Allstate Parkway, Markham, Ontario L3R 4T8.

Library of Congress Cataloging-in-Publication Data
Atwood, Nina.
Be your own dating service: a step-by-step guide to finding
and maintaining healthy relationships/Nina Atwood.—1st ed.
p.   cm.
"An Owl book."
ISBN 0-8050-4097-8
1. Dating (Social customs)   2. Man-woman relationships.
I. Title.
HQ801.A8255   1996   95-22964
646.7'7—dc20   CIP

Henry Holt books are available for special promotions and
premiums. For details contact: Director, Special Markets.

First Edition 1996

Designed by Paula Russell Szafranski

Printed in the United States of America

9 11 13 15 17 19 20 18 16 14 12 10

Contents

♥   ♥   ♥

Contents

Introduction

♥   ♥   ♥

Welcome to the world of modern dating! Whether you're newly divorced or you've been single for years, you've no doubt discovered the challenges of finding the right partner and creating a healthy, lasting relationship.

As a single person myself, I am acutely aware of how difficult this is. When I first conceived of writing a book like this, I began my research as much for myself as for my clients and future readers. I, too, wanted to know how to make dating a more rewarding experience and move myself closer to a healthy relationship.

Whenever I talk to groups of singles and field their questions, I hear the same ones over and over:

"Where are all the nice people to date? Where do you go to meet the right people?" and "Why is love so hard to find? Why are relationships so difficult?"

These questions reveal the problems that singles have in today's dating scene:

1.   Not enough choice—the sense that there aren't enough people to choose from.

2.   When we do meet someone new, we move too quickly into a relationship without a proper assessment of what the possibility is, and without good boundaries. Thus:

3.   We get our hearts broken, often unnecessarily; we get discouraged, become cynical, and withdraw from the dating scene, sometimes for months or years, sometimes permanently, or,

4.   We stay too long with the wrong partners, fearful of never finding anything better.

Given all the challenges, it's amazing that so many of us hang in there and continue to play the dating game. We do this for one simple reason: *the drive to connect in a meaningful way with a romantic partner is very powerful and not to be denied.* We try and try again, even though the problems sometimes seem insurmountable.

After a few years of being single, we begin to feel the urgent need for solutions. We go to workshops, we buy self-help books, we even go into therapy. We join dating services, thinking that this will be the answer.

Dating services provide introductions to other singles, but they do nothing to help us understand how to create good relationships. Most self-help books for singles offer advice on attracting and winning over partners, which is fine as long as you're content with just any old relationship.

If you're like me and like the singles I talk to and work with, you want more than that: *You want a compatible partner with whom you can create a loving, healthy, lifetime relationship.* This means that you'll need more than just tips on meeting, flirting, and winning people over.

This book is about healthy relationships and how to create them from the beginning. I view single life as an incredible opportunity: the perfect time to step back, take a new look at how we're going about the dating game, and learn about relationships *prior to getting into one.* Being single can be a powerful intervention point in getting the kind of healthy love we want.

This book offers solutions, but not with a particular result in mind. Instead of recipes for attracting and winning over a desired partner, this book provides steps that lay the foundation for healthy relationships.

Instead of an answer book, this book is more like an exercise book. Rather than saying, "Do this, do that, and you'll get the person you want," this book says, "Practice this, practice that, and you'll know yourself better, create a more rewarding life, and move yourself closer to a healthy love relationship in the process."

This book is actually a philosophy of dating designed to empower singles in their search for the right partner, so that they: 1) have more choices; 2) make better choices; and 3) thereby create healthier relationships that have a good chance of lasting. It doesn't offer any guarantees or magical solutions.

Instead, this book asks you to look at how you're going about the dating game, to examine your attitudes and views, and to make changes at the very heart of your approach to finding a partner. You will design and create your own personal "Dating Game Plan," customized to fit your personality, your needs, and your lifestyle. You will make a new assessment of what kind of partner you're looking for. Most important, you'll have the opportunity to use this plan for your own personal growth in every area of your life and in all your relationships.

Part I

Your Dating Game Plan

♥

1

❤   ❤   ❤

Love Myths, the Reality, and the Challenge of Love

Once upon a time, there was a princess . . . well, she wasn't really a princess, but she thought of herself as one. She was, after all, waiting for a prince to come and take her away from her boring life.

Day after day, the princess dreamed of the beautiful life she would have with her prince. He would be tall and handsome, strong and brave, yet sensitive to her every emotional need. They would live in a castle (or a very large suburban home) and do romantic stuff every day.

Because she was attractive, many suitors came to see if they could win her hand, or something else. Some of them wanted merely to gaze into her eyes and yearn secretly for her. Some wanted a good time but no commitment. Some wanted a relationship, but since they weren't handsome princes, she turned those away.

The princess was frustrated and complained daily, "I just never meet anyone I'm interested in. There just aren't any handsome princes out there anymore. What can I do?"

Finally, the princess got tired of waiting for her prince, so one day she decided to go out and look for him.

First she went to a bar where a lot of men hung out. But she didn't find any princes there, only a lot of married men, alcoholics, and more of those no-commitment types. Then she tried the personal ads, but that didn't go anywhere.

Finally, she decided that as long as she was out, she might as well do something she enjoyed. She went to a big art show, where she got to see her favorite artists' work. While she was there she met some new people and made some friends. Later, she went to a big dance where she had lots of fun and made some more friends. The next day, she found more fun things to do and made more friends.

After a while the princess forgot about finding her prince. She was having too much fun with her new friends, and her dreams of a perfect life in a castle began to seem less important. She became a lot more outgoing, and she noticed that the kind of men she used to like now seemed rather boring.

The princess began having more dates but found that she was no longer so worried about finding the perfect Prince Charming. Instead, she chatted about her life and her new interests and took the time to get to know the man she was out with. She quickly moved on from the no-commitment type because they didn't fit into her new life very well.

One day while the princess was taking a photography class she noticed a guy who was not a prince but looked interesting. She noticed that he noticed her. After class they talked and then they went for a cup of coffee. A few days later they had lunch, and later that week they had dinner together. She found out that they cared about a lot of the same things, like children being happy and having good relationships with friends. They talked a lot, laughed a lot, and held hands. Sometimes they got mad and had it out, and sometimes they cried. But they tried to always speak from their hearts.

Later, they discovered that they loved each other and decided to stay together. The princess realized that she hadn't felt bored in a long time and that having someone to love and be loved by was a lot better than having a prince. She threw away her tiara, and the two lovers got married.

Fairy-Tale Love and Romantic Love Myths

This story was written like a fable because it seemed appropriate. After all, so much of what we perceive to be true about romantic love has its origins in the stories we read in childhood. And so much of our disappointment has its roots in the inevitable differences between these fairy tales and real life.

How many women (real or imagined princesses) have felt the heartbreak of waiting for a perfect prince to come along and instead found themselves in love with the wrong men? How many men have felt the sting of rejection from women who were looking for an ideal and failed to see the real, available man in front of them?

This story has a realistic ending because that's the way healthy love is. Falling in love may be splendid and glorious, but *keeping that love alive is the greatest challenge we face.* Falling in love while keeping sound judgment in place is equally difficult.

Perhaps in no other area of life are we so prone to mythology than in the area of romantic love. With no precise definitions, we speculate endlessly on love's meaning. The boundaries between friendship, romantic love, and a dating partnership are often fuzzy. We ask ourselves: "Is this real love?" We want to know what love is and what we can expect from it.

We look to our family of origin for answers and often come up empty-handed. Many of us came from families that were not models of healthy relationships. Our parents may have divorced bitterly, or in a friendly way (which way is right?). Or they stayed together and fought bitterly. Or they stayed together in a dead marriage. We hope that ours will turn out better, but we're not sure of how to make that happen.

To add to the confusion, Hollywood and television present us with their versions of what love is. A popular one is:

Boy meets girl in the midst of spine-tingling adventure. Sparks fly. They hate each other at first, then fall into bed, then love each other.

Their instant relationship is now "true love." Often these characters know nothing about each other and have very little in common. Yet we are expected to believe that theirs is a lifetime love. And, sadly, we accept this in some way as a model for love relationships.

The Origin of the Mythology of Love.   Our lack of a precise definition of love, plus a lack of role models for healthy love and a good dose of Hollywood, gives us fertile ground for developing myths. In fact, at no other time in history have we been so prone to the invention and preservation of that mythology than now, in the latter twentieth century. Ann Swidler, among many authors, writes about our modern tendency to develop and maintain notions about what constitutes "true love."[1] These notions and ideas powerfully influence our attitudes, feelings, and behavior in relationships.

Often we are not aware of this influence, yet our lives and relationships are being colored nonetheless. Our impressions form the backdrop of our consciousness as we interact with others in our daily lives. Because so many of these impressions are inaccurate, we find ourselves kept from what we want by an invisible boundary. Nowhere is this more prevalent than in the modern singles dating scene.

Myth: Love Is Forever.   One of the first myths that we collide with is the idea of true love being forever. If it is real, then it is supposed to last. If it doesn't last, then it isn't real. The idea is that there is *one and only one true love* in each person's life.

This myth forces us to forever question whatever relationship we're in. Is this "the one"? How do I know? We second-guess ourselves instead of dealing with whatever it is that we have. Or we try to force the relationship into some idealistic mold that it may not fit into. Since I love you, this must be true love, and therefore it has to last.

Reality: Love is whatever it is and it lasts as long as it lasts. One person has the capacity to fall in love many times during a lifetime.

---

[1]Ann Swidler, "Love and Adulthood in American Culture," from N. J. Smelser and E. H. Erickson's *Themes of Love and Work in Adulthood* (Cambridge: Harvard University Press, 1980), pp. 120–147.

Today's singles are often men and women who have experienced the loss of a love (or more than one love) and who find themselves, contrary to expectations, back on the dating scene again. Many men and women are choosing to remain single until later in life. Others are divorcing or ending long-term relationships. Thus dating, once considered to be something you left behind after high school and college, is now commonplace for people throughout their life spans. Needless to say, we weren't prepared for this! And one of our difficulties lies with the abundance of romantic love myths that follow us into our dating lives, making it more difficult for us to get what we want. Let's look at more of these misconceptions and half-truths.

Myth: Dating Is Separate from Relating.   This is the idea that dating, an often frustrating and unrewarding experience, is something that we endure as singles in order to eventually find someone with whom we can have a relationship. It's uncomfortable and awkward, but it's the dues you have to pay until you find the right person, and then—whew!—you can relax and have a relationship.

In this view, dating is often a series of maneuvers in which the goal is to attract and "get" the object of our affections. If we wear this, say that, and behave just so, we can win over a desired person. *Dating is a game we play in order to get what we want.*

Many books and articles have been written on how to do this. Much of the advertising industry targets this wish to win a desirable partner. Once we accomplish our goal—getting the right person—we can then relax and begin a loving relationship.

Reality: Dating Is Relating.   From the first meeting, the first phone call, the first encounter, we have some sort of relationship with another person. How we relate with that person and the other people we date, how we go about meeting and getting to know others, how we determine whom to become emotionally and sexually involved with are crucial. These factors determine the kind of relationships we end up in. And the kind of dating relationships we have powerfully influence the kind of marriage we will have and, ultimately, the health and emotional well-being of our families. It looks something like this:

> HOW WE MEET others influences the KIND OF DATING RELA-
> TIONSHIPS we have
> HOW WE DATE influences the HEALTH OF OUR LONG-TERM
> ROMANCES, which influences the HEALTH OF OUR MAR-
> RIAGES, which influences the
> EMOTIONAL AND PSYCHOLOGICAL WELL-BEING OF OUR FAMI-
> LIES

If we are prone to falling in love too quickly while letting our rational minds fly out the window, we will find ourselves in skyrocket relationships that fizzle quickly. If we hide our true feelings from those we date, being afraid that we will "scare them off," we will end up in relationships in which we do not feel free to express ourselves fully.

If we date in a manipulative way, revealing only what we want people to know in order to win them over, we will find ourselves in relationships that lack true intimacy or are even exploitative, with both partners feeling cheated out of the experience of real love. If we focus solely on keeping a desired lover, sacrificing our own needs in favor of our partner's, we will find ourselves in addictive relationships, "hooked" on people who can never give us what we want and need.

How we date is how we relate. The two cannot be separated. In order to have healthier relationships, we need to focus from the very beginning on how we date and how we interact.

More Fairy Tales

Myth: Successful Relationships Are Accidental. This is the idea that true love always finds you when you're not looking. This myth says that if we just go about our daily living, then the right partner will find us, magically, and with no effort on our parts we will be blissfully happy ever after. A trip to your local movie theater will reassure you of the prevalence of this notion of romantic love!

Reality: Most Relationships Are Accidental in Real Life.   We don't usually make conscious decisions about relating to others. Most of the time we put little energy into considering what we are looking for and what kind of partner we want. We tend to rely solely on feelings of attraction to guide us when we meet someone new. We count on chance encounters. And for most of us this works, up to a point.

Yes, we do eventually meet new people and have dates. We do fall in love and have relationships. *What we don't often do is create healthy love relationships that have the potential for lasting a lifetime.* Just having a relationship is not enough. To experience true success, we need to feel that with a partner we've made a special connection that carries the possibility of a lasting commitment, and this does not happen by accident.

Myth: Finding the Right Person Guarantees a Successful Relationship.   Hand in hand with the last myth is the idea that all we have to do to have a great relationship is find the "right person." Again, this myth says that somewhere out there is the one and only perfect partner for us, and when the time is right we'll meet him or her. We'll fall in love, everything will fall into place, and we'll live happily ever after.

The problem with these two myths is that they leave everything to luck, chance, and fate, with no real power or control in our hands. Nothing could be further from the truth.

Reality: Successful Relationships Are Created.   We are only able to have healthy, successful love to the degree that we have put *conscious effort* toward this goal. Only by consulting ourselves about what we really want, on an intellectual, spiritual, and emotional level, are we able to choose the right partners. Accidental love is often unhealthy love. Successful love is created and is a direct result of how we go about meeting and dating potential partners.

This view is very much to the contrary of the expectations we have by virtue of living in today's culture. Erich Fromm remarked that most people see loving as easy, while finding a partner is viewed as difficult.[2] This belief is the source of much of the frustration that singles feel today. "I'm ready for love," we say. "I know how to love and be loved, I just need to find the right person to do that with. Where, oh where, can I find Mr. (or Ms.) Right? That would be the solution to my problems."

The truth is that finding someone to love is the easiest part of love, if you are willing to take a few steps to increase your social exposure and improve your social skills. Finding someone with whom we are basically compatible, creating a healthy relationship with that person, and being partners in a lasting love is the greatest challenge that we face today. The good news is that we can do something about it.

Singles feel out of control of their love lives because they are looking for answers in the wrong place. The answer isn't in the people we meet and date. No one out there is going to make romance easy or right for us. The real solution lies within, not without. It lies in our willingness to question ourselves about the problems of love and to diligently search for meaningful answers.

It's too easy to brush off our past mistakes in relationships as being a simple matter of having chosen the "wrong person." It is much more challenging, and infinitely more rewarding, to look to ourselves for the source of the problem. After all, what is the common denominator of all your relationships? You are, of course!

We can realize that regardless of how our past partners behaved (certainly we have lots of evidence about their flaws), we chose them and we entered into relationships with them. We can face the inner forces that influenced those choices, and we can make changes within so that we make better choices. We can question and challenge the romantic love myths that govern our attitudes and behaviors, replacing them with ideas that make sense in today's world. Most important, we can become more conscious of each step of meeting, dating, and relating, increasing our level of awareness and choosing appropriate behaviors.

---

[2]Erich Fromm, *The Art of Loving* (New York: Harper & Row, 1956).

In so doing, we are looking to ourselves for solutions, growing and becoming better partners for our future mates. Our lives and our relationships are in our own hands, not in the hands of some mythical perfect partner who may or may not come along someday.

Why Is Love So Challenging?

"But wait," you say. "This is beginning to sound difficult. Isn't love the most natural thing in the world? Can't we just sit back and let love find us and unfold the way nature intended it to? Why must love be so difficult to find and to keep? After all, our grandparents and their parents didn't have to read self-help books to find love."

In one of the seminars I lead on dating and relating, I asked the men and women in my audience to talk about what they wanted and expected from their relationships. We wrote the responses on the blackboard, and the board was filled very quickly. What they wanted included:

love	honesty
acceptance	open communication
romance	commitment
nurturing	doing things together
great sex	a loving family life
companionship	listening
friendship	sharing
understanding	intimacy
support	personal growth

Then I asked how many of them believed that their parents expected these kinds of things from a marriage or love relationship. A few hands went up. I queried further as to how many of them believed that their grandparents expected these things from marriage. Only one or two hands went up. Great-grandparents? No hands went up.

Even though this isn't a scientific survey, I think it indicates how dramatically our expectations of relationships, particularly the marriage relationship, have changed from those of previous generations. We want so much more than just a mate with whom to raise children and help with the chores or the family business. *We want all the goodies that a loving, intimate relationship seems to offer.*

Expectations Are Higher Than Ever. We want love, intimacy, sharing, acceptance, and nurturing from another human being. We want to know that we are valued above all others by our mate, and that they will be with us through thick and thin, good times and bad. We want open, honest communication. We want to know that we can share anything and everything with the person we love, and that they will still love us. We want support for our dreams in life and a partner to cheer us on. We want a relationship that allows us both to grow personally. Affirmation and positive feedback are wanted, and criticism offered in only the most loving way!

We want all this even though most of us are not prepared to deliver the goods. Not having grown up in loving, supportive, affirming environments, most of us are ill-equipped to love and be loved in the way we dream about.

In our imperfect families we learned ways of relating that don't necessarily help us as adults to have the healthiest of relationships. And these patterns began very early in life. Social scientists who have studied attachment behavior in infants have discovered certain patterns of relating that begin within the first few months of life and that profoundly affect the kind and quality of close relationships in adulthood, especially that between men and women.[3] These studies show us that the way our parents interact with us early in life sets the stage for our relationships throughout life.

For years as a single, I believed that most of my relationship problems were the fault of the current man in my life, that because I loved him so much, the problem couldn't be mine. After all, I was capable of love. It wasn't my fault that I kept choosing men who couldn't love me back in the way that I wanted to be loved. Not until I began look-

---

[3]C. Hazan, "Patterns of Adult Love," *Human Ecology Forum,* Spring 1990.

ing to myself, exploring my own family's legacy and its shortcomings, did I begin to realize how truly lacking I was in the emotional and communicational skills that it takes to have a healthy love relationship. I had to take responsibility for developing those skills in order to have a chance of getting the love I wanted.

Someone once said that no one escapes childhood unscarred. Even in the best homes, parents fail to give their children everything they need in order to grow into fully productive human beings who are capable of loving and being loved and accomplishing their goals in life. Why is this? Simply put, it is impossible for parents to be all things for and to satisfy all the needs of their children.

Parents are human beings who are imperfect, flawed, lacking in sufficient insight, and who make lots of mistakes. Additionally, most parents do not bother to educate themselves in the most important task they will ever take on; they "wing it" when it comes to child rearing, just as their parents did, and their grandparents before them, and so on. Thus, we have imperfect people parenting other imperfect people, with only the examples of their own parents to rely on. The result: We all have deficits from our childhood. We all wish for something that our parents didn't give us, or wish we were not saddled with something that our parents did give us.

Some of us came from homes where emotional or physical abuse and neglect occurred as well. There is no doubt that abuse of any kind sets up patterns of relating and emotional responses that lead to difficulties with relationships in adulthood. Regardless of the particular family legacy, from the benign and imperfect to the most profoundly abusive, we all carry the emotional scars of less-than-perfect childhoods.

The Promise of Love. Harville Hendrix, in his groundbreaking book *Getting the Love You Want,* describes beautifully how this sets us up for our romantic relationships in adult life.[4] Our unfulfilled

---

[4]Harville Hendrix, *Getting the Love You Want* (New York: Henry Holt & Company, 1988).

needs from childhood do not disappear when we become adults. They follow us, in a largely unconscious fashion, and influence our choices in relationships. Without realizing it, we choose partners who represent our parents in some way. Then, having always wanted that parent to give us what we didn't get, we look to our love relationships to supply those needs. By its very nature, romantic love offers the fulfillment of our deepest emotional needs. It is this unconscious drive that draws us together in relationships.

Our very high expectations of love, coupled with our unconscious drive toward fulfilling unmet needs from childhood, leave us in a double bind. We want and expect so much from love, yet most of us have few experiences of the kind of love we want. Human beings are rarely able to accomplish levels of intimacy and love that are beyond the level they experienced growing up in their families unless they are willing to face their own inner deficits and make conscious choices to do better than their parents did.

Personal Growth Is the Key. Because we want so much more than our parents and grandparents yet are left with their legacy, we have a unique challenge that no previous generation undertook. We are faced with the opportunity to educate ourselves about family and love relationships, to face our own deficits from earlier in life, and to make changes in ourselves and our lives. If we choose, we can embrace the challenge of moving beyond the models of love that we inherited and creating relationships that are more suited to our modern expectations.

If we are willing to examine ourselves, learn to know ourselves, and stretch the limits of our capacity to love and be loved, we can get the love we want. Will this take some effort? Yes! Will this be uncomfortable at times? Most certainly. Personal growth is almost always uncomfortable.

Is it possible to have a truly loving, nurturing relationship with mutual love, admiration, and respect? Only if we say so. The first step, therefore, is to affirm the belief that it is possible (even if it's not yet clear how to make it happen). Second is the decision to settle into the journey toward loving relationships, realizing that this won't happen overnight. It is important to give up on finding a perfect partner. In case you hadn't noticed, there aren't any! Instead, the goal is to *be our best possible selves, be open to personal growth, and focus on our own lives and what we want out of them.*

Why is love so challenging? Because we want the most out of love, and the obstacles to rewarding relationships have never been higher. However, the journey itself can be just as rewarding as the destination.

A Surprising Benefit.   The search for a healthy love relationship carries its own reward. By looking within ourselves for our own sources of happiness and fulfillment, we find the controls of our lives in our own hands. By facing our own personal barriers to love, and making changes within ourselves, we are able to live more productive lives.

The real reward in the search for a loving relationship is not some mystical destination. Happily-ever-after exists only in storybooks. In real life, there are no guarantees that love will last. Even when you do find the love of your life and create a healthy relationship, there is no promise that it will never end. The reward is in the journey itself, in the day-to-day struggle to face and conquer fears and insecurities, to become conscious of our innermost feelings, and to communicate in the most authentic and honest way to a partner. The opportunity for personal growth and the enrichment of our lives is tremendous when we resolve to look to ourselves for the answers to life and love.

Sharon, an attractive woman in her late thirties, approached me at the end of the second session of a workshop I was leading. Her eyes sparkling, she related how much fun she was having meeting men since being inspired at the previous session. When I asked her if I could include her story in my book, she responded, "Wait until I have some real success, maybe in a couple of more months." I pointed out to her that, even though she hadn't found the right man yet, her having a more rewarding and fun experience of life as a single looked to me like success.

So often as singles we completely overlook or discount the growth that is available as human beings in the process of looking for love.

Sharon's experience of being more outgoing and assertive in meeting men clearly helped her self-image as well as her sense of being in charge of her own love life. She was not passively waiting for love to find her. What a kick! No wonder she was thrilled.

Successful Dating: More Than the End Result. I believe that as we begin making changes in our dating lives, we can fall in love with the process itself. We can thoroughly enjoy practicing our social and relational skills. As we meet more people, find more of the right people to date, and have more enriching dating experiences, we can have a more fulfilling experience of life as a single, and this is valuable in and of itself.

I believe that the years we spend as single adults offer tremendous opportunities for personal growth if we are willing to look for them and not just step over them. Going to a singles dance on Friday night may look like just another one of those frustrating experiences in which you get all dressed up and don't find Prince Charming, but it could be much more than that. It could be an evening in which you resolve to work on your fear of meeting new people, the goal being to move out of your usual comfort zone, discover some things about yourself, and grow personally. Whether or not you meet Mr. or Ms. Right takes a backseat to the pride you feel at the end of the evening because you extended yourself, walking up to strangers, introducing yourself, and making new friends.

Being single does not mean that we have to be lonely and without joy, stuck in a holding pattern until the right person just happens along. The search for a rewarding relationship can be a true adventure, although not one without some risk!

If we can learn to enjoy the journey itself, looking for opportunities for personal growth along the way, we will be less focused on the end result and will be more likely to celebrate our successes along the way. We will also find ourselves happier and more fulfilled, and thus much more attractive to the kind of people we're looking for: other happy, fulfilled, and successful people.

2

❤   ❤   ❤

Stages of Love

*Sherry, a thirty-year-old executive secretary, described her up-and-*down, hot-and-cold relationship with Mark, a thirty-eight-year-old small-business owner. For five months they had dated without commitment. Finally, Sherry refused to see him again until he agreed to stop seeing other women. Faced with losing Sherry, Mark acquiesced to her demands, and their relationship became exclusive. Two months later, Mark's mother died suddenly. Grieving and not dealing very well with it, Mark pushed Sherry away, hurting her and damaging the trust between them. Soon they were engaged in a power struggle, with one pursuing and the other distancing, and then vice versa.

Sherry was obviously in pain as she told her story to me. When I asked her what was driving her to continue trying to make things work out with Mark, she said simply, "I love him." She went on to say that this had happened to her before; that she invariably ended up with men who were unavailable to her in some way. "All I want is someone to love me. I want to get married, have children, and have a good family life," Sherry said. "Why can't I find someone who wants that, too?"

In order to discover what was keeping Sherry from what she wanted, we explored her past relationships, looking for common threads. In so doing, we were able to identify her particular patterns of relating that were getting in her way, thus setting the stage for change and, ultimately, healthier relationships.

As we looked at Sherry's history, one thing became evident. Although Sherry wanted one partner in a lifetime relationship, the fact was that she had already had several serious romances, none of which had lasted forever. And although her current relationship appeared to be on the way out, the odds were that it wouldn't be the last relationship in her life.

Love Throughout the Life Span

Most of us have been in love more than once, and many of us have been in love many times. Gone are the days when couples met at an early age, married, and remained together until one of them died. Like it or not, we live in an age of what some have called "serial monogamy." This means that we are committed until the current relationship ends, and then we move on to someone new.

The majority of us are likely to experience more than one deeply significant and meaningful love relationship in our lifetimes. In fact, most of us will move through the three stages of love several times throughout our life spans (see Figure 2-1).

The top vertical line represents the end of a past love relationship, whether through divorce, death, or breakup. At that time, we enter the first stage.

Stage One: Grief, Loss, and Recovery.   In this stage we have many issues to deal with. First is the grief for the relationship that has been lost. Depending on the duration and the intensity of the relationship, there may be anger, resentment, sadness, and a whole host of other emotional reactions. Depending on how the relationship ended, it's possible to get stuck in some of those strong feelings.

THE THREE STAGES OF RELATIONSHIPS:
End of last relationship

STAGE THREE
Exclusive
relationship

STAGE ONE
Grief, loss, and
recovery

STAGE TWO
Dating around

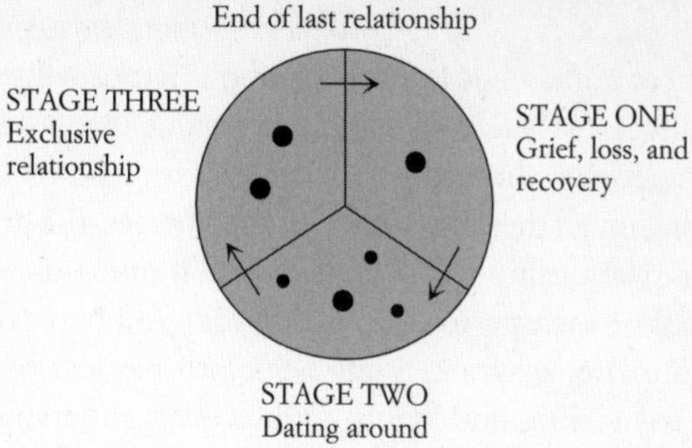

Figure 2-1

If there was a bitter divorce, especially with battles over children and money, anger and resentment toward an ex-spouse may be primary. If these battles are drawn out over months and years, ongoing feelings of anger and rage can lead to depression, physical exhaustion, the draining of financial resources, and many other negative consequences.

The death of a partner can leave a legacy of anger (Why did this happen?), guilt (Could I have prevented it?), and deep sadness. The grief can take months or even years to deal with fully.

The breakup of dating relationships can be every bit as painful and devastating as a divorce. A dating or live-in relationship may last for years and end with the loss of the person we love. Even very short relationships can bring painful endings, particularly regarding the loss of what might have been. Dating relationships are often filled with expectations of marriage and life lived happily ever after, and breakups often represent the end of those dreams.

The ending of a relationship can bring a wide range of feelings, from simple relief to intense pain and grief. Surprisingly, even when one chooses to end the romance, there may be surprising feelings of loss. There are no correct feelings to have, so it's important to validate whatever we experience.

At the end of each love relationship, there is usually the "One Who Leaves" and the "One Who Is Left." The person leaving usually feels some degree of guilt, while the person who is left usually feels resentment. In both cases there is an emotional residue that requires time to deal with, especially when one partner leaves for a new love interest.

Depending on all these and other circumstances, the grief issues at the end of a relationship will occupy a certain time frame in an individual's life. For each person this is different and may take a matter of days to a matter of years. Some deal with the loss by relying on supportive friendships and family. Others need a therapist or a support group.

Eventually, most of us move through the stages of grief and loss and discover that we are ready to move on. We come out of our self-imposed social hibernation and begin reaching out again. Even though we may tell ourselves that we never want to fall in love again, all of us are vulnerable to the enticement of love's promise. We want to believe in the possibility of love. So, against all the odds, we move back into the dating scene and begin again.

Stage Two: Dating Around. This is actually the stage of relationships that most singles spend very little time in or skip entirely. It is not unusual to find ourselves back in an exclusive relationship almost as soon as we come out of our cocoons of grief. Rarely do we take the time to assess our needs, meet lots of new people, and sort through them to find a partner who is good for us.

I call this the "Lost Art of Dating," and it goes something like this:

In the dating-around stage there is the opportunity to date various potential partners. This can be a time in which there is no serious relationship. We meet new people, we go out, we experiment with short relationships (one to several dates). Sometimes this means that we go out with a new person a few times, discover that they're not right for us, and move on to someone else. Sometimes we may date more than one person at a time, but none in a serious way.

Much of the first half of this book addresses the "dating around" stage and how to make the most of it.

The majority of singles eventually meet someone who particularly grabs their interest. We feel drawn to this individual and want to spend more and more time with him or her. Interest in other dating partners wanes, and if our partner feels the same, we eventually move into the next stage of a relationship.

Stage Three: Exclusive Relationship.   In this stage, all of our emotional energy is focused on one person. Whether spoken out loud or not, we have moved into a monogamous relationship and no longer date others.

Exclusive relationships may last anywhere from two months to twenty years, and even longer. Some monogamous partners move in together and agree that marriage is not for them. Others live together, with one partner hoping for an eventual marriage commitment while the other is content with the live-in arrangement. Still others live together, hoping to "test the waters" before making a commitment and marrying. (Unfortunately, studies do not bear out this idea. Couples who live together first have no better chance of a successful marriage than those who do not.) Other couples merely date exclusively, preferring to live apart until they make a marriage commitment.

In the early months of an exclusive relationship, both partners may agree that it is too soon to discuss marriage. Eventually, however, the question is raised: Are we going to get married or not? Are we going to try to spend a lifetime together, or is this relationship a dead end? Sometimes one partner demands an answer to this question while the other evades the discussion.

Deciding whether or not to commit to marriage is a process that varies greatly from one couple to the next. Sometimes both partners want marriage, and they will smoothly segue into an engagement and marriage. Sometimes one partner is unsure and will stall on the question in order to sort out confused feelings. In this instance, the other partner may find himself or herself in emotional limbo for an indefinite period. Some couples in this situation will take years to decide on the direction of their relationship.

Eventually, most couples arrive at a decision. They will either proceed into marriage or they will break up, at which point they begin again in the stages of love. Obviously, couples who marry may end up divorcing, so either way the process may begin again.

An Unpredictable Course

In real life, we don't progress through these three stages in a smooth, predictable fashion. Sometimes one exclusive relationship leads to another, with the grief stage and the dating-around stage skipped altogether. Sometimes we end an exclusive relationship, begin dating someone else, then find the old love back in our lives. Going back and forth between the exclusive and dating-around stages is very common.

After the loss of a love, some singles date around a little, then go back into seclusion. I see many singles in my practice who go back and forth between dating around and not dating at all. Sometimes we are like turtles, sticking our heads out and looking around for a bit, then withdrawing quickly when we don't find things (relationships) to our liking.

Sometimes a relationship is repeatedly ended, then resumed, ended again, and so on. This "On-again, Off-again Pattern" is actually a particular way of relating, not merely jumping back and forth between stages. These couples play a game of "pretending to break up," with the payoff being a gain in power, the pleasure of a romantic reconciliation, and the denial of the problems in the relationship. It is sometimes a way to continue a relationship that is too intense or that is a source of too much frustration and pain. The breakups allow for psychological relief so that the couple can get back on the roller coaster once again.

Linda was emotionally in the dating-around stage but was pretending to be in the exclusive stage. Having been through the breakup of a three-year relationship, she enjoyed dating John, who was nice and treated her like the special person she wanted to believe she was. Even though she knew he wasn't what she wanted, she continued to see him exclusively, but her heart wasn't in it. She found herself attracted to other men and wanting to go out with them, but she felt guilty about her feelings. Like Linda, we sometimes find ourselves in a kind of limbo, one foot in one stage and one foot in another. Eventually, though, she faced the fact that she was cheating herself and him, and permanently ended the relationship.

Some couples end an exclusive relationship, begin the grief process, and then later reconcile and go on to marriage. Some individuals carry on a seemingly exclusive relationship while still dating around, unbeknownst to their partner.

As you can see, the possibilities are endless! The stages of love are not smooth and well defined, but looking at this model offers us a greater awareness. Now we can begin to consider our needs as individuals, regardless of what stage we are in.

What Do We Need?

Dealing with Loss.   The loss of a significant relationship has a powerful impact on our lives. It is vitally important to not skip over the emotional reactions that are inevitable at these times. Whether the primary feeling is sadness, grief, anger, bitterness, relief, or a combination of the above, our hearts need time to heal.

If sadness is primary, then tears need to be cried. If anger is primary, then constructive ways of releasing the rage need to be found, such as hitting pillows or a punching bag. Writing letters (not for mailing) to the lost loved one is a popular technique that my clients use and that seems to aid in the healing process.

Grief has its own timetable and varies with each person and circumstance. It is important to allow grief all the time that it requires, regardless of whether this coincides with others' ideas of how long you should grieve. Well-meaning friends often want to distract us from our grief, not understanding that the healing forces, if left unobstructed, will work wonders.

Tracy, whose boyfriend of two years had just left her, numbly accepted a blind date that her friend set up in order to distract her from her overpowering grief. Her unlucky escort was probably a wonderful man who, at a different time in Tracy's life, might have been a terrific dating partner. She barely saw him, noticing him only at those times when she came out of her fog of misery long enough to compare certain traits of his with those of her lost love. Of course, he never stood a chance of measuring up.

It is crucial that we fully acknowledge the depth and importance of the loss. With death and divorce, most people understand that these issues have to be dealt with. We must realize that the same issues are there when a long-term romance comes to an end.

After the breakup of her four-year relationship with Jim, Ellen joined a divorce recovery group. She quickly discovered that most of her grief issues remarkably paralleled those of the men and women in the group who were going through divorce. Ellen's admission of the level of pain that she was suffering enabled her to deal with her loss and grief with the full range of emotional reactions and thus begin the process of recovery.

Stuck in Grief.   Sometimes we do not progress through grief but find ourselves stuck. Signals that we are stuck include deep resentment and rage that will not subside with time. If these feelings are accompanied by fantasies of harming the ex-partner, it is time to seek professional help.

Long-standing feelings of resentment are detrimental only to the person feeling them. They can sap energy, prompt unnecessary litigation, and even result in impaired health. They can also inhibit the movement forward into new relationships or can act as emotional baggage that negatively affects any new attempts to partner.

A year and a half after her husband left her for his secretary, Ann was still enraged. She had resolved to "get even" with him for her pain and had hired a bevy of lawyers to work on her behalf. Now, she witnessed the draining of both her and her husband's finances as they battled endlessly in court, accomplishing nothing. Both resisted mediation and counseling to resolve their differences. They were far more interested in being "right" about how badly they had each been treated by the other than in salvaging their dignity and getting on with their lives.

The boiling resentment and rage that Ann felt was primarily hurting herself (and their children) and giving herself no satisfaction.

Denial of Grief.   Sometimes we deny the feelings of loss at the end of a significant relationship. We rush forward, trying to "get on with our lives," failing to deal with the emotional residue that has accumulated.

Dorothy, a thirty-five-year-old advertising executive, had ended an eight-year relationship only six months earlier. Denying her feelings of loss and anger, she was dating furiously. "I date all the time," she said. "I bet I'm home only two nights out of the week." On the one hand, Dorothy wanted a good relationship, but on the other hand, she was nowhere near being emotionally available herself. By denying the extent of her loss, she was failing to take advantage of this time in her life to deal with her feelings and reach an emotional resolution of the last relationship. Without doing this work, Dorothy will have an unstable foundation on which to build a future romance.

Jenny's pattern had always been to replace the man currently on the way out. Since college she had had a continuous string of relationships, including a marriage, each one leading into the next with no break and often overlapping. By the time she came to see me at age thirty-four, she had enough emotional baggage to fill a stadium! Her first significant change was to resolve to deal with the ending of her current relationship without rushing into a new one. Jenny knew that she had to learn to slow down and give herself time to deal with her feelings and heal, rather than anesthetizing the grief by becoming attached to someone new.

In contrast, April resolved to take one year off from dating after her last relationship ended for her own healing process. She occupied herself with friends and singles' activities, creating for the first time an extensive support system. She read books, meditated, got therapy, and focused on herself and her own growth. Just as the year was ending, she met Charles, for whom she later realized she wouldn't have been able to be truly available without having taken time off like she did.

Other signs of being stuck in the grief stage include feelings of guilt that do not subside with time, fantasies of a reunion with the ex-lover (even when he or she has married someone else), depression, suicidal thoughts, or other self-defeating behavior that persists. Seeing a therapist or joining a support group can help the healing and recovery process. Many churches provide divorce recovery groups that offer the opportunity to share thoughts and feelings with others who are going through losses. The most important thing is to get help when stuck in the grief stage and to not put off doing so.

Reestablishing Old Ties.   Sometimes a love relationship is so all-consuming that we neglect other important relationships. After it ends, we may want to reconnect with friendships that have fallen by the wayside. This can be a time to rediscover those old ties and even form some new ones. Time spent with old and new friends can prove remarkably healing while dealing with grief.

Taking Inventory.   Once the grief reactions have subsided to some degree, this is a valuable time to reassess wants and needs for future relationships. Reviewing past romances may reveal patterns of relating that haven't worked. Taking another look at personal values (which we will explore in the next chapter) is critical in this stage. So often we compromise those issues that we hold most dear in order to have a certain person, only to find later on that there is a steep price to pay.

Reexamining what kind of relationship we want is also important. If we haven't gotten what we wanted in the past, then we may need to take a second look at what we're trying to get. We also need to realize what qualities we want in a partner and bring those into clear focus. These personal inventories require time and effort, and sometimes professional guidance, and I can't emphasize enough how important they are. *Empowered through more clearly knowing ourselves and what we want, we stand a far greater chance of having healthy, loving relationships.*

Dating Around.   As the desire to pursue new relationships resurfaces, a game plan is helpful. Rather than waiting for eligible singles to beat a path to our door (possibly a very long wait!), being proactive and creating opportunities to meet and date gives us two things. First, we have the sense that we are in control of our love lives, that they are not merely subject to luck and chance. Second, we develop an expanded sense of the possibilities for relationships, giving us greater confidence and less desperation. In later chapters, you will actually create your personal "Dating Game Plan" for meeting, dating, and relating.

Exclusive Relationships.   Most dating relationships just drift into the exclusive stage, with no formal declarations or an acknowledgment of what this means for the future. Because all exclusive relationships signal the possibility of marriage, we are in a better position if we understand that. Knowing that a discussion of permanent commitment is inevitable, we can be more discerning about whom we wish to become more involved with and date exclusively. In chapter sixteen we'll explore in greater depth the dynamics of exclusive relationships and how to deal with them.

Taking Inventory

At this point it may be helpful to take stock of where you currently are in the stages of love. In a journal or notebook, ask yourself and answer the following questions, being sure to include your thoughts and feelings:

1.   Where am I (Stage One, Two, or Three) *emotionally?* Where am I *behaviorally?* If these are different, is this causing me a problem, and if so, how?

2.   Where do I want to be? (Which stage do I want to be in?)

3.   What do I need in order to move or progress toward that stage? (Identify the areas of personal growth that you need.)

Awareness in All Stages

Armed with an awareness of the three stages of love in our lives, we can begin to take an inventory of ourselves and our relationships. We can identify problematic patterns and begin making changes to move closer to our goals. Is this going to be a challenge? You bet! Will personal growth be necessary in order to do this? I hope so!

Regardless of which stage of love you may find yourself in, opportunities for learning more about yourself and becoming more of the person you want to be are abundant. With awareness comes insight, and then comes the opportunity for new choices and change. Instead of stumbling blindly from one unsatisfactory relationship to the next, you can begin to design the life you've always wanted as a single: a life filled with people you like, activities you enjoy, and a rewarding search for the right partner.

3

❤   ❤   ❤

Who's Doing the Choosing?

"*I'm frustrated with the pace of our relationship,*" Angela said. "We've been dating for three months and I still have to wait until he calls, which isn't often, to see him."

"What do you want?" I asked, to which she replied, "An agreement to see each other on a regular basis, exclusively. And for him to open up more to me on an emotional level. I want an understanding that we've got a *relationship,* not just a matter of convenience. I want to know where I stand with him, whether or not he's falling in love with me like I am with him."

After stating her willingness to ask for what she wanted, Angela resolved to do so as soon as she could see Jeff again. A week later, she'd talked to Jeff, but still seemed confused about where she stood with him.

"What did Jeff say he wanted?" I asked. "He said he wanted what we have now: no commitment, no strings, just seeing each other every now and then. I couldn't get him to open up about his feelings. He said he wasn't interested in that kind of relationship; he just wanted to have fun."

"Sounds like you have your answer," I told her, and she began to cry. "Couldn't I give him more time? Maybe he'll change his mind and decide he wants more," she said almost desperately. But she already knew the answer. The truth was, Angela had chosen yet another man who wasn't emotionally available for a relationship. She was disappointed and hurt, but not yet so attached that she couldn't get out. She broke up with Jeff the following week and resolved to choose someone more available the next time.

Like most singles, Angela, age twenty-five and divorced once, chose her partners based solely on attraction, as she had chosen Jeff. She tended to go from one partner to the next in a thoughtless fashion, relying strictly on chemistry as a guide.

It feels natural to do this. Most of us don't stop to think about what to look for in the dating process, and yet the choice of who to go out with and continue dating is probably one of the most important decisions we'll ever make in our lives. It is also, all too often, one of the most *unconscious* choices made.

Making Love Choices

How do we decide who to date and who to pass by? Who to fall in love with and who to merely like? These decisions have a direct impact on our choice of partners and thus the kinds of relationships (and ultimately, marriage) that we tend to end up in. Naturally, it would seem that we would be very cautious about who we become involved with. Unfortunately, nature has other plans for human beings when it comes to romantic love.

How Biology Chooses for Us.   R. Rizley writes about the swiftness with which couples go from being strangers to being partners as evidence for there being strong biological and evolutionary factors in romantic love.[1] These factors allow human beings to fall in love

---

[1] R. Rizley, "Psychobiological Bases of Romantic Love," in K. S. Pope & Associates' *On Love and Loving* (San Francisco: Jossey-Bass, 1980), pp. 104–113.

with anyone, *regardless of similarity in background, culture, or beliefs.* This obviously had great evolutionary advantages: Human beings could reproduce with greater efficiency. Thousands of years ago, when there were very few human beings on the planet, this was important.

Nowadays, we are much more selective about our mates, yet the same old biological mechanisms are still in place. If we don't stop to think, nature takes over and makes the choices for us. In fact, our biology sets us up for making unwise choices in love.

This is because so much of human behavior has its origins in the deep recesses of our brains, where ancient impulses still reside. Romantic love is one of those. Studies show that when humans fall in love, the actual chemistry of the brain is altered for a time, making us think less logically and with a great deal more fantasy.

Eons ago, when there were few human beings in the world and those few needed each other for survival, this mechanism served to bring people together powerfully enough to allow procreation and to form communities. Without it, we might not have survived as a species. Today, our brains still work in much the same fashion, causing us to be drawn to certain partners, regardless of whether or not we're compatible.

There's more than evolution at work when it comes to romance. Most of us are equipped with a very powerful drive to bond with another human being in a sexual, emotional, and intellectual way. This serves many needs, among them being social, attachment, and sexual needs. We are social creatures, and we tend to seek out other human beings to socialize with. We have attachment needs, going back to infancy, and we look for people with whom we can bond closely. We have sexual needs, nature being wise enough to make the act of procreation feel very good. Thus, we seek out a mate with whom to enjoy our sexuality, bond, and enjoy intimacy and companionship.

Romantic love relationships offer the opportunity to meet all these needs in one person. Because these needs are so powerful, we tend to look for any reasonable (and sometimes unreasonable) way to satisfy them. As soon as we meet someone for whom we feel a strong attraction, our innate quest for closeness, attachment, and sex takes over, and we begin a new relationship. Unfortunately, because these needs tend to override our intellect, we are prone to making un-thought-out choices in mates. Biology and nature scream, "Go for it!" while good judgment whispers, "Wait and see."

How Personal History Chooses for Us.   As social creatures with a sex drive, we look for another person with whom we can bond closely and satisfy these very basic, powerful needs. Unconsciously, these drives influence our choice of dating partners. But there are other unconscious forces at work as well. Every person has a unique history of relationships, going back to the first and most important: those with our mother and father.

Whether aware of it or not, we all tend to look for partners who allow us to recreate the same relationship dynamics that we experienced with mother and father (or whomever our primary caretakers were). M. F. Weiner asserts that individuals in love idealize their partners, choosing someone who represents important aspects of their parents. This allows a style of relating that is familiar and therefore comfortable.[2] However, because all parents fall short in giving their children everything they need, we grow up searching for the missing pieces of those earliest relationships. In choosing partners who remind us of our parents in some way, we are able to experience, in effect: "Once again, I am close to someone who is _____ , who always _____ , and who doesn't give me _____ .* But, because I am so smart and capable, I will find a way to get what I want and need from this person, therefore righting the wrong that was done to me earlier in life."

---

[2]M. F. Weiner, "Healthy and Pathological Love: Psychodynamic Views," in K. S. Pope & Associates' *On Love and Loving* (San Francisco: Jossey-Bass, 1980), pp. 114–132.

*Fill in the blanks:

SOMEONE WHO IS:	WHO ALWAYS:	and DOESN'T GIVE ME:
domineering	runs over me	any freedom
undependable	leaves	security
hostile	yells at me	love and nurturing
controlling	tells me what to do	respect for my abilities

Of course, for the most part, these processes take place out of our immediate awareness. What we are in touch with is a powerful pull toward certain partners, along with a heightened sense of positive feelings, the experience we call "falling in love." What we are usually not conscious of is the deeper purpose that is being served.

That purpose is, quite simply, to address our need to heal from the pain of childhood losses and hurts in our relationships with our parents. In *Keeping the Love You Find,* Harville Hendrix indicates that this phenomenon is powerful indeed:

> What we unconsciously want is to get what we didn't get in childhood from someone who is like the people who didn't give us what we needed in the first place. When we meet an Imago match, that chemical reaction occurs and love ignites. All other bets, all other ideas about what we want in a mate, are off. We feel alive and whole, confident that we have met the person who will make everything all right.[3]

Becoming Conscious: The Key to Wise Choices. Even though these unconscious forces dictate our attraction to certain partners, we can begin to exert more control over our choices of mates by realizing that these forces exist. In fact, if we want healthier relationships

---

[3]Harville Hendrix, *Keeping the Love You Find: A Guide for Singles* (New York: Pocket Books, 1992), p. 21.

that last, we must acknowledge these dynamics and be able to look beyond them. We must first of all know ourselves better, gaining some insight into our own past and how it influences the present and the future. We must face up to the pull that we have toward certain kinds of partners and whether or not they will ultimately be good for us. We cannot afford to be driven solely by unconscious forces. We must seek self-awareness first and learn to date in a more thoughtful fashion.

Becoming conscious of the forces that drive us into certain relationships does not mean that we have to become perfect before we can have a good relationship. In fact, there are some issues that are best resolved within the context of a committed relationship.[4] *It does mean that by working on our own issues we can be healthier and therefore will tend to be attracted to healthier partners, thus allowing us to have better relationships.* We can never gain full control of the unconscious forces that determine who we are attracted to, but by focusing on our own personal growth we can influence those forces to serve us better.

Awareness is the first step toward change. Use the following inventory to see if your unconscious forces are choosing the same partner for you over and over again:

Relationship History Inventory

1. List the first names of all your past significant romantic partners. Use a separate sheet of paper for each person. *Significant* means that it was important to you, regardless of how short or long the time you spent together.

2. On the top half of the page, for each *person,* list as many positive characteristics as you can think of. Use descriptive terms: loving, giving, affectionate, neat and orderly, romantic, intelligent, etc.

---

[4]This is because there are some issues that simply don't arise when we're not in a relationship and therefore can't be addressed until we are. However, a great deal of healing can and does occur while still single.

3.   In the middle of the page, for each person, list as many negative characteristics as you can, using terms such as controlling, verbally abusive, sloppy, unmotivated, lazy, unaffectionate, domineering, avoidant, etc.

4.   At the bottom of the page, put words that describe how you felt in the relationship, both positive and negative, such as fearful, angry, loved, rejected, manipulated, esteemed, abandoned, abused, used, desired, and so on.

5.   Now, go back to each page and circle the words that you see repeated on at least one other page.

6.   On a new sheet of paper, write "I'm drawn to partners who are initially" and fill in the positive traits that you've circled; then write "and who turn out to be" and fill in the negative traits. "I do this so I can feel" and fill in the relationship feeling words that you've circled.

You now have a picture of your formula for romantic relationships. You've chosen a certain type of partner in the past in order to recreate the feelings you've felt each time, hoping that it will turn out differently than it has before. This is actually not bad, but is an unconscious strategy that helps us learn the lessons we need to learn in order to move closer to real, lasting love. Thus, each new relationship is an opportunity to learn and grow if we are willing to make conscious choices and corrections along the way.

"What can I do to change my pattern?" you ask. First and foremost: Make a commitment to do whatever it takes to *transform yourself*. Second, reach out for the tools you will need. Therapy, counseling, workshops, books, tapes, twelve-step groups, spiritual growth—all provide the means by which you can permanently alter your patterns.

Remember that the past does not have to dictate the future. We all have the ability to learn from the past and create a new future, as long as we are willing to intervene by becoming conscious, making a commitment to growth, and then using the available tools to accomplish that.

Other Challenges to Finding the Right Partner

Why do we have so much difficulty in choosing appropriate partners? Aside from the influences of biology and early home life, we must also remember that we live in a highly diverse culture. We don't as a matter of course live and work with people who happen to share our basic values, the way our grandparents did. We don't all adhere to one view of what marriage should be or what is important in life. The women's movement, the sexual revolution, and global communications have given us the awareness and freedom to embrace many different views of love, marriage, family, and purpose in life. The same is true of the people we meet.

Because we tend to have many love relationships over a lifetime, the odds are that most of the people we meet are already involved with someone else or are carrying unresolved emotional baggage from a past relationship. Thus, if we rely strictly on feelings of attraction to choose our dating partners, we are very likely to find ourselves attached to people who aren't really suited to us.

Kelly met her last boyfriend, Tom, while celebrating at a restaurant with friends. "He was tall and charming and absolutely gorgeous," gushed Kelly. "I wanted to meet him, so I sent a drink to his table." Soon they were talking and that led to dancing, which led to going to Tom's place, which led to spending the entire weekend together. After a couple of months of dating, Kelly wanted more commitment from Tom, who preferred to "keep his options open." Even though Kelly made demands for exclusivity, she continued to date Tom, who became very good at resisting her demands. "He'll come around if I give him more time," she thought. So she dropped the subject until her resentment built up and she felt compelled to confront him about being exclusive with her. Again, he refused to comply. Again, she adapted to his wishes and continued seeing him.

This became their pattern. Occasionally Kelly would find evidence that Tom was seeing someone else (lipstick on a beer can in his apartment) and would again demand exclusivity. Each time she backed down, until after two and a half years she had had enough. She ended her relationship with Tom, but her anger and rage did not disappear so quickly. Kelly had invested heavily in this relationship, and didn't get the return she wanted on her investment.

Like so many of us, Kelly chose Tom based solely on her feelings of attraction to him, never stopping to discover whether they shared common interests and goals or whether he was emotionally available for a committed relationship. Swept away on a tidal wave of love and hormones (and unconscious influences from her upbringing), she allowed herself to become attached to a man who could not or would not give her the kind of relationship she wanted.

Chemistry Isn't Enough.   In today's world, we need to balance our intellectual, physical, and emotional needs in choosing a mate. Being attracted to a person isn't enough to sustain a healthy relationship over years and decades, as any marriage counselor can attest to. Chemistry and falling in love feel good, but we need much more than these if we are to have any possibility of maintaining a romance over time.

Chemistry Is Necessary.   Although it may sound contradictory, being strongly attracted to another person, while not enough in and of itself, is actually an essential part of a healthy relationship. Falling in love is the glue that binds two people together. The memories of those earlier, delicious feelings give us incentives to work on our relationship when we enter stormy seas, which we inevitably will. But this alone is not enough. Other factors, combined with romantic love, create a strong foundation for a healthy relationship.

Five Factors for Healthy Love

After years of working with singles and couples, I've discovered that there are basically five essential relationship factors that must be present in order for a relationship to work (see Figure 3-1). If any of these factors is missing, a couple may initially be attracted and may even court and marry, but there will always be a sense that something is missing. When conflict arises (as it inevitably does) or the relationship enters a rocky time, there will be less to draw on in terms of remembering how good the relationship was and could be again. More often than not, a relationship missing one or more of these key factors will eventually crumble.

The most essential of the five factors are the two that I've shown at the bottom of the pyramid. These, I believe, form the foundation of a successful relationship. Remove one of these factors and you have a very shaky relationship that will not stand the test of time and conflict, just like a house built on a faulty foundation. They are *shared values* and an *equal desire for the relationship*.

Shared Values.   This means that we are basically seeking the same things out of life. Obviously, it would be impossible to find a partner with whom we share every single value in exactly the same way. However, when our most important values clash, love tends not to thrive and will usually deteriorate.

On a television talk show recently, the host interviewed Jerry and Cindy to try to understand why their marriage had failed. Jerry, a traditional man, wanted a wife who was willing to be a full-time homemaker. He did not support his wife in starting her own business and when she worked overtime, he felt cheated out of what he expected from marriage. He believed that their child suffered from not having

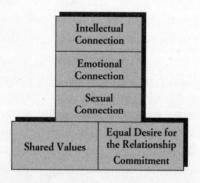

Figure 3-1

a full-time mother, causing Cindy to feel guilty. As she brought her business to a more successful level, Jerry felt threatened, and he pressured her to stop working and stay home to care for their child. Inevitably, the mounting stress of their discordant values about marriage and family life split this couple apart.

The talk-show host correctly pointed out that Jerry had the right to have a partner who shared his values about homemaking and that Cindy had the right to have a partner who could genuinely support her need to have a successful career. These two people were both good people, but the vast differences in their values kept them from being happy together.

Equal Desire for the Relationship. This is the foundation's other vital part, without which a relationship is sure to fail. I've shown the word "commitment" in the same box because without equal desire there can be no genuine commitment. This idea refers to the emotional as well as intellectual choice by two people to be together, to place their relationship as a high priority, and to work on maintaining their connection. It is *not* one person wanting the relationship really badly and the other person just going along. Nor is it simply an agreement to be together, spoken or unspoken. It is a *state of being,* coming from genuine desire on the part of both people in the relationship. Equal desire for the relationship cannot be faked.

This kind of commitment cannot occur without the true availability of both partners, both emotionally and in other ways. (We'll explore availability further in chapter thirteen.)

Carol and Patrick's relationship shows how important this is. Equally desiring their relationship, they were willing to work on the issues they had together and to resolve them in the best interest of both people, as well as they could. Neither of them was distracted by other entanglements, nor were they resistant to making a commitment. Their love wasn't perfect, but because they both wanted it and chose to be together, they were able to progress in therapy and achieve an even more intimate and loving relationship.

A couple desiring their relationship equally and strongly provides a powerful base from which to work through the inevitable problems that assault any modern love relationship. If we both want to be in a committed relationship together (as defined by both of us), then we will be more likely to confront our issues, working together as a team to resolve them.

Desire in a romance is often nothing more than the sentiment "I want you" or "I want to be with you" or "I want your body"! While this kind of desire is certainly part of a healthy relationship, it isn't the same as commitment. The two are very easy to confuse but are actually quite different. *The desire to be with someone may or may not be accompanied by commitment.* The fact that someone "wants you" does not mean that they are necessarily willing to invest in a committed relationship with you.

Equal desire for the relationship (commitment) serves several purposes. It helps to bind couples together, allowing them to form a psychological boundary around their relationship. This boundary prevents intrusions from others that might disrupt the couple's sometimes fragile and growing sense of intimacy. It also serves as a sort of safety net for the couple. Knowing that they are in it for the long haul and not just for some fun and games, couples are more likely to risk the sharing of innermost thoughts and feelings. They are also more likely to risk confronting each other and asking for what they need, all of which contribute to the development of a strong, healthy relationship.

Martin had recently ended a four-year relationship when he met Stacey. He'd loved his ex-girlfriend and wanted her but had never quite made the step to commitment, nor had their values meshed. With Stacey, he felt a powerful connection of chemistry as well as common values, which grew into a strong commitment on both their parts. He wanted the relationship just as much as she did, which helped him confront one of his deepest fears. Shortly before their wedding, Martin woke up one night in a cold sweat, sure that he was making a mistake. Terrified of telling Stacey, he nevertheless picked up the phone and called her at 4:00 A.M. to express his doubts. Stacey responded calmly, listening to his feelings and not offering any resistance. They were able to fully explore their anxieties about getting married and renew their commitment. Martin was elated when he shared the story several days later. Being fully committed to this relationship gave him the courage to confront his fears and express them, something Martin had never been able to do in his earlier, less committed relationships.

Intellectual, Emotional, and Sexual Connections. In addition to shared values and an equal desire for the relationship, we need a combination of other factors to create a healthy, loving relationship. We also need to connect at the level of the head, heart, and loins! Added together, these three factors contribute to that indescribable something that we call "chemistry," which we've already discovered is necessary for a good relationship.

Kevin and Lisa certainly shared an emotional and sexual connection. Within days of meeting they experienced a powerful emotional and sexual bonding. Eight months later they married, and within a year their troubles surfaced. Kevin worked in a factory and held only a high school equivalency degree. Lisa, on the other hand, had finished three years of her college degree, which she soon completed after their marriage. When she enrolled in graduate school, she felt the distance increasing rapidly between herself and her husband on an intellectual level. Even though she tried to dismiss the feeling that she was somehow mentally on another level than her husband, she could not make the reality disappear. Lisa and Kevin knew how to communicate with their bodies in the beginning, but like most couples, this dropped off in importance after marriage. Although they loved each other, they found their love waning in the face of their inability to communicate and understand one another intellectually. Eventually, Lisa moved out and filed for divorce.

Sometimes couples are drawn together strictly on sexual desire. While these feelings may be very exciting, they are clearly not enough on which to base a relationship. Yet often there is the attempt to turn great sex into the romance of the year, usually because of loneliness or the fear that there will never be anyone else that it's "so good with." The error is believing that great sex lasts forever; the truth is that familiarity always leads to the challenge of keeping chemistry alive. And when other essential factors are missing, there's usually no incentive to continue. These relationships almost always fail and can be quite painful when they end.

Other couples get together because of feelings of love and attachment but without a strong sexual bond. These couples usually suffer great difficulties later, especially if they marry. Never having had a good sex life together, they will often eventually show up in a therapist's office expecting to create one. Unfortunately, all the therapy in the world cannot restore what was never there. If sex is important to even one of the individuals in such a relationship, the satisfaction level will be quite low and the likelihood of divorce quite high.

Some couples attempt to pair up strictly on an intellectual understanding. Tired of being hurt in love, they try to be totally logical in their choice of a new mate, hoping to prevent the heartache that they have suffered in the past. On paper, it looks as if they've made a good choice, but there's always the sense that something's missing. Without the vital connection at the heart, what we call love, these couples have an almost impossible task. Being in love in the beginning of a marriage provides the fuel for the engine of the relationship. We need those warm and powerful feelings to fondly remember and strive to reach again when we are in the midst of conflict. Without love, modern couples either live their lives feeling cheated of their birthright or they break up. Good or bad, right or wrong, our culture strongly emphasizes the importance of romantic love. If we don't find that, we tend to keep looking. In our culture, marriage without romantic love and chemistry carries a high probability of affairs and not much chance of success.

Five Factors: A Good Beginning. The five ingredients for a healthy relationship are *shared values, equal desire for a committed relationship,* and *intellectual, emotional,* and *sexual connections.* With all of these in place, a relationship has a good shot at succeeding. What?! You mean, this doesn't guarantee success? Absolutely not. These ingredients are necessary but are not all that a couple needs. If I could tell you what to do so that you could guarantee a successful relationship, I would no doubt be the world's wisest person. I can tell you that not having these things in place is like trying to drive your car with no gas or oil. You certainly won't get anywhere. Gas your car up and fill it with oil and you will be able to get somewhere, but you will still have to drive the car, consult a map, and take your chances with flat tires and accidents.

Remember Angela? Four months after she broke up with Jeff, who refused to commit, she sparkled as she talked about her new relationship with Jason. "We just connect so well. We talk about our feelings and we talk in terms of a future together. When he talks about his work, I can tell he's inspired by what he does, by the creativity involved, not by money and power. Also, he appreciates my desire to work and be successful. That fits with my values. And," she continued, blushing, "the sex is wonderful! I never knew a relationship could be like this." Angela and Jason clearly connect intellectually, emotionally, and sexually. And, they both want the relationship and are willing to work to make it as healthy as possible. Their values mesh. All the ingredients are in place, and what a difference it makes. Angela was finding a new level of emotional safety and security for the first time, enabling her to express feelings that she never thought she would be able to share with a man. This gives them a strong foundation from which to deal with the problems that will emerge later in their relationship or marriage.

Romance can encounter circumstances that are not foreseeable, like a car that gets a flat tire on your vacation, but with the right ingredients at the beginning, there's something worth fighting for and there's something to fight with. *Couples who share values and both want their relationship strongly, who connect emotionally, intellectually, and sexually, tend to stay together.* They may have conflict, they may encounter hard times economically or in terms of health, but they tend to work out their problems as partners. These couples stand a very good chance of being together for a lifetime. And you, as a single person, can *consciously choose* someone to have a relationship with when all these factors are in place, someone with whom there's the *strong possibility* of a lifetime relationship.

4

♥ ♥ ♥

Looking for Love

Time and again as I sit with clients who express pain about dating relationships that aren't working, I ask, "How did you decide that you wanted to go out with this particular person?" and get responses like, "He was attractive and he kept asking me out," "She was the most beautiful woman I've ever met," "He made me laugh," "I felt different with her than with other women I've dated," and so on.

"How did you decide to continue dating this person and get involved with him or her?" I'll often ask. I hear answers like, "I don't know," "We just kept going out and I fell in love," "I just felt so good with him," "I wanted to be with her," and so on. Almost never do I hear something along the lines of: "I felt attracted on several levels, but also our values are very similar. I checked him out and decided that there weren't any major red flags and that he was emotionally available for a relationship."

We now that know most men and women rely on attraction to choose potential partners, often not using logic at all. Some say that's just the way it is: You can't dictate love with logic. You just have to go with what your heart says and hope for the best.

I say that's a major cop-out. I say it is possible to choose with both the heart *and* the brain; that, in fact, a balance of emotion and logic are essential if wise choices in romance are to be made. To hold out for someone in whom all five of the necessary ingredients are present takes some work, and some of those ingredients are easier to find than others. Finding someone with whom we can connect intellectually, emotionally, and sexually is actually the easiest part, given a fair degree of social life and exposure to new people. What is difficult in today's world is finding someone with whom we share common values and have an equal desire for a relationship (both people are available and willing to commit). Add all of these ingredients together and we have the foundation for a lasting, healthy relationship. However, this is not the kind of partner we will run across every day. In order to find someone that we can have all these things with, we need to conduct more than a casual search. We must expand our social world so that we are meeting lots of new people. We need to be savvy and efficient in weeding through new people, able to quickly determine whether or not someone is a good candidate for a relationship. Later we'll explore how to take these dating steps to intensify your search for a right partner. The most important part of the search, however, is determining exactly what you want.

Beginning the Search

Let's imagine for a moment that you're about to buy your dream house, the one that you've worked hard for all of your adult life. You approach a real estate agent and you say, "Please find my dream house for me. I want it to have everything I've ever wanted in a home and be within my budget. I'm sure I'll recognize it when I see it. Let me know when you have some houses for me to look at." End of instructions. This may seem silly, but suppose that's the way you did it. How long do you think it would take your Realtor to find this house for you? A year, ten years, twenty years? If you guessed a lifetime, you're getting close. With no idea of what you want in a home, your Realtor would be show-ing you houses for a lifetime and then some.

What We All Look For.   Now think about how you've searched for your special romantic partner in the past. If you're like I was through most of my single years and like most of the singles you know, you never really stopped to think about exactly what you were looking for. You probably assumed you would "just know" when you met this person that he or she was "the one." Like our fictional agent, you could search for a lifetime and possibly not find this person. No wonder so many of us have the experience of having looked forever for the right person, only to be disappointed time and time again.

Maybe 5 percent of singles have actually asked themselves this question: What am I looking for? They may even have started a list. If so, they're definitely off to a good start. If you have started a list, you may find that you have written down or thought of things such as:

> *fun to be with*
> *likes to do the same things*
> *good sense of humor*
> *good communicator*
> *honest*
> *intelligent*
> *good personality*
> *attractive*
> *sexy*

Look over this list. Who wouldn't want a partner with these attributes? Perhaps it is safe to assume that we all want someone who has these qualities. These might be called the *minimal requirements* for a mate. Let's also assume that anyone whom you would be very attracted to would probably have these qualities, in your eyes. Remember that these are all subjective qualities, meaning that each individual might see them in a different way. I might think my friend David has a great sense of humor, while you may think his jokes are real duds. I think my boyfriend is very good-looking and sexy, but you might find him just so-so.

It's true that there are some people who have mass attractiveness appeal, who so closely fit the ideal standards of beauty for our particular culture that almost everyone finds them attractive. These are our movie stars, models, television stars, and even many of our politicians. For the majority of us, however, beauty and other attributes like the ones listed above are truly in the eye of the beholder. What is really important here is how *you* see your prospective mates.

Going for "The Package" Versus Looking at the Person. Most singles stop with their lists at this point. Because our culture emphasizes the most superficial aspects of relationships, we tend to look only for those qualities that add up to the old cliché, "a good catch." So, driving the right car, looking like a model, making a certain income, having intelligence and being successful, having a good body—these are the things that make up a good "package." If the packaging looks good and we feel attracted, we go for it. If the packaging doesn't look so great or we don't feel instant fireworks, we pass it up.

Furthermore, there's also the tendency to look at a potential partner and measure them against an internal picture of the "right partner" (which is a compilation of good qualities we've observed in significant others and people we meet), instantly judging them as right or wrong for us.

This is not only erroneous and inefficient, but we are overlooking the qualities that actually do have an influence on the success of a relationship. One of the most important is our values, or the things we hold most dear in life, without which we cannot function effectively.

"I always go for the most striking man in the room," Cheryl told me, herself an attractive woman in her mid-thirties. Invariably, she wound up dating men who wanted a more casual relationship than she did or who were unavailable in some way. With more questioning, Cheryl revealed that she really wanted a guy who would go to church with her and who shared her values about marriage and family life. Cheryl was having trouble looking beyond the packaging of the men she met (handsome and charismatic). Failing to focus on her own values and include them in her criteria of an acceptable mate, Cheryl found her deepest needs going unmet in her relationships.

We must get beyond the packaging as we look for a partner to spend our lives with. There are individual qualities and aspects of a relationship and person that are far more important than having a sparkling personality or looking like a centerfold. Wanting most of the same things out of life; feeling connected spiritually, emotionally, and sexually; having a deep sense of understanding of one another—these form a far more powerful bond than simply knowing that you got a "good catch." Catherine Johnson, in interviewing happy couples, found that the majority of them felt a ". . . sweeping sense of connection, of shared values."[1] These couples felt that they understood each other and shared much more than simple attraction. And they felt it from the beginning of their courtship. This kind of connection is the fabric from which lifetime relationships are woven.

Visualizing Your Right Relationship. Psychologists have known for years that a very powerful way to play a better game or deliver a great keynote address is to visualize yourself succeeding. By seeing yourself perform a difficult task well, you actually create the brain chemistry needed to make it happen.

The same is true for creating great relationships. It's important to visualize a successful love first, unconsciously paving the way for you to make it happen.

Before we get to specifics, it's important to take a snapshot or two of your general ideas about the relationship you want. This is an important step in finding your right partner, and it takes some time and thoughtfulness. The idea is to actually create and write down your own personal "Vision Statement" about the partner you imagine yourself spending your life with. While you could write strictly about the personal characteristics of your future mate, it is

---

[1]Catherine Johnson, "Secrets of Lasting Love," *Reader's Digest,* May 1992, p. 141, condensed from *Lucky in Love* (New York: Viking Penguin, 1992).

actually much more valuable to write about the relational aspects that are important to you. (This, by the way, is much more challenging and difficult to do and will probably require more effort on your part.)

Gina, thirty-four and divorced once, created this vision of her ideal relationship:

"I am married to a very loving man, my best friend. We are sharing a committed, healthy, nurturing, and honest relationship in which we experience joy, affection, and harmony. We communicate and work out problems and issues to solution. I feel safe with him and trust him. We share mutual respect, inspiration, appreciation, values, and trust. We have individual interests and lots of common interests. We enjoy doing things together (movies, cuddling, social events, dinners, cooking, making a home), and we enjoy making things happen together. I have the experience of nothing missing in this relationship."

How to Create a Vision Statement.   First, choose a quiet time and place so that you can focus fully. Put on some of your favorite relaxing music and find a comfortable place to sit or recline. Have paper and pen close by. Now, close your eyes and begin to imagine yourself in the future with your ideal partner. What do you see the two of you doing? How do you see the two of you interacting? What is your emotional state and mood with this person? Remember that it isn't important to see clearly what the person looks like, only the setting, the mood, and the quality of your interactions.

While you can still see the scene in your mind, take your paper and pen and begin writing, just letting the words flow. Later, you can go back and edit to make it more understandable.

Some important things to include in your Vision Statement are:

• relationship-quality words, such as love, trust, respect, honesty, nurturing, etc.

• action statements, as if you were seeing yourself and your future mate on video, such as, "We enjoy doing things together, such as playing raquetball, taking walks, cooking dinner together, listening to music"

- feeling words, such as happy, joyful, loving, safe, etc.

Take your time when composing your Vision Statement. This will form the backdrop for everything else you put together in your search for the right mate. Think of it as setting the stage for your future relationship.

Once you have written your statement, keep it handy so that you can add to it, revise it, and change things as you move out in the world on a day-to-day basis.

Taking Inventory

Now let's move on to some very important lists: your personal values inventory. After writing down your Vision Statement, you will create two lists below it, labeled Negotiables and Non-Negotiables. These will be very crucial in your search for the right partner. Both refer to qualities in a mate and in a relationship. Before you begin writing, read this section carefully.

Negotiables: Wishful Thinking

These are the wished-for aspects of a partner or a relationship but are ones you could live without if all the other things add up to what you want. They may be fanciful, or they could be practical. For example, my friend, who I'll call Jane, was puzzled about her attraction to Henry. "He doesn't look anything like the way I imagined my partner would look! He's short and has a funny-looking face. But I feel more chemistry and common values with him than with anyone I've ever met." Jane had always wanted someone tall, dark, and handsome, but this turned out to have nothing to do with what she needed to make a relationship work. Tall and handsome was definitely a Negotiable on Jane's list.

Some examples from my own Negotiables list show how this works. One is "close to the same age." Studies have shown that people who are close in age are more likely to feel a connection of similar backgrounds and common values and therefore to be more successful together. So, I've put this on my Negotiables list. But if I met someone with whom all else was what I wanted, a difference in age would not be insurmountable for me.

I also discovered that studies indicate that having a similar background (e.g., both from small towns) tends to increase compatibility. Again, I didn't rule out potential partners with backgrounds different than my own. But wanting the odds to be more in my favor, I added similar background to my Negotiables list.

Negotiables may also be fantasies that you have about your future partner, but which you know you may never find and could certainly live without. *We need to express these wishes and fantasies.* They are very much a part of us and deserve validation.

An example of a Negotiables list might be:

> *tall and slender*
> *blue or green eyes*
> *close to my age*
> *similar background*
> *shares my religious beliefs*
> *likes to read thrillers*
> *loves going to the movies*
> *enjoys the arts*
> *prefers the beach to the mountains*
> *likes to cook*
> *vegetarian*
> *works out regularly*
> *. . . and so on.*

Negotiables are the expression of your desire for the perfect "package." The qualities in a potential mate that matter most are values, but the packaging is still pretty enticing. You need a place to express these desires, even though you will learn to look past them and consider what really counts in a relationship. So, indulge in your desire for the right package, but realize that if these things are Non-Negotiable, you're in big trouble. The odds are against your finding a perfect package with a compatible partner inside.

Your Negotiables list will fluctuate with time and is the place where you record your wishes, fantasies, and wants about a relationship. While you may find someone who has these qualities, you know that the success of your future partnership with the right person will not be determined by them. These are things you can live without, some of which you know are probably quite unrealistic. Nevertheless, we all need to indulge in these fantasies, if only to be able to express them. Then we can put them back into perspective and continue to look for a partner who shares our most important values.

Feel free to play with your Negotiables, adding to the list (which may be very long) and taking items off. As you meet more new people and have more dates, this is the place where you can record your own progress away from looking for a certain package. As you indulge in your fantasies, realize them for what they are, and let them go, you will find that you are viewing yourself and others more tolerantly and realistically. You will be able to look beyond the package and explore the qualities of a mate and a relationship that actually offer the possibility of a fulfilling love.

Non-Negotiables: Building Blocks of Compatibility

These are the things that we know we can't do without in a relationship. These are not just wants. These are qualities in a mate that reflect our most deeply held values. These are things that, if we compromise on them, will cause us to lose a very basic part of ourselves. *Non-Negotiables are the building blocks of compatibility in a relationship, without which all the love, chemistry, and great packaging in the world will be useless.*

The following are examples of Non-Negotiables, most of them my own. Feel free to borrow any of these that seem right for your list. At the same time, use them as take-off points in your discovery of your own Non-Negotiables.

> *nonsmoker*
> *very light drinker*
> *drug-free*
> *treats animals and children with kindness*
> *respects and supports my work*
> *stays present to deal with conflict*
> *lives in the same city*
> *non-abusive, verbally and physically*
> *committed to personal growth (workshops, books, therapy, etc.)*
> *committed to spiritual growth*
> *handles finances with integrity (pays bills, files taxes on time, etc.)*
> *knows self and what he wants out of life (has a career that inspires him, knows where he's headed, and knows what he wants)*
> *makes a home of his dwelling place (i.e., reasonably clean and neat, comfortable; he's not ashamed to invite people over)*

When I created my Non-Negotiables list, each item was thought out carefully, based on my own self-awareness and my values. Let's look at each item, how I arrived at it, and the particular value statement each makes.

Nonsmoker. I knew I had to have a nonsmoker, not just because I don't smoke, but because I can't stand the noxious clouds or the smell. Even the sight of cigarette ashes makes me feel a little ill. Knowing myself, I realized that I would never cease in my quest to get the smoker in my life to quit. I also know that addicts don't often stop their addiction just because their lovers want them to. For me, this would ultimately prove draining and self-defeating, and would most likely alienate my partner. (For some nonsmokers this isn't true. They are able to tolerate a smoker in their environment. For this person, "nonsmoker" would not be a Non-Negotiable as it was for me.)

Value Statement: *a commitment to health and well-being in life, starting with taking care of my body.* It is difficult for me to see a smoker who is not getting treatment as having that commitment, and I want a partner who shares that value with me.

Very Light Drinker; Drug-Free. As far as alcohol goes, I knew that I needed someone for whom drinking is not an issue. If we go out to dinner and I want us both to remain sober, for whatever reason, I want a partner for whom this isn't a problem. Knowing my own tendencies toward codependent behavior (trying to change, fix, or control), I knew that a heavy drinker or an alcoholic would never work for me. I would be trying to fix or change him, driving both myself and him crazy and only adding to the problem. For the same reasons, I would obviously never be able to live with a drug user.

Again, the value statement is the same as in the first Non-Negotiable: *a commitment to health and well-being,* which, to me, is inconsistent with alcohol and drug abuse (unless the person is solidly in recovery).

Treats Animals and Children with Kindness. This is one Non-Negotiable that anyone who has pets or children should put on their list.

I've had my cat Biscuit for fifteen years, and she's like a member of my family. Pet lovers will appreciate this. It would be intolerable for me to live with someone who mistreated any member of my family, including my cat.

Many of my single clients have small children, and I always coach them to choose potential partners who are kind and gentle with little ones. This may sound like just common sense, but you'd be surprised by how many single parents become involved with people prior to finding out about their attitudes toward children. Tragically, some of these people will put their attachment to the partner above their children and will fail to protect the children.

Value Statement: *a shared respect for weaker and smaller creatures, such as animals and children.*

Respects and Supports My Work.   Some people believe that psychotherapy is a lot of mumbo jumbo and a waste of time and money. While I obviously don't agree with this view, I can respect the fact that some people hold it. However, I know that I could never live with someone who devalues my chosen life's work. I absolutely must have a partner who believes in what I do and supports me fully in it.

Value Statement: *Having self-respect and good self-esteem, I expect a partner who loves and supports me for who I am and what is valuable to me.*

Stays Present to Deal with Conflict; Lives in the Same City.   Looking over my past relationships, I realized that I had suffered agonies over men whose style of dealing with conflict was just to leave. Knowing myself to be extra sensitive to abandonment, I decided that I needed a partner who *stays put* when there is conflict and works through problems with me.

I also know that I can't tolerate a long-distance relationship (especially knowing that this kind of relationship has less probability of success). I need a partner who is accessible to me.

Value Statement: *Knowing myself and where I am vulnerable, I choose a partner and circumstance that I am more likely to succeed with.*

Non-Abusive, Verbally or Physically.   Again, this item may seem obvious. I've always known that I would never tolerate any kind of physical abuse. However, there are other kinds of abuse that are just as damaging to a relationship and to one's self-esteem. Any kind of abusive situation is unacceptable to me. (For example: chronic lateness, verbal put-downs, arriving drunk for dates, canceling at the last minute, infidelity; I'm sure you can think of many more.) Having this as a Non-Negotiable, plus my own personal growth and therapy, helps me steer myself toward men who are inherently kind and non-abusive.

Value Statement: *Having self-respect and good self-esteem, I choose a partner who will act in ways that also show esteem for me.*

Committed to Personal Growth. I've seen many couples go to battle over the issue of personal growth. I believe that there are many ways to grow personally, and I enjoy finding new ways to challenge and better myself. Some people are threatened by this approach to life and adamantly oppose going to workshops or to therapy. I need a partner who is as open as I am to personal growth and who is willing to explore the many ways of doing so, some individually and some as a couple.

When couples who are committed to personal growth hit rough spots in their relationship that they are unable to resolve themselves, it is understood that they will see a marriage therapist together as soon as possible. Sharing a commitment to personal growth gives a relationship a safety net and provides an immense source of comfort both individually and as a couple.

Value Statement: *As a human being I view myself in the process of constantly becoming a better person, more able to contribute to the world around me, and I seek and welcome the input of other resources to this process. I choose to share my life with a partner who feels the same.*

Committed to Spiritual Growth. While I don't require a partner who shares my exact religious beliefs, I do need a partner who is committed to spiritual growth of some kind and who actively seeks it in a way that I can understand and connect with in some manner.

Lots of seemingly great relationships have broken apart over the question of religious and spiritual beliefs. The breakdown usually occurs once the relationship has become more routine and the practices of each person's religion begin to interfere. Greg came from a fundamentalist Christian background, while Lucy was a practicing Christian Scientist. While neither objected to the other's different beliefs, the fact that they couldn't attend church together without one being uncomfortable became a huge stumbling block.

With differing religious beliefs, there are three things to consider: first, how the practice of those beliefs will affect your time together and your psychological comfort; second, whether you can both truly be tolerant of differences (not secretly hoping to convert each other!); and third, whether you can agree about how to handle your children's religious training.

Value Statement: *I seek a partner who respects my beliefs and whose beliefs I can be equally respectful of.*

Handles Finances with Integrity.   For me, this means someone who pays their bills, files their tax return each year, maintains a satisfactory credit rating, and puts some thought and action into financial planning. This sounds basic, but again, it's surprising how many adults of all ages don't operate with an even minimal level of responsibility with regard to money.

Typically, one of the main areas of conflict in marriage is money: how to spend it, save it, plan for retirement, handle bills, and so on. Couples with vastly different ideas about financial management will engage in endless power struggles unless one is willing to completely hand it all over to the other.

Value Statement: *Knowing my own sense of responsibility with regard to money, I must have a partner who feels the same.*

Knows Himself and What He Wants Out of Life.   For me, this means someone who has a career that inspires him, knows where he's headed with his life, and knows what he wants. In the past, I've chosen men who don't know themselves very well and therefore don't know what they want. I've discovered that this makes for a very shaky commitment. How can someone genuinely and fully commit to a relationship when they don't know who they are or what they want? How can we plan a life together when one person doesn't know what he wants and therefore can provide no input?

Value Statement: *Knowing myself and my wants and needs, I choose a partner who is equally self-knowledgeable and equally interested in interaction about life goals.*

Makes a Home of His Dwelling Place.　This means someone who is reasonably clean and neat, who lives in a comfortable environment that he wouldn't be ashamed to invite someone in to share.

This is another basic and important requirement. Mental health professionals know that how one cares for one's home reveals a lot about self-esteem and the ability to function in the world. Also, the ability to create a pleasant home environment is a cornerstone of basic maturity.

Value Statement: *Being a stable person with a comfortable home environment, I need a partner who is equally mature, stable, and self-caring.*

Knowing Yourself Is Vital.　The key to putting together a list of Non-Negotiables is knowing yourself and your basic values in life. As you can see from my personal items, you must know what is important for you in a relationship and in your life. You don't have to justify your Non-Negotiables (e.g., "I think most people want this"). It is enough to say that these are the things that *you* can't live without, and it is essential that you resolve to find a partner who fits these needs.

As you list your Non-Negotiables, keep asking yourself: Is this something that I can't do without in a relationship? Would I be making a serious compromise if I tried to do without it? If it is something that you want but could do without, put it on your Negotiables list.

If you are currently in a relationship as you're reading this, you may be discovering that you and your partner do not share some of your values. Or you may be unsure that you do. I encourage you to do this exercise with your partner: Each of you do your own lists separately, then review them together. If you discover that there are vast differences, it may help to seek out couples' counseling to find out if they can be resolved without a serious compromise to one of you individually.

If you're having trouble coming up with any Non-Negotiables at all, you may want to talk it over with a good friend or a therapist. Having someone off whom to bounce your thoughts and impressions may help you realize that you do have values but are perhaps not in touch with them.

Areas of Major Importance to Consider for Your Non-Negotiables

Religious Beliefs. Do you need someone who has the same religious faith? Some individuals know that they must have someone who shares their religious beliefs. For others, differences in beliefs are acceptable, as long as neither partner needs to change the other.

One couple I counseled hit an apparent impasse three months into their engagement, over religious differences. Keith, a devout believer in his own faith, knew that he had to have a wife who shared his spirituality with him. Charlotte, having attended Bible study with him for several months, found that she could not fully embrace the views of Keith's church. They came for therapy that night in despair, having called off their engagement but still loving each other very much and wanting to find a resolution.

With some exploration, Keith revealed that the key to his values was "spirituality." He needed a partner who was spiritual (which he considered Charlotte to be) but who didn't necessarily agree with all of the teachings of his church. Together, they realized that studying the Bible together, praying, and exploring their spirituality were what they each wanted and valued. When I next saw this couple, the engagement was back on, the wedding date was set, and both their faces glowed as they talked about their spiritual journey together.

What brought this couple back together was the realization that their values were actually quite similar, even though they had very different religious backgrounds. Both valued openness and exploration with regard to spiritual matters; neither was locked into a rigid belief system that excluded the other's way of thinking. This made for great compatibility for this couple, along with the fact that they both clearly wanted the relationship very much and were willing to work together to resolve their issues.

Children. Do you want them? Not want them? Not want to raise someone else's? Are you undecided? Knowing what you want on the issue of children is vitally important in your search for a mate. This can be a relationship-breaking issue if it goes unaddressed in the beginning.

Most important is realizing if you have strong feelings one way or the other. For instance, if you know you want children and your life would be unfulfilled without the opportunity to be a parent, then one of your Non-Negotiables will be a partner who wants children. If you know you don't want children, then the reverse is true.

Many couples are in the gray area on this issue, especially older couples who have been married before. Some already have children who are grown. You may know that you don't want to parent again, or you may be open to the possibility of having more.

Career and Family Life.   Do you need a traditional home life in which the man works outside the home and the woman inside? Or do you need a flexible home life in which the traditional roles are negotiable?

Patrick had very traditional ideas about marriage and men's and women's roles. For two years he had dated Katie, an independent, strong-willed career woman. Their relationship was fraught with difficulties. Finally, he realized that they were fundamentally incompatible and ended the relationship. Within months he met Susan, a woman who shares his values. Eight years later, their marital roles are clearly defined. Patrick works outside the home and doesn't mind being the sole breadwinner. Susan works inside the home, raising their three boys. While some may think this arrangement old-fashioned and even distasteful, it works perfectly for this couple.

Again, the important thing is finding a partner who shares your values about career and family life. By knowing what you want, and whether that is Negotiable or Non-Negotiable, you stand a far better chance of finding a partner who is compatible.

Smoking, Alcohol, and Drugs.   As we've discussed above, it is important to know where you stand on these issues. If you are abstinent and you choose a partner who drinks or uses drugs, you are at great risk of falling into codependent patterns (trying to fix, change, or control your partner). This is a formula for a very unhealthy pattern of relating.

If you come from an alcoholic family, it may be very difficult for you to feel attracted to someone who doesn't drink. Therapy helps with these issues, and there are other solutions as well.

Pamela, thirty-two, had three relationships in a row with men who either drank or used drugs or both. Coming from an alcoholic family, she found herself irresistibly drawn to these kinds of men. With some personal growth work on her part, she was eventually able to pass up the addicts she met. Jim, thirty-four and sober for the past two years, was the perfect partner for her. As a recovering alcoholic, he was safe for her to date, and he brought an understanding of the issues to their relationship. This turned out to be a very powerful and healthy bond for them both, enabling them to work together in healing their childhood wounds.

Personal Growth/Therapy. How important is it to you to have a partner who shares a commitment to personal growth? The chances are that if you're reading this book, you have some degree of interest in personal growth. Realizing whether or not you need a partner who shares this with you may be crucial to the success of your future relationship.

Eric was almost compulsive in his pursuit of personal growth. He attended workshops and had been in therapy more than once. When he met Norma, he was certain he had found "the one." They shared similar backgrounds and values and connected on all important levels but one. What they didn't share was a commitment to personal growth. In the beginning this didn't matter, as they fell in love, moved in together, and planned a wedding.

Like most couples, though, Eric and Norma eventually hit some rough waters. As they battled over the issues in their relationship, they realized that they were at an impasse. Eric begged Norma to go to counseling with him but she adamantly refused. No one in her family had ever relied on a therapist to help with their problems, and she wasn't going to be the first. This became the stumbling block they could not surmount. Their relationship ended painfully, but Eric emerged from it sure of one thing: He absolutely must have a partner who would be committed to personal growth and therapy when faced with difficult problems.

Your Non-Negotiables list should be fairly short, and it should contain items that are a statement of your deepest values. These should be things that are easily understood. If your items sound vague or difficult to define, they are probably Negotiables and should be shifted to that list. For instance, Paul commented that he needed someone who is "neat and orderly." At the same time, he was willing to allow for the possibility that someone might become more orderly as a result of living with him. Since he couldn't exactly define the term, and he wasn't adamant about a partner having this quality, I suggested that this might be a Negotiable for him.

You may find that some things that seem Non-Negotiable for you may be very limiting. For example, Richard wanted a woman who worked out as regularly as he did. Since he ran every day and worked out at the gym five days a week, this limited him to a narrow population of women. Some time later he did find someone who fit his criteria, but he found that in many other ways they were far from compatible, and the relationship ended rather painfully after a few months. Too much focus on satisfying this one need of Richard's left him vulnerable to becoming involved with women who were wrong for him in other, more meaningful ways. After all, how often one works out really has little bearing on a relationship, except in the obvious extreme. Clearly, someone who works out regularly and is very fit is going to have little in common with someone who is overweight and inactive. However, as long as both people have a genuine commitment to being healthy and fit, differences in how regularly or how often they work out can be tolerated.

If you suspect your Non-Negotiables are limiting, you may want to work with a therapist in sorting them out. You may decide that you want to stick with your criteria, knowing that this restricts you to a very small segment of the population. If so, then you know you're going to have to be very active socially in order to find these rare individuals. On the other hand, you may decide that some of your values could use some revising in order to expand your scope of possible partners. Values, of course, can change with honest introspection and the decision that those changes would benefit your life.

Compromising Non-Negotiables: Built-in Failure. Beware of compromising your Non-Negotiables just because you've met someone who doesn't meet them! This should be a very large red flag that a relationship may have failure or struggle built into it. Stella and Robert discovered in the first few weeks of their relationship that she didn't want children and he wanted them very badly. Because they were so enamored of each other, they continued dating, each hoping that the other would change their position. Four years later, they are still unable to commit to marriage because of this stumbling block. Now, however, they have built a great deal of their lives around this relationship and find themselves unable to either let go or move on.

Spend as much time as you need doing this list—remember, you're looking for a lifetime relationship, and these issues are vital to building the foundation for healthy love. Choosing a partner with whom you share your most fundamental and most important values allows you to better accept your partner as he or she is rather than having to change them to suit you. Trying to change your partner's most basic values is worse than useless. It is emotionally draining and can lead to an unhealthy, addictive way of relating.

Sharing Values—Not Being Clones. At this point you might find yourself wondering if finding someone who fits your Non-Negotiables means that you'll be looking at a mirror image of yourself in your partner! Actually, this would make for a very boring relationship, and I wouldn't recommend it to anyone.

Values are only a part of who we are. As human beings, we manifest our uniqueness in many ways. Our individual temperaments, likes and dislikes, ways of dealing with problems, and differing views of the world are only a few. Partners may share values yet have very different personalities. In fact, this is desirable if you want a relationship that carries the opportunity for growth. Healthy couples have a mix of similarities and differences.

D. E. Orlinsky asserts that each person in a love relationship brings qualities that are essential to the personal growth of the partner, thus creating an environment in which both persons can grow and experience love.[2] Differences in personality and temperament allow each partner to benefit from the other's perspective. If a couple shares values and wants personal growth, these differences can enhance their relationship tremendously.

Lori was Felix to Steve's Oscar. Compulsively neat, she was always straightening and cleaning around the house. Steve seemed unable to move without leaving a trail of litter behind him. Once they were married, however, each began to open up to the other's way of doing things. Steve became more orderly as he helped Lori clean the house on the weekends, and Lori discovered that leaving a few dirty dishes in the sink was less important than taking a walk together in the fresh air and sunshine. Both modified their behavior, each benefiting from being married to someone different.

Having interests that overlap but are not identical also allows for personal growth. Before meeting Jack, working out and being fit was always something that Becky wanted but found she had difficulty following through on. Being in the gym with all those machines was intimidating, and she was sure she was doomed to be a perpetual couch potato. Jack, with a degree in physical education and a love of the gym, turned out to be the perfect partner for Becky. With his encouragement and support, she overcame her fitness phobia. She learned to use the equipment, became comfortable in the gym, and now actually enjoys working out. This shared value—a commitment to health and well-being—gave them a foundation from which to grow, even though they were different.

Sharing values provides a stable base from which to work out differences in other areas. Having these other differences is inevitable, and having these differences is growth-enhancing if there is a foun-

---

[2]D. E. Orlinsky, "Love Relationships in the Life Cycle: A Developmental Interpersonal Perspective," in H. A. Otto's *Love Today: A New Exploration* (New York: Association Press, 1972), pp. 135–150.

dation of shared values providing a basic compatibility between two people.

Using These Lists. Look back over your Vision Statement and your lists. You might notice that the partner you are looking for is not someone you're likely to run into every day. You might say, "Maybe I'm being too picky." Your friends and family have probably already told you this. I would rather see you being a little too selective than settling for someone who doesn't share your most basic values in life. Without this kind of compatibility, your relationships aren't going to succeed or be emotionally healthy for you.

Since you are being so selective, however, all this means is that you have to meet lots of new people to choose from. If you're going to find the right partner, you need to "be your own dating service." That means taking advantage of every opportunity to meet eligible singles, discovering the ones that might be right for you, and choosing one with whom you can have a loving relationship.

5

♥　　♥　　♥

Successful Dating:
A Journey, Not a Destination

Having a successful relationship often seems like the ultimate end we are all striving for. If we believe the myths that prevail, we expect that the way to a great love lies in somehow managing to encounter the perfect person, the one and only right person for us. Just finding this one great person is the answer to the pain and frustration of all the relationships that haven't worked in the past. Nothing could be further from the truth.

The perfect partner doesn't exist, any more than a perfect person is sitting here reading this book. If you can figure out a way to be a flawless, all-loving, all-wise, all-giving partner, then you have the right to expect to find someone like that. If you're like me, however, you're a human being full of quirks and flaws. Like me, you have an imperfect relationship history, and you come from a far from perfect family. Like me, you bear the emotional scars of having lived a blemished and often painful life. Like me, this makes you a less than perfect partner.

The key to successful relationships doesn't lie out there in the "right partner." *It lies within you and me, in our own hard work to learn about ourselves and grow personally.* It lies in our ability to be realistic in our expectations of others, to communicate fully our thoughts and feelings, and to ask for what we want, realizing that we probably won't get everything we ask for.

The key to successful dating is the same. Rather than focusing solely on finding and winning over that one and only right person, use this time in your life to learn about yourself and about relationships and to become a better partner. Being single can offer a unique advantage in the pursuit of good relationships. You have the opportunity to step back, take an inventory, learn and grow, and be far more ready for a healthy relationship. Instead of leaping headlong into the next romance, slow down and make some personal discoveries that will increase your chances of having your future relationships be more successful.

By slowing down and focusing on the process of dating and relationships, you can become far more insightful about yourself. Knowing yourself first and foremost is essential to successful relating. By going out with lots of different partners for a short period of time, you can learn about communication, men and women, and what it takes to have a romance that works. You can be successful in your dating life to the degree that you are willing to fall in love with the process itself, realizing that as you do so you are becoming a better partner and therefore moving closer to the relationship you want.

There are no perfect partners. We can never find someone who is all things that we want and none of the things that we don't want. We can find someone, however, whose particular quirks and flaws we can live with. A human being, like us, with whom we share values and who is available for a relationship; a person who is willing to grow and who will be a companion on life's journey.

Just as our lives are enriched by accepting ourselves as we are, our relationships are enriched by the capacity to accept others as they are. As you can see, this is a circular process. By learning to meet and date lots of potential partners, we can become more knowledgeable about ourselves and our needs, which opens the door to more self-acceptance and acceptance of others.

In order to do this, we need to consider how to go about meeting lots of new people, for it is from this large social pool that we draw our dating partners and thus our potential mates. The larger the pool, the greater our opportunities for dating, and thus for learning more about ourselves and about relationships. Learning how to use the Dating Around stage of relationships is therefore very important.

Dating: A Lost Art

"I don't know how to date," Jill admitted. She spoke for most of the class. "I've always gone from one relationship to the next, never stopping to consider more than one potential partner at a time. How do I break this cycle?"

Invariably, in my classes and in the counseling groups that I lead, this subject comes up. Most of us have never experienced a time of life in which we dated several potential partners with no serious involvement before carefully choosing one partner with whom to move into a committed relationship.

Singles today run from one relationship to the next, never stopping to consider whether or not this partner is truly available for a commitment—or whether they themselves are. We have forgotten, or were never taught, how to date more than one partner for a short time, choosing who we really wish to become more involved with. In fact, rarely do we have a sense of having actually chosen our partners. Our romances seem to be a fluke or happenstance. No wonder we're not satisfied with them!

Even though I didn't date much in high school, I had friends who did. I remember one girl's mother trying desperately to keep her daughter from "going steady" with just one guy, encouraging her to date lots of boys. We laughed at her old-fashioned ideas then, but there was actually some wisdom in my friend's mother's ideas. She knew that we all need time to not be committed to any one person, to date lots of people, and to learn and grow from these experiences.

In our hurried, instant-gratification culture, we have fallen out of touch with the capacity to take dating relationships at a healthy pace.

Just as we try to fill our empty feelings of loneliness with too much booze, television, work, or food, we try to fill the same vacuum with hastily entered into, un-thought-out relationships. We are afraid to confront those feelings by spending a few of our Saturday nights alone with ourselves. We accept dates with people we don't like, we have sex with partners we don't love, and we trap ourselves in long-term dating relationships with people we know we don't want to marry or who will never marry us.

These periods of dating to avoid loneliness are often interspersed with periods of isolation and discouragement. If we have enough negative or unfulfilling experiences in the dating game, we may withdraw and declare ourselves out of the ring. "I've had enough of the games and the pretense," we say. Disgusted with ourselves or with the kinds of partners we've been seeing, we lose hope and stop trying.

In order to make the most of the Dating Around stage of relationships, we have to become friends with our feelings of loneliness. These feelings are an essential part of life and don't go away even when we are in close relationships. Part of the discomfort we feel is that we are much too unfamiliar with the closest person in our lives—ourselves. Being alone can be an opportunity to know ourselves better. When we are our own best friends, we feel less desperate to find someone to keep us from feeling so lonely. In fact, when we genuinely know, like, and appreciate ourselves, we can begin to actually enjoy a certain amount of time alone. Time spent with ourselves can then become nurturing and revitalizing, enabling us to bring more to our interactions with other people.

When our alone time or time spent with friends is positive rather than painful or an escape, we are more likely to take our time with the dating process. We can concentrate on our social skills, developing the ability to establish and maintain rapport, to set up and go out on lots of dates with potential partners, and to choose those with whom we might become more involved. When we sense that someone isn't right for us, we are able to pass them up, knowing that there will be other opportunities. We can feel confident that even if we don't have a date for Saturday night, there's no huge loss. If a date that appears to hold so much promise doesn't lead to a great relationship, that's okay, too. There's disappointment but not devastation. Comfortable with ourselves, we can fully enter the Dating Around stage and embrace those experiences.

In the next chapter we will be creating your own personal "Dating Game Plan"—your road map for the journey to a healthy, empowering love relationship. We will rediscover the lost art of dating. It is vitally important that you put your energy into the journey itself and trust that you will find what you want as you go, not at the end of some imaginary road. A healthy focus for this journey will involve a strong commitment to your own psychological, emotional, and physical well-being, and making that your number-one objective.

Keep your focus on what you're learning as you meet and date a variety of different people. Only by interacting with others can you learn about how you relate, what works and what doesn't work about that, and what you need to change and work on within yourself in order to have better relationships. Remember that it's not your destination that is most important, but rather what you do and learn along the way to create positive, growth-enhancing experiences.

Staying in the Game Is Primary. Remember that we're paying attention to the *process* of dating, not just whether or not we get a particular result. What we're striving for is positive, growth-enhancing experiences as we meet and date potential partners. This enables us to stay in the game. We may feel disappointed from time to time, but if we're feeling overall that we're learning and growing from our dating encounters and that there isn't too much damage, we will continue our efforts and not become too discouraged.

In my less-educated single days, I paid very little attention to my own internal gauge of satisfaction and reward when it came to the meeting and dating game. Like most of my friends, my only gauge was: Did I or did I not get asked out by that really cute guy? If I did, did he want to see me again? If he did, did he want a relationship with me? And so on.

I didn't stop to ask myself: Is this a rewarding experience? Am I truly enjoying my interactions with the men I'm meeting here tonight? Do I feel good about myself for being here? Do I feel good about my actions here? Are my positive experiences reflected in the faces of those around me? What do I really want here?

Without reflecting on my own inner experience in a social or dating situation, I was left with no way to determine what I wanted or what was appropriate for me. Thus, I often found myself in very uncomfortable circumstances, putting up with an almost nonexistent level of satisfaction and reward. Sometimes I found myself in circumstances in which I did not feel good about myself, my behavior, or the behavior of those I was with. These negative experiences left me feeling bad about myself and discouraged about dating. No wonder I frequently withdrew and gave up!

Out of sheer frustration, my friends and I occasionally went to bars. We didn't know that there were numerous other, more positive ways to meet singles. We had little hope of meeting anyone nice, and this became a self-fulfilling prophecy. At the end of the evening, we invariably went home disappointed and with a hangover to deal with the next day to boot.

Why Can't I Find Prince/Princess Charming at a Bar?

Before I present the downside of meeting other singles at bars, let me say that this is not an absolute. We all know or have heard of couples who met at a bar, fell in love, got married, and are living happily (or so it would appear) ever after. So, to begin with, let's agree that meeting in such places is not completely out of the question.

The main problem with meeting other singles in bars is the prevalence of excessive alcohol consumption. Drinking distorts reality and creates a high degree of illusion. We've all heard the jokes about meeting someone in a bar, taking them home, and then being shocked the next day to wake up with this person. Unfortunately, these jokes, like all humor, contain a good measure of reality. Even if we don't go home with someone or take someone home, the disappointment abounds when we see the person we met in the bar in the cold light of day on our first real date with them.

Another problem with meeting singles in bars is the tendency toward false personas that prevails. This may be because of the alcohol again, or it may be the carnival-like atmosphere. For whatever reason, we tend to behave differently in bars than we do in other environments. The social phobic has a few drinks and becomes the life of the party. The wallflower gets caught up in the excitement and dances with every man who asks her. Mixed messages are the rule of the day. What you see is often not what you're getting.

When we meet someone in a bar we also tend to question the integrity of the person we are meeting. After all, if they are picking us up at a bar, who else and how many have they done this with in the past? We're a little suspicious, and we sometimes carry that forward into the relationship. We forget entirely the fact that we were there in the bar meeting others as well!

Trying to meet someone with whom to explore the possibility of a meaningful relationship becomes very difficult in these circumstances. And the opportunity for negative experiences abounds. Someone who's drunk makes a pass. Someone else becomes obnoxious and belligerent. Boundaries aren't respected. Courtesies are forgotten by people who ordinarily are quite well-mannered. And, let's face it, many alcoholics hang out in bars!

Most singles openly admit that, even though they go to the bars from time to time, as a whole they don't enjoy those experiences. Some are more blunt and simply say, "I hate the bar scene!" Why do we resort to this? Because we've not made ourselves aware of the many other, more enriching opportunities for singles to meet.

The Waiting Game.   Another standard method we use as singles is the waiting game. This means simply waiting and hoping that someone will come into our lives who will be the right person. This stance is encouraged by the popular belief that we are more likely to meet someone if we aren't looking. And it does eventually work. It's difficult to live any kind of life and never meet anyone new. Sooner or later, the waiting game will pay off and we'll meet someone who is a potential partner. The problem is that if weeks and months have gone by since the last date, we often feel compelled to grab this person, whether or not they are right for us. The waiting game also leaves us paralyzed in our ability to pass up a potential partner we don't feel good about. The opportunities are so few and far between that we can't afford to say no to any that come along.

Assertive, Not Desperate.   To break out of the waiting game, we need to give ourselves permission to take a more active stance in our dating lives, realizing that conscious dating leads to conscious relationships, which are far healthier. Being assertive in looking for and creating opportunities to meet other singles is not the same as being desperate. We need to separate those two concepts once and for all. Desperation comes from a lack of abundance of dates and a lack of good feelings about ourselves. If we don't believe we deserve the best and if we believe that there are very few good people out there, we will feel desperate to latch onto any possibility that comes along. Assertiveness, on the other hand, comes from the belief that we can influence the direction of our own lives, and from the strong sense that what we want exists and that we deserve to have that.

Going to bars and playing the waiting game leaves us with feelings of frustration and a lack of positive dating experiences. Oddly enough, we don't tend to question our method or strategies. What we find is that there is a shortage of good people in our lives to meet and date. So, we erroneously conclude that:

There Just Aren't Any Nice People to Date!

The biggest mistake that most singles make is failing to have an adequate amount of positive social exposure. We go to work, go to the grocery store, go home and watch TV, play the waiting game, and occasionally go out with our other single friends to bars. We accumulate negative experiences in our efforts (or lack of) to find and meet other singles. Our world and our viewpoints become narrow. We fail to notice the people we do encounter in our daily lives, we fail to extend ourselves to meet them, and we feel frustrated that there "just aren't any nice people to date!"

Relationships Don't Happen in a Social Vacuum.   When we have limited social experience, a couple of things happen. First of all, it's easy to believe that there just aren't any good people to date out there. (How many times have you said this to yourself and to your friends?) After all, you haven't met anyone great lately, have you? Second, this becomes a self-fulfilling prophecy. Not believing that there are any available, desirable people out there to date, we stop extending ourselves to try and meet them. In so doing, we find ourselves sitting home alone, feeling lonely and discouraged. Feeling so discouraged, we lack the incentive to get out and try to meet new people. So it becomes a vicious cycle.

When we expand our social experience, several significant things happen. First of all, we begin to get some of our social needs met and this enriches our lives. We meet new people, often creating new friendships along the way. Second, as our lives fill up with people we enjoy being with, we feel less needy and less desperate for a new lover. Although friendships are no substitute for a romantic relationship, they help us feel a sense of belonging and stability, which lets us feel more whole. Feeling more whole, we have more to bring to a relationship, making us a better partner. This, then, is a positive cycle.

Abundance and Choice.   Third, as our social world expands we begin to get a sense of the abundance of good, worthy people out there. With this comes a feeling of certainty that it is possible to find a partner. This sense of certainty about our ability to find someone cannot be underestimated. It is essential that we feel this way overall if we are to exercise choice in our dating lives. I must feel sure that the right person for me is out there somewhere, that, in fact, there are probably lots of right people for me in this world, if I am to be able to pass up the ones who aren't right for me. *Until you can powerfully say no to the relationships that aren't right for you, you can never fully commit yourself to a relationship that is.* We will return to this idea again and again, because I believe it is vital to being able to have healthy relationships.

How to Enhance the Development of Meaningful Relationships

Our social lives must allow us to create the opportunity for developing meaningful relationships. We must feel good about ourselves and about the friends we are finding. Going to bars and playing the waiting game won't get us where we want to be: enjoying a rich, fulfilling life as a single person, content to choose potential partners carefully and enjoy dating until we find the right person.

Where We Go Is Important. Where we go to socialize is vital to our sense of being alive and feeling of joy in life. If we keep going where we feel bad, collecting more negative experiences, we will continue to carry a negative, limiting attitude about dating and relationships. If, on the other hand, we can begin to look for activities and events that we enjoy, where we can begin to create positive experiences for ourselves, we will find our attitudes brightening. Even more important, though, is what we do in the places we go.

Practice Versus Instant Results. This is one of the most important concepts for successful dating. A common experience for singles goes something like the one Nancy related. "After months of meeting no one interesting, my friend Sally and I decided to go to the big singles dance at my church. We got all dressed up and went, and almost as soon as we got there we looked around at the other people and began forming judgments in our minds. Right away I could tell that there *just weren't any men that were my type* there, except for this one really cute guy and, of course, he was *already taken.* We stood around for an hour or so and eventually left, concluding, once again, that there *just aren't any nice people around to date.*"

What's wrong with this picture? First of all, rather than being proactive, Nancy and Sally were passive, waiting for others to approach them. Second, and most important, they made the fatal mistake of judging men from afar, not taking the time to get to know anyone. Third, they expected too much by going there hoping to meet someone to date, completely overlooking the opportunity to meet new people and make some new friends. Nancy and Sally were looking for instant results rather than focusing on practice.

The idea of practice allows us to have a healthy focus as we expand our worlds and become more social. If I *must* find "the one" at each singles event I attend, I will find myself continually disappointed and discouraged. Remember that we're looking for a very special person who fits our Non-Negotiables and who is genuinely available for a relationship. The odds are not in favor of our finding this person overnight or at the next party.

If I instead focus on my own personal growth and development, I will always feel a sense of accomplishment. So I didn't meet "the one" tonight. What I did was expand my social world, not to mention my self-confidence. After all, I went to the party, even though I was nervous about meeting all those new people. I made a new friend. And I practiced walking up to people I don't know and introducing myself. I practiced starting conversations and building rapport. I practiced listening to my gut responses to people, building my confidence in my own intuition. I practiced self-disclosure, developing my comfort in letting myself be known to others. What a rewarding opportunity this party was!

By keeping a focus on practicing behaviors that enhance social desirability and relationship savvy, failure experiences are minimized and successes are maximized. *There is no failure in practice,* for it only builds skills and improves self-confidence. In the dating game of the nineties, the winners are those who resolve to be the best possible people they can be, to have the healthiest possible relationships, and to have the most rewarding lives possible, whether in a relationship or not. A focus on practice (I'm getting better as a person) rather than results (I've gotta have a date/lover/relationship) creates this winning attitude, which actually contributes to great results!

Focus on Real People.   We all carry mental and psychological images, or "pictures," of the ideal partner. Motion picture and music stars add to these images, and the real people we meet out in the world rarely measure up. While it's natural to have our mental pictures of the ideal partner, it doesn't work to adhere fixedly to them. Chances are, we're not going to find our ideal at the church picnic this Sunday. In fact, most of the people we meet are just regular folks, like you and me.

Rather than looking for the ideal mate each time we venture out into the singles marketplace, we can focus on meeting and interacting with the people we do meet. With no particular agenda other than to expand our social worlds and enhance our own ability to interact in a meaningful way, we are open to all kinds of people, not just the exceptionally beautiful or charming ones. Focusing on discovery about other people, finding and making new friends, and enjoying our social interactions frees us from the burden of having to find the ideal partner today. Without this cumbersome pressure, we find ourselves having more fun, reaching out to more people, and being ourselves.

Shed of those desperate longings to find the ideal mate, we relax and cease to appear desperate. Enjoying ourselves just meeting and interacting with other interesting people (young or old, married or single, available or not) actually puts us in a more favorable light. *People tend to be more attracted to those who enjoy themselves and have fun.* In fact, studies show that we are more drawn to those who are positive and interactive (even though physically plain) than we are to those who are not (even though physically beautiful).

Focus on Activities You Enjoy.   All of this is possible when we choose activities and events that we enjoy for themselves. If you enjoy sailing, look for the meetings of your local sailing clubs. If you like biking or tennis or whatever kind of sport, there are groups that get together to meet others who are interested in the same. If you're a reader, there are book clubs you can join. If you enjoy the arts, find other people who also do.

All too often as singles we neglect to develop our real interests, thinking we have to concentrate only on singles activities that are designed specifically for finding dating partners. We joke about singles "meat markets," yet we've all found ourselves going to a party or other social event strictly for the purpose of finding someone to go out with. This means that we walk in with an attitude that is less than relaxed. We've already started pressuring ourselves to get results.

On the other hand, when we go to an event because it is centered around an interest or activity that we enjoy, we are automatically more receptive and relaxed. If we happen to meet someone who's a potential dating partner, well, that's just the icing on the cake. Furthermore, in this way we are more likely to meet people with whom we share common interests.

Now, let's begin putting together your plan for creating opportunities to meet lots of people, make new friends, expand your world, and have lots of dating partners to choose from.

6

♥   ♥   ♥

Be Your Own Dating Service

In today's world, being single and trying to find the right relationship is one of the greatest challenges we face. We can't afford to leave this to luck and chance, not if we truly intend to have every opportunity to have the most satisfying relationships possible.

When we look for a new job, we don't sit at home and wish and hope for the right career opportunity to come our way—not if we hope to succeed! If we are truly committed to having a good job, we put a considerable amount of effort into it. We may begin by creating a résumé. We may go back to school to further our education, making ourselves more marketable. We will undoubtedly comb the employment section of the newspaper, perhaps contact an employment agency or hire a "headhunter." Once the research is done, we call and inquire and go on interviews.

Finding a great relationship is similar in many ways to this process. It's important that we see ourselves as desirable, that a fair number of the people we meet will find us attractive (marketability). We need avenues for meeting people (the want ads) or for getting introductions (employment agencies, headhunters). At some point, we initiate contact, ask for a date (making inquiries), and meet prospective partners in person to get to know them (the interview). When we find the right "fit," we invest more in the budding relationship (asking for the job, getting hired).

Obviously, this analogy isn't perfect. Generally we don't have as much on the line emotionally in the job market as we do in the singles market. But many of the feelings are quite similar in the beginning. Who hasn't felt rejected when turned down for a job or a date? Who hasn't wanted a particular job or person, only to be disappointed when it doesn't quite gel? Most important, isn't the quality of our personal relationships at least as important as that of our careers?

Having a Plan Is Vital.   If having a fulfilling personal life, having people to spend time with who you like and share values with, and having quality relationships is as important as having the right career or job, then it's worth having a "Dating Game Plan." This means taking the time to review current social opportunities, look for new ones, and begin expanding your world. It means taking charge of your dating life and making it what you want. It means being as savvy and assertive in your personal life as you are in your career. The following exercise will get you started in creating your new, improved Dating Game Plan.

Exercise: Expanding Your World

Without knowing where you are, it's difficult to plan where you're going. Let's begin by taking a look at how much opportunity to meet new singles currently exists in your life. For this exercise, take a blank sheet of paper and make a circle about the size of a nickel and put a "W" in the center of it, symbolizing work, whether you have a career or are in school. Now, thinking about your acquaintances at work (defined as someone you've met—you know their name, they know yours), put a small x outside the circle for each person you know. This includes same sex, opposite sex, old and young, single and married. If you work for a very large company and know hundreds of people, put "200" or "350" or some approximation of your acquaintances at work.

Now, in another area on the same page, draw another circle and put a symbol inside it to represent another social sphere of your life. Perhaps you attend a church or a synagogue. If so, repeat the same as above. Remember to include all sexes, ages, and marital status.

Continue the exercise until you have drawn a circle for each social sphere in which you participate in your life. Some categories might be clubs or organizations, the gym where you work out, your apartment complex or neighborhood, volunteer work that you do, a restaurant you go to regularly (and meet people there), school or other educational environment, and so on. Refer to Figure 6a to see how this exercise looks.

If you find that you've only drawn a couple of circles and there are very few *x*s around them, don't despair. The purpose of this exercise

EXERCISE: CIRCLES AND ACQUAINTANCES

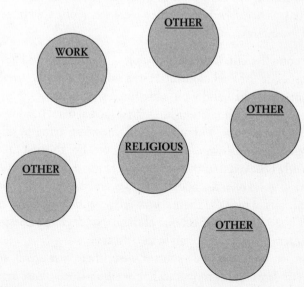

Figure 6a

is to help you be more aware of just how large or how small your networking opportunities are. We have very little influence over that which we are not aware of, so the important thing is to find out where you stand.

The first time I did this exercise, I had two circles and a total of about thirty *x*s around them. This is nowhere near enough social exposure for a single person who's looking for the love of her life! I knew I had to have more opportunity to meet new people, and I resolved to do so. One year later, I had five circles and more than two hundred *x*s around them! I had succeeded in building a sizable social network, and, most important, my attitude had changed with it.

The First Benefit: A New Attitude   Gone were the days when I went to work, to the grocery store, and came home to sit alone and watch TV. No longer did I rely on outings to the local singles bars in order to meet men. My evenings and weekends were filled with plenty of opportunities to indulge in my interests and expand my social world. I was doing things I enjoyed with people I liked and respected. When I had dates, they were more often with men who shared my interests.

The Second Benefit: Less Desperation.   No longer did I feel lonely and desperate for a relationship. I was satisfied with the friends and acquaintances I had and with a life filled with activities I enjoyed. I still knew I wanted a relationship with a special man, but I no longer felt as if I would die without it. And, most satisfying of all, I had developed a *sense of abundance* about people. For the first time in my life, I truly believed that there were lots of good people in the world and lots of good men to choose from. I even believed that there were probably lots of men out there who were potentially right for me, and that all I had to do was meet one of them. Not feeling so desperate, I was content to let this happen in its own time.

From an impoverished point of view (there just aren't any nice people to date) had sprung a feeling of abundance (there are lots of single, available, desirable men in the world). Anxiety and fear about social situations (I just couldn't possibly speak to that attractive guy) had given way to feelings of self-confidence and poise (I think I'd like to meet that interesting-looking person). The old dread about singles' events and about dating that had once paralyzed me had become transformed into a sense of opportunity for personal growth. Mistakes were no longer miserable failures but were learning opportunities.

I had experienced a positive, upward cycle of personal growth. Making the decision to expand my social world while focusing on *practice* allowed me to take some new risks. As I did so, I found myself learning powerful new information about myself and my relationships. I had to stretch beyond my old comfort zones, which gave me more self-confidence. And this was key to my feeling better about myself and more deserving of a good partner.

Where to Begin

Now that you've got a visual picture of your current social opportunities, you may want to ask yourself some questions: Am I giving myself sufficient social exposure to have a rewarding experience of single life? To develop my social skills and self-confidence? To be assured of the abundance of quality, available singles? If your answer to these questions is yes, then you can probably skip this section. If your answer is no, then read on.

For this next exercise, give yourself permission to be as creative as possible. Remember, you're doing these inventories only for yourself, and you'll benefit to the extent that you are able to explore as many options as possible. On a blank sheet of paper, write the following heading:

ACTIVITIES I AM OR COULD POTENTIALLY BE INTERESTED IN

Then just brainstorm, listing as many as possible. Did you always want to take a French cooking class? List that. Do you like sailing? Write down "find a sailing club." Do you love reading? List "book club or reading group." Are you a professional in your chosen career? Write "attend professional group meetings." And so on . . .

It's important to list as many ideas as possible, not necessarily singles-oriented activities, but things that you might find enjoyable in and of themselves. Enlist the aid of a friend to brainstorm further. Remember, you don't have to *do* all of these, you just need a lot to choose from.

Next Step: Get Started. Once you have listed as many as you can, take a moment and look over your list. Now, choose one item that you are willing to take action on within the week and put a star by that item. That's all you have to do to get started. Make a commitment to get started this week on one of your ideas for expanding your social world. Maybe you've chosen pottery making, and getting started would mean calling the various community colleges in your area to find out about the schedule of pottery classes.

Remember, you are making a commitment for yourself, to begin expanding your social world and creating positive experiences in your life as a single. You may find a certain amount of discomfort in doing this. If that's true for you, it's normal. In fact, the less accustomed you are to taking assertive steps to meet new people and enjoy new activities, the more uncomfortable this is likely to be for you. Even if we are doing something positive for ourselves, it will feel scary if it is new and different.

A Special Note to Workaholics. At forty-two, Sheila was looking back on her life and wondering if it was time to make changes. For fifteen years—ever since her early, short marriage had failed—she had put almost all of her energy into her career. She was very successful, but she was also not very available for a relationship. Spending 80 percent of her time traveling and fourteen-hour days at work even when not traveling didn't leave much room for another person in Sheila's life, let alone a significant other. At the same time, she had put stock in her self-esteem mostly through her work. Yet she was missing something, something that only a relationship with a special other human being could fulfill. Sheila had some difficult choices to make.

If you can identify with Sheila, then you're probably wondering where you're going to find the time to do all this social stuff. Like Sheila, you, too, may have some difficult choices to make.

The truth is that if there's no time for socializing, then there's probably no time for a relationship. It is a myth that we can do it all. The reality is that there's only so much of our time and energy to go around, and we have to choose where to make that investment. If you have invested primarily in your work and very little in relationships, including friendships, then you will have to make substantial changes in your approach to life in order to have a life more filled with people you like and to find a special person.

The offices of therapists are filled with single people who reach midlife and realize that they've made no room for a loving relationship in their busy lives. The reasons for this are many. Working to the exclusion of all else may be a way to avoid intimacy; it may be an escape from painful realities, such as loneliness, fear, grief, or despair; it may be an attempt to build self-esteem from the outside (I must be worthy if I can do so much or make so much money).

Of course, these attempts are doomed to failure; eventually, even the busiest person slows down enough to feel the painful feelings and the loneliness. And true self-esteem is never built on accomplishment but is a function of inherent self-worth.

Sometimes confronting those feelings provides the incentive to make changes. If that's you, then read on. The chances are that if you're reading this, you're at least considering a rearrangement of your priorities. And, like Sheila, you'll face many challenges and the changes won't be easy. But, like so many others who have chosen to open up the room for relationships in their lives, you may well discover that the rewards are plentiful and are worth the effort.

Outside Our Comfort Zones

Remember that in order to be satisfied and fulfilled in our lives as singles, we need to concentrate on personal growth, trusting that at some point we will find a partner. And in order to grow, we have to take some risks—try some new things, experiment with new behavior. This means that we will be moving outside our "comfort zones": our familiar and previously determined lifestyles and behaviors. If I have been accustomed to going to work every day at 9:00 A.M. for the past five years and I change to a job that requires me to arrive at 8:00 A.M., I'm going to feel uncomfortable with my new schedule for a while, even if I'm getting paid twice as much at my new job! Eventually, though, if I stay with my new work schedule, I will adjust, and one day a workday that begins at 8:00 A.M. will be comfortable, the "norm," to me.

Animal behaviorists know that if a dog, for instance, is kept in a small cage all of his life and then one day is let out, he will shiver in fear of the outside world and will actually seek to return to the cage! Even freedom is uncomfortable to those who have been confined.

With human beings the same is true. Even positive, growth-enhancing change is frightening because *all* change is frightening. Psychologists know that human beings seek a balance of change and stability. If that balance tilts, as it does when we are faced with too much change too fast, we become stressed and will seek to return things to stability, or "the norm." On the other hand, if we have too much of the same-old-same-old, we will become bored and will seek change, something new. Therefore, without being conscious of it, we all seek a balance of stability and change, which keeps us in our comfort zones.

My friend Susan was sharing with me about the changes that had recently taken place in her and her husband's lives. He'd been transferred in his work (a change that was positive and full of new potential for him), they'd moved to a new city (that they both liked), and they were building a new home (that they absolutely loved). Their kids were adjusting well in school and had already made new friends, and Susan had experienced a severe stress reaction. "Out of the blue, I started feeling so jittery and nervous, I thought I was going to have to call my doctor for some Valium!" she told me. After a few days of this, she made some dietary changes that relieved the nervousness.

But we both were struck by the paradox. We tend to associate negative stress reactions with negative life events, yet Susan's experience tells us that even positive experiences, when there's a lot of change in a short period of time, can produce the same reactions.

Expect Some Discomfort.   As you begin making changes in your life as a single, seeking out new activities with new people, you will find the balance of stability and change in your life tilting toward change. This will inevitably feel uncomfortable, so the best thing to do is to welcome those feelings of discomfort; this only means that you have stepped outside your comfort zone and are heading for some positive, growth-enhancing experiences. Remember that discomfort isn't always negative. It can just as easily mean that you're taking positive action in a new way. Someone wisely said that if it makes you uncomfortable now but you know it will bring you joy in the long run, then it's good for you.

Creating Your Dating Game Plan

What do dating services provide? For a fee, they provide you with introductions. That's all, regardless of any claims to the contrary. Even so-called matchmaking services are capable only of making educated guesses about who is a potential partner for you, and they frequently foul up.

"I couldn't believe it. I had asked for a nonsmoker and here he was, blowing smoke in my face at the dinner table. I asked for someone with at least a bachelor's degree and this guy didn't even finish high school!" As Shelly described her date, provided through a matchmaking service that charges a rather hefty fee, her words were punctuated by her obvious indignation. "And, to add insult to injury, he revealed that his divorce wasn't even final yet. And I specifically asked for someone who had never been married, like myself." Even with obvious factors that are quite easy to screen for, this dating service had wasted Shelly's time, money, and emotional energy.

Matchmaking services make mistakes, which isn't surprising. After all, they are run by human beings like ourselves. They're limited, as we all are, in their capacity to accurately determine in advance which two people will be suitable for one another. They can look over interest surveys and even values inventories, and match people on the basis of that kind of information. Even with in-depth profiles, they will never be able to predict one thing: the chemistry that either happens or doesn't happen between two people. Chemistry, or the intellectual, emotional, and sexual connection that just seems to occur between certain people, is as unpredictable as falling in love. None of us knows when or where it will strike. We can't make ourselves fall in love any more than we can force ourselves to be attracted to certain people.

Before meeting someone new, we can never know ahead of time whether that chemistry will happen. We take our chances when we go on a first date with someone. In fact, the mystery of whether or not it will occur is what makes dating so exciting—and sometimes scary.

Another thing that dating and matchmaking services can't do is screen for people who are dishonest about their lifestyles and personal relationship histories. All they have to rely on is the questionnaires that people fill out and their word that they are accurate. Again, that is something we all take our chances with.

The main thing that these services do, therefore, is provide introductions to new people. It's up to us to screen potential partners for compatibility (our Negotiables and Non-Negotiables) and to take our chances that even if all the factors match up there may be no "spark."

Create the Magic.   Being your own dating service simply means finding your own ways to meet and date prospective partners. It means getting introductions for yourself, because this is, after all, the first step. But being your own dating service offers much more.

Being your own dating service means expanded social horizons, finding enjoyable activities filled with likable people. And it means looking for opportunities to "network" within those social circles, thereby obtaining introductions to new, potential dating partners. Along the way, of course, opportunities abound to practice social and relational skills, to grow and become more attractive, to find desirable partners, and to make lasting friendships. Even better are the chances to learn more about oneself, about relationships, and about creating healthy connections with other human beings. This is the magic of being your own dating service: not just getting introductions to potential dating partners, but the opportunity for life enrichment and personal growth, something no dating service can provide.

Networking: Friendships and Dates

Now that you've listed some activities that you could enjoy, and you've gotten started by committing to take action on one of those, let's fast-forward to the future. Let's say you're at your pottery class, which you've been attending now for a few weeks. You've made an effort to meet some of your classmates. The odds are, you've gotten mixed responses. Some people are friendly in return, while others are more reticent. You've been able to strike up a rapport with a couple of your classmates, or maybe only one. You've made plans to attend an art show outside class time and you had a good time with your new friend.

At some point you feel comfortable enough to share relationship stories with your new friend. After this, you open up and tell your friend that you're actually interested in meeting new people to possibly date. One way you might express this would be:

"You know, Martha, I'm really interested in meeting someone new, possibly to date. Do you happen to know anyone who's late thirties to forty-something and into personal growth, and who's available?" Your friend says, "As a matter of fact, I do know someone like that." And you say, "Well, if you're comfortable with this, I'd like to ask you to pass my card along and just tell your friend that I'm someone single looking to meet new people and that I'd like to meet them for lunch or coffee one day, if they're interested." At this point you hand over your phone number and your friend pockets it.

Your new friend now has a choice: to either pass the number along or not. If she's uncomfortable with doing so, she can always just "lose" your number or forget about it. There's no pressure for her to have to do this. (It's important not to pressure people beyond this point.) Or, she may give your number to her other single friend, who then has a choice. He or she may or may not call you; there's no pressure on anyone in this way.

What makes this way of getting introductions work is that it's really up to the other people to act only if they choose to and are comfortable doing so. There isn't the discomfort that's often associated with contrived "I'll fix you up with my friend" scenarios, wherein your friend would be expected to arrange a meeting for all three of you. Your friend is only briefly in the middle, and then it's up to the other party to do what's comfortable for him or her. Your risk is minimal because you don't lose anything, even if the other person never calls.

Trigger the Relationship Connection.   The other important thing is to be sure to say something about what you're looking for. This serves two purposes: It does some preliminary screening for you, and it triggers people's memories of their friends and acquaintances. Saying "Do you know anyone you can introduce me to?" is too broad and general. With that question, most people don't immediately come up with a face and a name. Saying "Do you know someone who's maybe late thirties to mid-forties, into personal growth, and is available?" is likely to trigger thoughts of specific people your friend knows.

The idea is simply to get introductions to lots of new potential dating partners, to *network*. Be careful that you don't invite your friends and acquaintances to be your dating service for you. Remember that the responsibility (and opportunity) for screening new people lies with you. No one else can even begin to know who is right for you.

"But I don't want to waste my time getting introduced to people who aren't right for me" is a common concern I hear. We would all like guarantees that everything will turn out great, but this just isn't possible unless you have a good crystal ball! It's not important to know ahead of time if this person is going to be your dream date. It's much more important that you have the opportunity to meet someone new and practice your dating and relationship skills.

Practice Is Most Important.   Remember that we're not trying to find Mr. or Ms. Perfect. The goal should be to get as much practice as possible in meeting new people, getting to know them, and determining if you want to invest more time and energy in a possible romance. This focus allows a more casual, less desperate approach to people and to new relationships. It allows you to focus on personal growth rather than the ups and downs of whether or not your first date in six months led to the romance of the century!

If practice is the goal, then I will welcome the opportunity to meet the friend of a friend. This doesn't have to be "the one." This may simply be someone with whom I enjoy a lunch date and decide to go no further. Or, this person may turn out to be someone with whom I share lots of interests but no sparks. I may also meet someone who ends up being a lifelong friend. Or, I may make a friendship that one day takes a romantic turn. Any way, I don't lose. Even if I never want to see this person again, I had the practice of taking some risk in asking for an introduction, setting up the date, and interacting with someone new, paying attention to my feelings and thoughts about the date. This way, I was able to improve my relational skills and build my confidence in my ability to sense and determine who is or isn't right for me.

So far, we've looked at expanding your world through finding activities you enjoy with people you like. This creates the opportunity for making new friends, providing the kind of fulfilling life experience that only the magic of friendships does. With these new friends and acquaintances, doors are opened to meet the people in their lives. The doors are opened through your own assertive behaviors: being honest about the fact that you're looking for a relationship and asking for introductions. Viewing these introductions as opportunities to make new friends and to practice relational skills, these experiences add to the developing sense that dating can actually be fun and rewarding! With that sense, a more positive attitude prevails and desperation begins to wane. Now, let's "up the ante" and add some new challenges to your Dating Game Plan.

The Meeting Game

If you wanted, you could stick with the networking that we've covered so far, and that would be enough to eventually bring you in contact with your right partner. Or, you could add something else to your plan, something that requires a little more risk-taking. Of course, along with the risk comes even more opportunity for personal growth!

Singles Events: More Ways to Meet.   Another way to meet potential dating partners is to participate in activities that cater mainly to other singles and to learn to introduce yourself to new people at those events.

This way of meeting potential dating partners is a lot riskier, mainly because of *the rejection factor.* Everyone at a singles event knows that people are there looking for potential dating partners. Hearts beat faster, palms sweat, we get tongue-tied, or we come across as too slick. Embarrassment may send us in retreat. All the words fly out of our heads and an awkward silence ensues. No matter how many times we play the game, it's still difficult. Standing face to face with a stranger and trying to establish rapport, determining whether you're interested in them and vice versa, and then making an overture that could lead to a date is probably one of the most intimidating experiences we could ask for! Because if the person doesn't return the same level of interest, it feels like a personal rejection. And, let's face it, that hurts! Most of us don't welcome chances to feel rejected. In fact, we usually do everything we can to avoid it.

Both men and women take the risk of rejection when they approach a stranger in this way. Even though men generally have more practice in making the first move, I'm told that it never gets any easier no matter how many times they do it. For women, the role may be more passive, but it's still a challenge to try to send the right signals so that he'll know she's interested, and if he doesn't respond, it still feels bad. Additionally, the rejection factor gets stronger with higher levels of attraction. The more I'm drawn to you, with butterflies in my stomach and sweaty palms, the more it hurts when you don't return the feeling.

Dealing with Rejection: The Key to the Meeting Game. Remember from chapter three that chemistry, the intellectual-emotional-sexual connection between two people, is a vital part of a healthy relationship. You might also picture this as the sparks that fly between two people who are strongly attracted to each other. Romantic sparks cannot be explained with any degree of scientific accuracy. Most psychologists agree, however, that they are the result of meeting someone who offers the opportunity to resolve old childhood issues. Biologists tell us that they have evolutionary significance: Strong attraction binds two people together long enough to allow procreation to occur. Of course, we aren't necessarily thinking about any of that when we feel these sparks!

Whether or not attraction and chemistry occur between two people is not something that can be dictated. It is, to put it quite simply, a fluke of nature! We cannot force it to happen; it either does or it doesn't. Once it happens, we cannot simply erase the feelings, although we certainly have choices about whether or not we act on those feelings.

It would be nice if chemistry always either happened mutually or not at all. Unfortunately, it often happens that one person will feel strongly attracted to someone who doesn't feel the same way in return. This is one-way chemistry and is no picnic for either party. In order to avoid feeling devastated when this occurs, it's vitally important to remember that *it's not personal!* Whether or not someone is attracted to you is no reflection on your worth or inherent attractiveness. It is, in fact, merely an accident over which you have no control one way or the other.

Have you ever met a couple and found one of them to be so unattractive (to you) that you wondered what the other person saw in them? And yet, their partner was obviously madly in love. This is because the psychological factors that dictate attraction are far more powerful than physical beauty or the lack thereof. (It must also be said that we know that people tend to seek out partners who are of the same general level of attractiveness, by the standards of our society.)

If you're like me, you fit in with the majority of ordinary people who are liked by some and not by others, who are attractive to some and not to others. This is reality: Some people will be attracted to you and some will not. A very small number of them will be powerfully attracted. Learn to not take it personally and you will free yourself from the self-consciousness and fears of rejection that, to one degree or another, stymie most of us socially.

Practice: Setting Reasonable Goals.   Playing the meeting game is much easier when we take the pressure off ourselves. Rather than hoping to find "the one," get a date, be the life of the party or the belle of the ball, resolve instead to make this a growth-enhancing experience.

Pick an event and set a goal, for instance: I will meet two new people tonight. Not necessarily people I want to date, but people who seem interesting and likable. As part of this goal, I will practice introducing myself to people, establishing rapport, and getting to know new people. I will also practice noticing my gut responses to people and situations, paying attention to interactions that I am uncomfortable with, and taking care of myself at all times. I will practice being myself, letting down my guard, and reminding myself that it's okay if someone doesn't return my interest.

As you can see, the possibilities for your goals are endless and are an expression of your desire to grow.

These kinds of goals are practical, realistic, and, best of all, *you can't fail!* Remember the importance of collecting positive experiences. With goals that you have control over, goals that enhance your personal growth and eliminate failure, you can't help but feel good about yourself at the end of the evening.

Dating and Matchmaking Services

These services, as we've already discussed, are never a complete answer because of their limitations. They can, however, provide an important, though not essential, part of your Dating Game Plan. There is a difference between them that needs to be discussed.

Matchmaking services attempt to make discernments about who is and isn't right for you. They look at the information they gather about their members and make judgments, pairing certain individuals who they feel would be compatible. You are then given a choice about whether or not to meet the person whose name is given to you by the service.

There are several problems with this approach: 1) the presence or lack of chemistry can never be predicted, so even if you're completely compatible on paper you may have absolutely no sparks and therefore no possibility of a romance; 2) there may be members of the service whom you will never get the opportunity to meet, who may be perfect for you but who don't look compatible with you in the eyes of the service; 3) because matchmaking is so time-consuming and limiting, you aren't likely to get very many introductions, so the return on your investment may be minimal.

Dating services, on the other hand, operate in an entirely different fashion. These services allow you to make as many choices of potential partners as you want. You are responsible for looking through books or watching videos, reviewing the profiles, and selecting those whom you wish to meet. If you utilize the service well, you can literally have as many dates as you have time for.

The advantage of dating services is that you are in control of the choices and the quantity of potential dates. Therefore, you have the opportunity for lots and lots of practice at meeting, screening, dating, and relating. There are no limits imposed by anyone else.

A matchmaking service is not a bad option, if the fees are very reasonable. Because you will get fewer introductions, it doesn't make sense to pay thousands of dollars for this kind of service.

Regardless of which you choose, matchmaking and dating services can be a part of your Dating Game Plan, but should not be the entire plan. Singles who participate in rewarding activities and belong to a dating service are usually more well-rounded people. Those who never socialize except with the latest person they've picked from their dating service are usually more limited in relational skills.

The value of expanding your world and networking can't be emphasized enough, as they are the keys to being less desperate and therefore able to draw in other happy, fulfilled people.

Your Dating Game Plan

Let's review your Dating Game Plan so far:

- Expand Your World: Activities You Enjoy
  Look at social circles
  Brainstorm new activities
  Commit to one and follow through
- Network: Friendships and Dates
  Make new friends
  Ask for introductions
- The Meeting Game
  Attend singles events
  Practice introducing yourself, developing rapport, etc.
  Keep the rejection factor in perspective
  Set reasonable goals

7

❤   ❤   ❤

Better Choices, Better Relating

Beth, forty-one and divorced, was describing her way of looking over potential dating partners. "Basically, I go out a couple of times with them, and if there's anything about them I don't like, I don't go out with them again. I just don't have the time to put up with men who aren't what I'm looking for." She was matter-of-fact and conveyed the no-nonsense attitude that had gotten her the success she enjoyed in her business. As we reviewed her personal history, however, Beth's voice softened, and there was a slight quiver in her chin from time to time. An abusive father, an alcoholic first husband, and a business partner who ripped her off had all left Beth more than a little wary. "I guess I'm wondering if I'm a little too hasty in my judgments," she finally confessed. We agreed that the term "gun-shy" fit her very well when it came to men and romance.

Joel, thirty-one and divorced twice, had the opposite problem. "I don't even think about who may or may not be right for me," he said. "If she's interested in me, I go for it. Sooner or later we end up involved, and I don't even know why I'm with the lady I'm with." When he talked about his most recent breakup, tears ran down Joel's face. All of his relationships had ended for basically the same reason:

Joel was unable to assert himself with his partners. If they wanted to know how he felt or what he wanted, he couldn't answer. When the time came for important decisions (e.g., getting married, buying a house), he left everything up to them. Joel's partner, wanting to feel that he *was* a partner, felt like she was grasping at air in her efforts to know him and feel his presence in the relationship. She felt frustrated, and Joel, unable to express his needs and feeling dominated, felt more and more trapped. Eventually the women left, triggering his fears of abandonment, which drove him straight into the arms of the next available woman. Joel came to realize that his compulsiveness in going from one relationship to the other came from his deep-seated fears of being alone and facing the real issue in his life: discovering who he really is and what his needs are, and rebuilding his self-esteem.

A Balance of Good Judgment and Choice

For different reasons and in differing ways, both Joel and Beth were having difficulty making good judgments about their potential dating partners. Beth's fear of being abused made her avoid relationships altogether. She couldn't make good choices because she was really choosing to be alone. Joel's fear of abandonment and aloneness drove him to jump from one relationship to the next, with no sense of choice. His was a choice to *not* be alone, regardless of the consequences.

Making Good Judgments. Both Joel and Beth had some work to do before they would be able to approach dating with balance: being able to make good judgments without being too judgmental. Their stories tell us something about what is needed in order to do this. First, a certain amount of caution is needed, but deep-seated fears of intimacy will make us too cautious. Thus, our fears about intimacy and the risk it entails must be confronted. Second, an active dating life is wanted, but not when it is an avoidance of the fear of loneliness. In order to be able to turn away partners who are inappropriate, the fear of being alone must be confronted. I can't say no to you if I'm afraid you're my last chance or if I can't face going home alone tonight.

Avoid being only a critical observer. Being proactive when you have an opportunity to meet people is essential. Standing on the outside at an event and looking in is no place from which to make judgments about potential dating partners. Being passive and waiting for others to make the moves is no way to build self-confidence. Judging people by the "package" they present (looks, clothes, and other superficialities) is no way to practice establishing rapport and building relationship skills. It is also very inaccurate; people are almost never what they appear to be at first glance, and we do ourselves and them a disservice by not looking beyond initial impressions. After all, Cinderella only looked really good at the ball! If the prince had judged her by the way she looked at home, he would have missed his true love.

The Freedom to Choose.   Looking over potential dating partners with a balance of wanting a relationship yet being okay alone allows a healthy perspective. With an active social life filled with friendships and rewarding activities, meeting new people is just one more opportunity to expand my world. You don't have to instantly be "the one" for me, and I can take my time getting to know you. I can afford to be discerning about whom I spend more time with, choosing only those people with whom I feel comfortable. I no longer have to settle for dates with just anyone in order to avoid loneliness. This easygoing view of dating removes a lot of the anxiety and discomfort. I am more attractive because I'm having more fun! And I am empowered because I have the freedom to choose my potential partners carefully.

What to Look For

With an expanded social world, more opportunities to date, and a sense of choice, the next step is knowing what to look for in potential dating partners. The key word here is *potential*. At this point there is no way of knowing for sure who will be a compatible partner and who won't. At this stage of the game—just meeting new people—the main objective is to practice noticing whom you might ask out or accept a date with. This doesn't mean you have to make a move. It means that you're paying attention to your own internal monitors about what you feel toward certain people.

Attraction: The First Ingredient. The very first thing you'll notice is that some people are attractive to you and others aren't. Remember that this is a fluke; it's not something you have any control over. You do, however, have control over whether or not to act on your feelings of attraction.

For instance, you might feel attracted to Joe, but upon meeting him you discover that he's living with someone and is therefore unavailable. If the attraction is very strong, you might be tempted to believe that you have no choice: If he's interested, you're going to respond. But, of course you do have a choice. No matter how powerful an attraction is, we always have the choice to not act on it. And we must be able to exercise that choice in circumstances such as this that might be a setup for a lot of emotional pain later on.

Attraction is the first feeling that draws us to others. Without it, we might never get far enough to even form relationships. So it's a good thing that we're wired in this way. Attraction is a force of nature that has very little to do with physical beauty. As we've said before, psychological and emotional factors are by far the most potent determinants of attraction. This is a very strong force indeed, and it's worth understanding since we are all subject to its power.

There are many kinds of attraction. There's the attraction that says, "This person is my kind of person, and I'd like to be friends." This kind of attraction often takes place in the beginning of new friendships that don't hold the possibility of romance, such as between same-sex heterosexuals or opposite-sex persons who already have a satisfying, committed relationship with someone else. Attraction of this type lacks romantic overtones, although in many ways it may be as intense as a romantic attraction.

Another kind of attraction is the one that says, "I feel drawn to you and I want to spend time with you, but not necessarily in a romantic sense." This often occurs between opposite sexes and leads more toward friendship. However, at some point in the future, this kind of attraction can grow into romantic love.

Yet another kind of attraction is the one that says, "I feel drawn to you, it feels like romance, and this could be the start of something really special." When mutual, this kind of attraction obviously often leads to marriage.

Then there's the kind of attraction that says, "Wow! I see stars when I look at you, and all I can think of since I met you is you!" This kind of attraction (when mutual) leads to intense romance and often marriage, although it also can be like a giant firecracker that goes off and then fizzles or leads to an unhealthy, addictive romance.

Do You Feel What I Feel?   Attraction may or may not be mutual. Sometimes only one person feels any attraction at all. Sometimes one person feels one kind of attraction and the other person something else.

When Linda first met Bob, she felt immediately that he was the one for her. She began falling in love with him from the first date. Bob, on the other hand, felt drawn to Linda but not as powerfully as she was to him. He knew he wanted romance, but not necessarily a committed relationship or marriage. Bob and Linda dated for two years before Bob's feelings caught up with Linda's. When he realized he was in love with Linda, he proposed and they were later married.

When Larry met Nicole, he felt his heart leap, and nothing was ever the same after that. Certain that Nicole was the one for him, he pursued her with phone calls and flowers. Nicole did not return his feelings. In fact, she felt so little attraction to Larry that she couldn't even accept a date with him. Their would-be romance never had a chance.

Gina and Ted met in night school and wound up studying together. Their friendship slowly turned to romantic interest and later to love. Their feelings for each other were mutual and, luckily for them, always on the same level. They were married on the anniversary of their first date.

Cindy felt drawn to David from the beginning but not like he was to her. David was sure he had found his future wife and refused to give up, even though he knew the feelings weren't mutual. Cindy went out with David because he was fun to be with and she genuinely liked and cared for him. But she never felt that he was "the one." David believed her feelings would grow if he was persistent enough. After six months, Cindy dropped David for another man whom she subsequently married.

As is painfully evident, there are no guarantees when it comes to attraction and love. We take our chances; sometimes it works and sometimes it doesn't. Knowing the different levels of attraction, we can make better judgments about potential partners.

Rather than taking an all-or-nothing stance (either fireworks go off immediately or I pass you by), we can afford to enjoy different levels of attraction, realizing that those feelings may grow one day. Since attraction is a potentially bonding force between people that has very little to do with physical beauty, we can focus more on getting to know people, which is where real relationship potential lies.

As our stories illustrate, it's vitally important that we be able to feel and understand our own and other people's levels and kinds of attraction. If I feel strongly attracted to Jim, yet I sense that he doesn't return the same level of feeling, I have some choices to make. Do I go out with him and hope his feelings grow? Do I pass him by because I'd rather not get involved with someone who may never feel the same intensity that I feel? These are sometimes difficult choices, but as with all important choices in life, the more we understand about relationships and about ourselves and what we want, the better our choices are going to be.

Who's Attractive and Who's Not?   Realizing that levels of attraction vary between people and over time, a more casual approach to looking over potential partners is possible. Maybe no fireworks will go off immediately, but that's okay. Practice noticing the different levels of attraction that you feel for different people. Go ahead and meet them even if your interest is only mild. Focus on practice and it won't matter if the relationship leads to something more.

Practice just making friends and noticing, too, how your feelings of attraction may grow with time. First encounters do not immediately have to lead to dates, and first dates don't have to lead to true love. Sometimes it's enough to just get to know someone without the pressure of an intense romance. Often this leads to friendship with the possibility of a romance later on.

By the same token, some people you meet are simply not attractive to you at all, in any way whatsoever. *It's okay to not date someone you feel no attraction to at all.*

Lucie, twenty-seven, joined a dating service and found that sometimes she was picked by men for whom she felt no attraction. Not wanting to hurt their feelings and thinking she should give everyone a chance, she accepted dates with these men. Invariably the dates were awkward, especially at the end when she was asked out again. Being too careful of hurt feelings, Lucie often pretended to have a good time even when she didn't. This charade was convincing, and she found herself with an even greater problem: How do I say no to a second date when I've already accepted one that I didn't want and acted like I enjoyed it when I didn't?

In her therapy, Lucie learned to be more honest with herself about her feelings and to reflect those feelings in her behavior. She learned that most people would rather be turned down than go out with someone who doesn't want to be with them. It was a great relief for Lucie when she finally gave herself permission to say no to men she wasn't attracted to.

Lowering Expectations Without Compromising. Remember that "picture" of the ideal partner that we all carry around? The one who looks like our favorite movie star and has all the most positive characteristics of our favorite people? When we set out to meet and date new people, there's a natural tendency to compare everyone to this internal picture. To some degree, this is healthy. It is a way of saying,

"I am a worthy person, and I deserve to have everything I want in a partner and in a relationship." This is a positive self-esteem message and in that sense is generally good.

But when we take it too far, comparing new people to our internal pictures of the ideal partner can also be limiting. After all, how many men look like Mel Gibson, have Ross Perot's billions, and have the sensitivity of a Father Knows Best? No man can measure up to icons such as these, nor would he want to. Women also resent being measured against *Playboy* centerfolds and movie stars. As human beings, we all want to be appreciated and loved for who we are. Most of us have real flaws and shortcomings. So our pictures of the ideal mate should be considered in just that perspective: They are fantasy images we enjoy, but we don't expect the people we meet to measure up to them. It's sort of like that old admonition about people in glass houses. If we don't want to be measured against perfect standards, it would be wise to not measure others against them.

Healthy Love: The Ingredients, Not the Package.   Remember that the ingredients to a healthy, happy relationship have very little to do with images, real or imagined. Attraction springs from a psychological and emotional kinship, love grows in an atmosphere of mutual love and respect, and commitment is a choice that two people make based on an equally strong desire for a relationship together. Shared values provide the foundation for all of these factors to flourish, and honest, open communication is the fertilizer that nurtures a budding relationship and allows it to grow and thrive over the years.

This can happen no matter how poor you are and no matter how plain you or your partners are. Likewise, no matter how rich and beautiful people may be, without the ingredients for a healthy love there will always be a despairing search for a lasting relationship with the right partner. All we have to do to see this is to follow the romances of some of Hollywood's most beautiful and famous.

So allowing attraction, in many forms and at many levels, to grow over time (or noticing that sometimes it doesn't) is essential to the kind of self- and other-awareness that needs to be developed in the dating game. Refraining from holding people up to impossible standards and taking the time to appreciate them for their own unique, attractive qualities isn't a compromise. Rather, it is a realistic approach that will open the door for lots of real people to come into your life; these are people you might otherwise have passed up, one of whom may be the right person for you.

How Do I Relate with You?

Attraction is the recognition of a feeling that draws people together. Relating is the behavior that turns that feeling into a possibility. This means communicating on many different levels: eye contact, body language, and conversation. How we go about this process of relating is vital to the development of healthy relationship possibilities.

Dan wanted to ask a question in the workshop, not just of me but of the other women present as well. "I was just wondering," he said, "if I could get some feedback about what kind of lines a guy could use with women that they would like." A groan was heard from several of the women present. Katie responded out loud and the other women nodded their agreement. "The answer is, no lines," she said. "The truth is, we can tell if it's a line, and that turns us off."

I asked the class what kind of communication is unspoken but heard when someone hands us a line. "That they have an agenda," they answered, meaning that something is wanted from the other person but rather than ask for it outright, the line is used to try to manipulate in order to get what is wanted.

In the movie *Tootsie,* Dustin Hoffman's character, Michael Dorsey, made this classic error. In a moment of candor, Julie, his love interest, shared to his alter ego (Michael disguised as a woman) that she would prefer a man who would be honest and straightforward about wanting to go to bed with her rather than playing so many games to get her to have sex. Later, dressed as himself, Michael approached Julie and repeated the same line to her, word for word, that she had said she wanted to hear. Of course, it sounded exactly like that, a line. Offended and outraged, she poured her drink on his head, leaving him astonished and more bewildered than ever!

What Michael didn't understand yet was that simply parroting words wasn't the same thing as an honest expression of feelings. Julie wanted a man who would be honest with her. If Michael had been honest, he would have told her that he was pretending to be her female friend in order to get close to her because he wanted a relationship. He would have said that he was falling in love with her and hoped they would be lovers someday. That wouldn't have been a line. In the last scene of the movie, he finally dropped all his facades and spoke from his heart. This got through to Julie, and they strolled off together, bantering like good friends, with the *possibility* of love at last established.

Remember the myth that dating is separate from relating? The reality is that how we relate from the first moment we meet someone lays the foundation for the future relationship, if there is one. Our first encounters with people can either set the stage for open, honest communication or they can signal a pattern of game playing and manipulation. The one creates the possibility of a healthy, lasting love, and the other results in destructive ways of relating that lead to emotional and psychological pain.

It is essential, therefore, that the focus in the early stages of the dating game is on practicing healthy interpersonal relating skills. Practice being as open as possible with new people. Practice speaking from the heart. Notice if you have an agenda with someone (e.g., I want a date or sex with you), and practice being honest about that. Practice *being here now,* which means paying attention to your gut responses to people and situations.

What to Say First: Establishing Rapport.   When an approach by or toward a new person is made, we all want to know what to say first. A friendly "hello" is always a good opener rather than some cute remark such as "hi there" or "hey babe." "Hello" never offends anyone, unless the intonation carries an added meaning. It's important to remember that *how* you say something is every bit as important as *what* you say. After saying hello and introducing yourself, the next step is establishing rapport.

Rapport is the sense of connecting with another person, through shared feelings, shared experiences, and even shared interests. Generally, most people like to begin with shared interests and progress to shared experiences and, later, to shared feelings. This is because the level of intimacy increases, respectively, as we move from interests to feelings. With a higher level of intimacy comes a higher degree of vulnerability, which may not be comfortable right away.

Thus, beginning with conversation about the interest you happen to be sharing is usually safe and comfortable. John might ask Mary, "So, how long have you been a cycling enthusiast?" Tina might ask Jay, "How did you get interested in computer graphics?" and so on. Try to ask open-ended questions that begin with *what* or *how.* This allows for a more elaborate response than a simple yes or no question such as "Isn't this class great?" or "Do you like water skiing as well as snow skiing?"

If you're at a singles event where the sole purpose is to meet potential dating partners, your opening lines are more difficult. Avoid clichés and focus instead on your own feelings. In this case it's sometimes best to jump all the way to shared feelings, such as "I enjoy these parties, but I get really nervous about trying to meet so many new people. How about you?" or "I wanted to meet you because you look like an interesting person, but I felt kind of shy about just introducing myself to you. I'm not very good at this, are you?" and so on. When feelings of shyness and nervousness are spoken from the heart (again, not just parroting lines), it can be very disarming and engaging. Often this will lead to a similar disclosure on the part of the other person, and then you'll be off and running.

Body Language: Other Signals. Besides conversation, there are other ways of letting people know that we're interested. Eye contact and body language sometimes speak far louder than the words coming out of our mouths. The study of Neuro-Linguistic Programming (NLP) shows us how to establish rapport simply by mirroring another's stance. If you tilt your head to one side and smile, and I tilt my head the same way and smile, we feel a certain connection. If you want to add body language to your repertoire of rapport-building skills, there are numerous books on NLP that you can find at your library. The danger, however, might be relying on the use of this or any other rapport-building skill strictly as a way of disarming other people rather than learning to be more honest and self-disclosing yourself.

Rapport Is More Art Than Science. There is no way I can teach you with a book how to establish a connection with a stranger in five minutes or less. For one thing, some people are innately better at it than others. My friend Ben was one of those people. He had the ability to connect with people in an incredibly short period of time. He seemed to look right into my heart from the first moment I met him. Most of Ben's acquaintances considered him to be one of their best friends. When he died suddenly in an accident, he left many grieving people behind. Hundreds of people came to his funeral, all of them feeling as though they'd lost their best friend. I felt a keen sense of loss, which was almost embarrassing considering that I'd known Ben for only a few months. But he had a special gift with relationships, and I realize now that his ability to put me at ease instantly, along with his caring and compassion, created the kind of close feelings that normally take much longer to develop.

Unfortunately, we're not all like Ben. In fact, few of us are. But, depending on our goals, we all have the *capacity* to develop our interpersonal skills to a greater degree. And there is only one way to do this: yes, through practice. *Learning to establish rapport is more art than science and can only be developed through the practice of the art itself.* If I want to be a good portrait artist, I can read all the books in the world and they won't substitute for simply picking up the brush and applying paint to the canvas, and doing that time and time again, honing and perfecting my skills as I do so.

While developing the art of rapport, keep in mind that what you're really working on is healthy relating. This isn't just some skill that you can pick up overnight and use to get what you want, like classes on how to make a sale. Slick lines and a charming persona won't get you a healthy, happy relationship with the love of your life. Honesty, openness, and integrity in your dealings with other human beings will. Knowing the right thing to say won't lay the foundation for a good relationship nearly as well as will connecting with people on a feelings level.

Social Shyness. If you're like most people in the world, getting out and mingling socially is a lot more easily said than done. Adele's story is a good example.

When Adele first came to see me, she had so much social shyness that she was barely able to interact with other people in public. What we discovered was that she was carrying around several universal misperceptions that were inhibiting her ability to relax and be herself.

The first error most of us make about socializing is thinking that others are focused on us, paying attention to every detail of our appearance and manner. Second, that they're busy judging and assessing our social performance. Third, that they're obviously far better than we are at these things and that we therefore can't measure up. This all rendered Adele so self-conscious that she was unable to relate effectively with new people.

With some re-framing, she was able to set aside these misperceptions and resolve to "try on" some new ideas about socializing:

• The truth is, everyone else is just as focused on themselves, wondering: "How do I look? Am I acting like a jerk? Will anyone like me?" and so on.

• With all this focus on themselves, they had no time to focus on her and how she was doing. This is like driving on the freeway: It takes all of one's focus and attention just to get oneself down the road and stay alive, leaving no time to worry about anyone else and where they're going.

• The most important thing is practice; what Adele is learning and how she's growing.

She also resolved to try new practices, such as:

- *Noticing* people who look interesting
- *Approaching* people who look interesting or sending signals so that someone else will approach (eye contact, open body language, smiling, saying "hello")
- *Establishing* rapport—starting with the here and now ("How often do you come here? What do you know about this group/class/organization?") and building toward personal information (work, hobbies, ever been married, kids, etc.)
- *Paying attention* to her own gut response (Is this someone I want to be around?)
- *Moving on* if her gut says she doesn't want to be around that person
- *Saying no* to those who aren't right for her or whom she doesn't want to be with

With her new focus and with these new steps, Adele's social life changed tremendously. A couple of months later she glowingly reported her social success at a gala event that she had helped put together. "I had so much fun just meeting new people and talking to them. I wasn't afraid at all. It was such a difference from a couple of months ago!"

Practice, Practice, Practice. While you're venturing out into the world, meeting new people and opening the doors to a larger social life, now is the time to develop your self-awareness and relationship skills by practicing all the techniques and new ways of relating discussed. Now, watch your fun and enjoyment in the dating game grow. As you develop your relating skills and feel more confident, watch yourself relax more with new people. As you become more honest and self-disclosing with people, watch your relationships become healthier and more rewarding.

Bill's eyes sparkled as he talked about the woman he'd met over the past weekend. "I actually managed to strike up a conversation and just enjoy chatting with her, without feeling like I had to make a move on her. This is a lot different and feels a lot better than my old ways—either too shy to speak or just blurting out some kind of come-on." Bill was developing the art of healthy relating, and the pride he felt in himself was obvious.

Relating in a healthier, more open way with others takes practice because it isn't the natural inclination for most of us. We've been inundated with messages that say that the key to romance is in applying the right makeup, wearing the right clothes, the right perfume or aftershave or deodorant, and having, of course, the perfect hairstyle atop the sleekest body. Hollywood movies and television follow up these messages with portraits of dramatic entanglements between beautiful people who only have to walk into a room in order to find romance.

With so much pressure to focus on our appearances and our snappy dialogue, we've gotten out of touch with just being ourselves and trusting that *that is enough.* My best friend, David, called one day sounding discouraged about his efforts to find someone for a relationship. "I don't know if I'll ever be able to compete with these other guys," he said (referring to the other men in the dating service he had joined). "They're doctors and lawyers and they look great besides. How am I going to measure up to that?"

"David," I said, "it doesn't matter about these other guys. What matters is the person you are inside. The right woman for you will respond to *who you are.*" And I thought to myself, "Why is this so difficult for people to understand?" I knew the answer, of course. It's not easy to drown out all the old programming and discover the reality of what makes good relationships.

The most effective way to do that is to get out there, practice meeting new people, noticing your levels of attraction and theirs, listening to your own feelings, and practicing self-disclosure when appropriate, thereby establishing rapport and creating friendships. As your life fills up with people who like and enjoy you for who you are, you will gradually put away your concerns about doing and wearing the right things, and you'll be more comfortable with who you are and more certain that that truly is more than enough to attract the right partner.

Your Dating Game Plan

Let's review your Dating Game Plan so far:

- Expand your world by doing activities you enjoy
- Network for friendships and dates
- Get involved in the Meeting Game
- Maintain a balance of good judgment and choice
  Be less critical
  Remember that you have the freedom to choose
- Know what to look for
  Understand attraction
  Remember the ingredients for healthy love
      —focus on the whole person, not just the package
- Practice healthy relating
  Establish rapport
  Open up to others
  Be yourself

8

♥　　♥　　♥

Who Makes the Moves?

Welcome to the world of modern dating! In case you haven't noticed yet, there are no longer any rules for the dating game. Virtually anything goes, and probably will. But it wasn't always this way. At one time, there were unspoken "rules" for dating and courtship. Even though everyone didn't necessarily adhere to them, they at least established general parameters that we could take for granted. This lent a certain amount of clarity to the game of courtship. But those rules have all gone by the wayside, leaving many of us confused. Love, romance, and relationships are more mysterious than ever. How did this happen?

Love and Marriage: Changing Roles

In the process of moving from a rural, agriculture based society to an urban, technology based one, our families, men's and women's roles, and, in particular, the pursuit of love have changed dramatically and permanently. The roles that men and women used to take for granted are no longer so clear. The assumption that men will take charge in love and in the family is only partly true. Yes, there are still men and women who prefer this arrangement, but there are many more who are striving for a more egalitarian relationship, one in which men and women function as partners and as equals.

Of course, equality isn't a thing, like a sofa, that you can just go out and obtain. It is a state of being that arises from the context of the culture (for example, compared with American women, Iranian women are still in a kind of slavery), the belief systems of the two individuals involved, and the definitions of their relationship. Given that we're in America and we know that equality between men and women is, at the very least, something we're striving for in this culture, there are still individual beliefs that come from our family backgrounds that must be considered.

Those who come from strictly role-defined families (he brings home the bacon, she cooks it) may decide that they'd like to continue those roles in their own families. Others want something more in keeping with today's values (they both bring home the bacon, and who cooks it depends on whose turn it is that day). The vast majority of today's couples have a sort of blend between the old and the new. One of the great challenges of today's relationships is figuring out where you both stand on these issues and negotiating your roles so that the beliefs of both of you are honored.

The Pursuit of Love

With marriage relationships and the roles they define in a state of flux, it's only natural that the old rules for dating and courtship have gone by the wayside as well. Men used to be expected to make the first move and to pursue women. Courtship was watched over by older family members and chaperones. Premarital sex was considered taboo (although this didn't prevent it from happening!), and women were not ever supposed to do the pursuing. They were supposed to be passive and virtuous, waiting like little flowers in the field for men to come along and pluck them. To repeat an old cliché, we've come a long way!

One of the most dramatic changes in the dating game is our expectations about who does the pursuing. Like modern marriage, modern courtship is now much more egalitarian. It is now *really okay* for women to make the first move in dating!

It is okay in the sense that society, as a whole, no longer frowns on women being assertive in the pursuit of a mate. At least theoretically, women do not have to wait for men to ask them out for the first time. No more waiting by the dance floor, praying that some guy will come along and ask for a dance. No more standing on the sidelines casting meaningful glances in the direction of attractive men, hoping that they'll catch a clue and approach. A woman who's willing to be assertive has the right to approach a man, initiate contact, and even ask for a date.

This doesn't mean that we have completely abandoned our old standards. In my workshops with women we explore this issue at length. Most women admit that even though they know logically that it's now okay to approach men, the old messages are still resounding unconsciously, messages such as "only loose, amoral women pursue men," or "only a woman who's desperate would ask a guy out." For some women, these messages came directly and verbally from Mother. "I was taught that a girl never calls a guy," Cathy shared in the workshop. "My mother would have killed me if she thought I was doing that. I always had to wait for them to call, and even now, I can still hear my mother telling me that only 'bad' girls pursue guys. To this day, I hang back and hope that the man I'm interested in will take the initiative."

So, even though we live in the age of women's liberation, we are still fighting ingrained stereotypes about men and women and their roles. This means that there will inevitably be a certain amount of confusion in the dating game. One distinction that helps is knowing the difference between *assertiveness* and *aggressiveness*.

Assertiveness Versus Aggressiveness.   Traditionally, men have been defined as aggressive and women as passive. Obviously, this has never been really accurate. There have always been passive men and aggressive women. Until recently, there hasn't been permission for men and women to exhibit varying degrees of passivity and aggressiveness. Again, we're trying to change from the old to the new, and we're finding that there are no easy solutions.

With the changing roles in our culture, we are now considering new words like *assertiveness,* which is supposed to be a gender-free term, one that infers a state somewhere in the middle of the extremes of passive and aggressive. But what do these terms mean within the context of relationships?

Aggressiveness in a relationship means taking action in pursuit of a goal, *without regard to the effect on the other person(s).* For instance, a woman might pursue a man who is already involved with someone else, regardless of how intrusive this feels to him.

Another example might be the guy who approaches a woman who's obviously not interested, inundating her with calls and flowers even when she clearly tells him to go away. For any woman who's been through this, it is a frightening experience. This kind of unwelcome aggressiveness is clearly the behavior of someone who lacks insight into and compassion for other people's feelings.

Passivity in a relationship means taking no action in the pursuit of a goal or on one's own behalf, even when something is wanted. Passivity is the manifestation of the *lack of belief in one's own power* to have an effect on other people or in one's own life. A passive stance is often the downfall of a potentially good marriage. Individuals who feel that they have no power over the direction of their relationships may do nothing to ask for what they want or to request changes. In the meantime they collect all sorts of negative evidence about their partners until one day the passive partner simply walks out.

Assertiveness in a relationship means taking action on one's own behalf or in pursuit of a goal, *while taking into account the effect on the other person(s) involved.* Linda noticed an attractive man while eating lunch in the cafeteria one day. Mustering up her courage, she approached him and introduced herself. Realizing her intent, he showed her his ring and told her he was married. Slightly embarrassed and apologetic, she withdrew. Linda respected the boundary that this man established with her, even though she was very drawn to him. At the same time, she didn't allow the incident to dissuade her from being assertive in approaching and meeting new men. Linda believed in her own personal power to influence the direction of her life and knew that she was capable of finding the right man for a relationship. She was persistent yet sensitive to the feelings and boundaries of those she encountered, taking those into account in her behavior.

Passivity leaves us stalled at the starting gate of relationships. Aggressiveness is offensive and potentially hurtful. Assertiveness moves us forward toward our goals in a way that invites healthy relatedness.

Practicing Assertiveness. Both men and women need an assertive stance in the dating game. An active pursuit of social connections, friendships, and potential dating partners will promote a feeling of influence and personal power. With a focus on practice, it's really okay if an overture doesn't lead to a date or a friendship. The important thing is exercising the capacity to take control of your life, taking little steps to expand your world and your dating possibilities. At the same time, you're learning more about yourself, developing your relating skills (listening, self-disclosure, developing rapport), and reinforcing your self-confidence.

One of the things I usually ask the men in my workshops is how they feel about women asking them for dates. Unanimously, they all say that they like it. Most men have felt the burden of making all the moves for too long. They welcome the chance to feel how flattering it is to be asked out. They enjoy the good feelings of affirmation that being approached by someone else brings on.

Of course, we should bear in mind that men who participate in workshops such as mine are more likely to be open to personal growth and to more equal male/female relationships. Certainly, not all men will welcome advances from women, just as not all women will be comfortable making the first move.

If you're female and single, however, and you don't want to grow old waiting for the right person to come along, then being the one to make the first move might be worth considering. Maybe developing some assertiveness skills and learning to approach men will move your search for the right partner ahead at a faster pace.

If you're female and already consider yourself assertive, you may still be concerned about those men who would not welcome your making the first move. Nancy spoke for several of the women in the workshop when she said, "I don't have any problem being assertive, but what if it scares the men away? What if they think I'm desperate and are turned off by that?"

"Are you desperate?" I asked her.

"Certainly not!" she said and laughed. Nancy was quite attractive, intelligent, and successful. Of course she wasn't desperate. I pointed out to the women, "If you're not desperate, and it's part of your personality and the way you live your life to be assertive, and some guy doesn't like that, what does that tell you?" After a moment's reflection, Nancy said, "That tells me he's not the right man for me. That tells me to move on and keep looking."

Because many women have been showered with messages to be passive in life and in love, it's quite tempting to adopt a demure stance in the dating game, to sit back and let men make all the moves. The message that men receive from that is, "I'm content to let you be in charge." The problem is that sooner or later, an assertive woman's true personality will emerge. This can lead to a lot of power struggles in a relationship as she tries to assert herself (which is how she really is) and he tries to keep her frozen in his original image of her as compliant and passive.

Creating healthy relationships means allowing ourselves to be our real selves from the very beginning. If you're naturally assertive, why not bring that into your dating life? Why not be your real self, dynamic and assertive, and let those who don't like that fall by the wayside? The right person for Nancy will be someone who appreciates her for who she is, someone who values assertiveness in a woman, who treasures her real personality. Even if you're not naturally assertive but value equality in a relationship, then practicing these kinds of skills will bring you closer to a mate who shares your values.

Making the Moves

Now that you have given yourself permission to be assertive in your dating life, where do you begin? Since we're practicing assertiveness, it's important to take into account the responses from other people in order to determine how much interest they have in us. Remember that communication is the fertilizer that nurtures our relationships from the very beginning. I may be saying, directly or indirectly, "I'm interested in you." But what are you saying to me?

Reading Signals. Communication isn't just words and language, with ears to receive. We communicate in hundreds of small ways, in addition to what comes out of our mouths. We must be able to read these other, more subtle forms of communication in order to have a successful dating life and to create happy, healthy relationships.

Eye contact (or the lack thereof), body language, and verbal responsiveness, including intonation and inflection, are all signals that give important information about someone's level of interest.

If I approach you and begin a conversation with you, what signals would you send if you weren't interested in connecting with me? You might avoid eye contact, even to the point of looking past me as if searching for someone else. You might stand with your body slightly turned away from me. You might cross your arms (signaling that you're closed to input) or glance at your watch periodically (signaling lack of interest). In response to my efforts at conversation, you might give monosyllabic answers. You might attempt to kill the conversation by not assuming a role in the dialogue.

On the other hand, if you were interested in connecting with me, what kind of signals would you send? You would probably stand with your body facing me and your arms uncrossed. You might make lots of eye contact (signaling interest) and respond to my conversation animatedly, nodding your head, laughing, and smiling. You would engage in a dialogue with me, responding to my questions with self-disclosing answers.

When approaching someone new, it's important to take these signals into account. When someone responds with little interest, as in the first scenario, what does that tell you? Possibly that person is already involved with someone and not seeking a new relationship. Possibly they are not feeling drawn to you (remember to not take that personally!). Whatever the reason, the bottom line is: *It's time to move on!* In your search for the right partner, it's wise to keep moving on when people don't respond. Why waste time trying to connect with people who aren't interested? Learning to read these and other signals will help you conserve your energies for those who are real possibilities for friendships or dates.

Sending Signals.   Not only is it important to be able to read other people's signals, it's also vital to pay attention to the signals we send out. If you want to convey interest, use body language that shows interest. Lots of eye contact, an open posture, really listening and responding to the other person all send the message "I'm interested in you." If you're working to get better at your social skills, these are the kinds of signals you need to practice.

Discerning to whom you wish to send "I'm interested" signals and to whom you don't is also important. A friend of mine laughingly told me the other day that she was often accused of being a flirt. "I don't really mean to flirt," she said. "I'm just very friendly, and I laugh and have a good time when I talk to men. Sometimes they think that means I'm interested." In this case, no harm was done because my friend is married and definitely not looking for a romantic relationship outside that. She also has very clear boundaries and is quite capable of making them known.

If you're single and in the dating scene, however, sending "I'm interested" signals to anyone and everyone can invite a lot of unwanted attention. It's okay to reserve your brightest and friendliest smiles for people you have a real interest in connecting with. It's okay to be merely polite to those you don't.

What if you're sending "I'm not interested" signals to someone else and they fail to read them? This often happens in the dating scene. Remember that most people are there with the expectation of meeting someone. This can lead to feelings of desperation that may color people's perceptions. Some people are less adept at reading body language and subtle signals. He might be thinking, "Since she hasn't screamed, thrown up, or run away, she's probably interested," while you are thinking, "Why doesn't this guy see that I'm not interested?" In this case, you need to know how to politely disengage from people you aren't interested in.

Saying No to the Wrong Ones

Molly told a familiar story. "There I was, trying to find a way to meet someone nice, when this really obnoxious guy came up to me and started talking to me. I instantly didn't like him and I wanted him to go away, so I tried to let him know I wasn't interested. I didn't make eye contact, and I was really cool to him, you know, just barely polite. It seemed like the harder I tried to shake him off, the more he clung to me. I ended up trapped next to this guy for the whole evening, and of course no one else ever asked me to dance. I was so angry."

Both men and women have had experiences like this. In Molly's case, she was suffering from a common disease in our culture. I call it Too Nice Syndrome (TNS). Most of us have been conditioned to be too nice, to be afraid to say no, and to be far too cautious about hurting other people's feelings. (In its more severe form, we call this co-dependency, which is the compulsion, regardless of the consequences, to take care of someone else at our own expense.) In the dating world, this results in the inability to set boundaries (which we'll explore further in the next chapter). We hang out with people we don't like, as Molly did, and wonder why we feel so bad at the end of the evening.

I asked Molly why she allowed her evening to be ruined in that way. "Because I didn't want to hurt his feelings," she answered, looking miserable. Like so many of us with TNS, she was willing to sacrifice her own potential to have a fun evening in order to spare a perfect stranger the discomfort of learning that his companion just wasn't attracted to him. Keep in mind that this was probably no picnic for him, either. How much fun could he have been having with someone who refused to look at him and answered his questions with monosyllabic answers? Meanwhile, both were missing out on other opportunities to interact with people with whom they might have connected.

Being too nice, not saying no when it's appropriate, doesn't spare bad feelings. In fact, it leaves both people feeling bad. I have counseled people on both sides of this scenario, and no one walks away feeling good. Paul's story might very well be that of the guy Molly described. "I just don't understand it," he said, looking downcast and puzzled. "She was friendly and nice, and we talked for two hours at the dance. When I asked for her phone number, she gave it to me. Then when I called, I got her answering machine. I've left messages for two weeks, and she doesn't call back. I've given up. But I just don't understand why she would be so nice to me and then just ignore me later." Paul was genuinely hurt and confused by the apparent mixed messages he had received from the woman he'd met two weeks earlier.

In our efforts to be too nice, we inadvertently end up causing more pain, both to ourselves and to the people we interact with. And if we can't be honest with ourselves and those we meet, we may very well have difficulty with being honest in our relationships. TNS doesn't stop once we meet someone we like. It continues in other forms as involvement deepens, such as the inability to express anger and other negative emotions or to set boundaries.

To set a healthy course for relationships, we need to learn to be more honest with ourselves and those we meet, right from the beginning. Practicing saying no to people who don't interest us lays the foundation for difficult communications when the right person does come along. Practicing walking away from the wrong people allows you to develop strength in taking care of yourself and being more authentic.

It is really okay to tell someone, "I appreciate the opportunity to talk with you, but I'm not interested in going any farther than that.

I'm really here just to mingle and meet lots of new people. So, if you'll excuse me . . ." If someone doesn't catch your nonverbal signals, it's okay just to tell them you're not interested. If you don't want to be that direct verbally, it's okay to simply say "nice meeting you" and *just walk away*. Remember that the other person is there to meet someone who is interested in him or her, and while it may sting a bit to be rejected, that's much better than wasting time on a lost cause.

Sending the right signals creates the freedom to choose people with whom you want a connection. Reading other people's signals can save time and energy. Being direct when you're not interested allows you to move on and meet the people you want to meet. Being assertive takes you down the road toward the love you're wanting. Practicing these skills builds confidence in the control that you have over your life and your relationships.

New Roles: New Dating Skills

Because there are no longer fixed roles in the dating scene, both men and women must define for themselves the behavior that's best for them. Assertive women can be themselves early in relationships by asking for dates. Women who want to be assertive can learn to be and can get better at it by practicing these skills. Men who don't want to make all the moves can relax a little and allow women to do some of the pursuing. But what are the appropriate moves?

Asking for Dates. Remember that to be your own dating service you must focus on practicing good relational skills—making friends and building confidence in yourself and your ability to choose better relationships. From this perspective, you can afford to relax and enjoy meeting and getting to know new people, whether you're at a singles party or your book club meeting. You don't have to ask for a date the first time you meet someone you're attracted to. In fact, timing is very important in the pursuit of romantic love, and that begins with knowing the best time to ask for a date.

Some relationships need to develop slowly, beginning with friendship. Maybe it's enough to go to brunch with the gang and sit near the person you're attracted to, taking the time to get to know him or her. If you're in the same cycling group, you can afford to find out first if the object of your desire is friendship worthy. In cases like these, it's sometimes best in the beginning to refrain from a formal date. Why not take the time afforded by being part of a mutual social network, getting to know the person through your common interests? Again, you can set your own pace, since there are no real rules. Of course, the person you're interested in may ask you out first! If you feel comfortable accepting the date, then go for it.

Knowing whether now is the time to ask for a date is a judgment call that isn't always easy to make. Attraction can happen instantly with a complete stranger, but that doesn't necessarily mean that the way is clear for a date. The instant after meeting someone new is sometimes too soon to ask someone out or to accept an invitation. Consider the following scenario.

Terry and Suzanne first met when their church threw a big singles get-together. As they stood there talking, Terry felt attracted to Suzanne and wanted to ask her for a date. She seemed interested in him, although it was difficult to tell. She was friendly to everyone. Thirty minutes after meeting her, Terry said, "How about going out to dinner sometime?" Suzanne, wanting to be polite and not wanting to hurt Terry's feelings, responded, "Okay, sure." Terry asked for and got her phone number. Suzanne, not wanting to hurt Terry's feelings by telling him that she wasn't interested, accepted his invitation even though she wasn't sure she wanted to. The next day he called to confirm their plans. He got her answering machine, left a message, and waited for a return call. Two weeks later he was still waiting, even after leaving two more messages. Suzanne, after some reflection, realized that she didn't really want to go out with Terry and decided that he would get the message if she just didn't call him back. Terry was hurt and confused. She accepted a date with him and then completely ignored his calls. What happened?

Several things may have happened. Perhaps Terry failed to read Suzanne's body language, overlooking important clues about her level of interest. Possibly he moved too quickly for her, asking for a date so soon after meeting her. Maybe she felt pressured to say yes rather than being given the space to ask herself what she really wanted. How could Terry avoid this in the future? Let's look at a new scenario.

Terry and Julia meet for the first time at the church dance. Terry realizes he's attracted to Julia but isn't sure how she feels about him. He has some choices to make. He can: 1) do nothing but spend some time talking and dancing with her, and look forward to seeing her at other church functions, taking his time getting to know her, or 2) after talking and dancing with her, say, "I've really enjoyed spending this time with you and would like to get to know you better; maybe we could go to lunch or meet for coffee one day soon, if you'd like. Here's my phone number. You can call me if you're interested, or we can just talk on the phone, whichever you're more comfortable with."

Option number one gives Terry a chance to get to know Julia a little better before asking her out. He can spend more time talking with her, getting a sense of whether or not she's attracted to him and whether or not she's available. He can also explore the possibility of a friendship if that's more appropriate.

Option number two makes a clear statement of interest but doesn't pressure Julia to respond. There's also no pressure for her to give out her telephone number to someone she doesn't know, which she may be uncomfortable doing. This is a nonintrusive way to assertively express interest, while leaving the other person a way to save face. Three days later, when he calls her back, she can gracefully decline, having had time to think about what she wants, or she can accept without having felt pressured. If she elects to take his number and decides she doesn't want to pursue the relationship, she can simply throw the number away. Again, no pressure.

Most important, this kind of nonintrusive approach sends a message of respect and non-desperation. By moving more slowly and giving the other person a way out, this says that I care enough about myself to only want a date with someone who's interested in me. And because I care about and respect myself, I of course respect you enough to allow you time to reflect about what you want. I am secure enough to be okay if you decide you're not interested. I don't have to rush you, fearful that I may lose my one big chance. I know that there are lots of wonderful people, many of whom would love meeting me.

How do you make these kinds of judgments? The most important information you have is your basic gut feel for a situation and an interaction with someone else. There are always choices to be made, including some that I haven't thought of here. Some questions to ask yourself in order to choose what to do when asking someone out are:

1. Have I known this person long enough to make a choice about asking them out? If not, how might I get to know them better in a nonthreatening way?

2. What kind of signals am I getting from this person? If I'm not sure, how can I explore that further without putting undue pressure on them or me?

3. Will I have other opportunities to get to know this person better as a part of our social network? Would I rather do that or go ahead and ask for a date?

4. How can I express interest without putting the other person on the spot by expecting an immediate response?

5. How am I feeling about being with this person? Am I relaxed and calm or do I feel afraid of losing my chance for a relationship? If I'm feeling a little desperate, how can I take the time to get my perspective back, rather than come across that way to my prospective dating partner?

I'm sure that you can come up with other questions to help you sort out the appropriate action to take in a given situation. There are no right and wrong answers to these questions. The important thing is that you're being *aware* of your feelings, thoughts, intentions, and wants. By being aware, we make better choices. Of course, you may not have time to think all this through! In that case, an offer of a phone number may be all that is needed. Later, you can sort out your feelings before you call the person or receive a call from them.

Accepting Dates.   When you are being approached (whether you're male or female), there's lots to sort out in order to make an appropriate response. Looking back at Terry and Suzanne's scenario, what happened with Suzanne? Suzanne, another victim of TNS, was afraid to tell Terry she wasn't interested. Perhaps she failed to read his signals, which might have told her how drawn he was to her. Realizing how attracted he was, she might have prepared herself mentally for the possibility that he would ask her out. Or, she might have chosen to simply move on and gracefully exit rather than waste her time and allow him more opportunity to frame an invitation. When he did ask her out, she might have given him a more straightforward response rather than leading him on. How could she avoid this in the future?

Paying attention to Terry's signals, Suzanne would have realized pretty quickly that he was interested in her. She then had some choices to make: 1) She could have decided that since she wasn't interested, she would simply move on. She might have said something like, "It's nice meeting you, Terry. I'm going to go look for my friends now. Maybe we'll run into each other another time. 'Bye," or maybe, "Thanks for taking the time to talk with me. I've got some other people to talk to. See you later," or some version of the two. This option would have allowed her a graceful exit. While Terry might have felt a little rejected, she would still be doing him a favor by not leading him to believe that she had feelings for him that she didn't.

2) If she didn't end the interaction sooner and Terry asked her out, she might have decided to be honest rather than letting him build up false expectations. She might have said something like, "I'm really flattered but I'm not interested in pursuing this further, so I'll say no. Thanks for the invitation, though," or even simply, "Thanks, but no."

What if it was just too soon for Suzanne to know what she wanted? In that case she might have gone with a third option: Since she didn't really know if she wanted to accept the date or not, she could have decided to put off her answer. She could say something like, "I don't know what my answer is, but if you'd like to call me in a couple of days at my office, I'll look at my calendar and we can talk about it." In the intervening time, Suzanne could assess her feelings and, if negative, just decline when Terry called back, or accept if positive.

Questions to ask yourself when being asked out:

1. Have I known this person long enough to make a choice about going out with them? If not, how might I get to know them before having to make that choice? How would I communicate this?

2. What is my gut response to this person and do I trust that response? Would having a date help me get clear about how I feel about this person?

3. Am I wanting to accept because I want to go out with this person or in order to avoid hurting their feelings? If it's the latter, how could I communicate my lack of interest in a respectful way?

4. Do I need time to reflect on my feelings before answering? How can I give myself that time and how would I communicate that?

Obviously, there are no right and wrong answers to these questions. There's no easy way to know for sure what will come of a first encounter with someone new. Sometimes an initial impression is incorrect and sometimes it is very accurate. Sometimes it's worth exploring and sometimes it's not.

The First Goal: A Good Relationship with Yourself

No one, no matter how attractive, is your last chance for a great relationship. Remember that there are lots and lots of possible partners for you. It's okay to make mistakes, to misjudge. It's okay to decline a date based on your gut feelings and find out later that you passed up a wonderful person. It's okay to take a risk and accept a date in order to find out how you feel about someone. The important thing is that you're listening to and respecting your own feelings, then acting on them. This builds self-respect and self-trust, which allows for respect and trust in relationships. I can't emphasize enough how important it is to use your dating experiences to build a positive relationship with yourself first.

Caroline shared an important insight. "I've been crying for two days now, and it's mainly grief and loss about how I've handled my relationships in the past," she said. "For as long as I can remember, I've given up myself in order to be with someone I was really attracted to. I stopped listening to my own feelings and respecting my own needs. I tried to be what I thought he wanted me to be and not who I am. *I failed myself,*" she said as her eyes teared. Caroline had worked diligently in therapy on the issues she had inherited from her family. An alcoholic, distant father and a controlling, critical mother had contributed to her problems with men. "I realize now that in spite of the problems in my family growing up, I am the person who has kept me from having a good relationship. I've sabotaged myself, and I've got to take responsibility for that. It's up to me, and only me, to take care of myself in my relationships, to listen to my feelings and respect them, to ask for what I want, and to trust myself first and then my partners."

Being able to take care of yourself in relationships begins with the first encounter. Are you listening to your own feelings when you meet someone new? Do you respect those feelings? Is your behavior consistent with what you feel? These are skills that don't necessarily come naturally to all of us; they have to be developed. And being your own dating service means practicing and developing these skills. By knowing and respecting ourselves first, we are able to make better choices when we meet new people. Asking someone out or accepting dates then becomes an opportunity for furthering awareness, of oneself and others, all of which contributes to healthier romance.

Your Dating Game Plan So Far

- Expand your world: activities you enjoy
- Network for friendships and dates
- Get into the Meeting Game
- Maintain a balance of good judgment and choice
- Know what to look for
- Practice healthy relating
- Practice assertiveness in meeting new people
- Read and send appropriate body language signals
- Say no to the wrong ones
  Be honest, walk away, send correct signals
- Know when to ask for a date, when to accept
  Pay attention to your own feelings
  Give yourself time before responding

9

♥　　♥　　♥

The First Three Dates

Creating and maintaining healthy relationships begins with the first encounter. Depending on how that goes, the foundation may be forming for a romance that enhances the lives of both partners and that is loving and nurturing, or for one that is unhealthy and dysfunctional. The kind of relationship being formed is determined by the quality of the interactions of the partners over time. How we relate from the very beginning establishes important patterns that are not easily changed later.

Boundaries: Building Healthy Relationships

A healthy relationship begins with the building blocks we discussed in earlier chapters. How we relate (e.g., communicate, listen, understand, resolve differences, etc.) determines whether those blocks will hold up over time or will crumble under pressure.

One vitally important concept in healthy relationships is that of boundaries. The word, in a psychological and relational sense, refers to the invisible place where one person ends and another begins. All

131

human beings have the need to feel special and unique. We feel that way by constantly defining ourselves from infancy until death. The way we walk, talk, laugh, gesture, and emote; our wants, fears, and hopes; our talents, our ways of being creative—all are part of who we are.

Who you are and who I am are different, even though we may share similarities. Our psychological boundaries allow us to experience our separateness and our sameness, without one of us feeling swallowed up or lost in the other. What I want may be different from what you want, and we must find some common ground if we are to have a relationship of any kind.

Boundaries allow us to test the limits of our relationship without exploitation. If Joe loves going scuba diving and Joan is terrified of being underwater, a respect for each other's boundaries would necessitate a compromise. Joe could go diving while Joan snorkels or sits in the sun on the beach.

If Joe and Joan have damaged boundaries, Joe might expend his energy persuading Joan to dive with him, ignoring her fears in favor of getting what he wants. She might give in and go, but the aftermath would be diminished self-respect and resentment toward Joe.

Healthy boundaries entail a deep and abiding self-awareness and self-respect. I know what I want for the most part and I know my feelings, needs, fears, hopes, and desires. I respect those feelings, and I expect my partner to respect them as well. When your wants and needs are damaging or hurtful to me, I am prepared to say no and to stand by that.

Healthy boundaries also mean a profound respect for other people and their differences. I am willing to listen to your feelings and to negotiate our needs together rather than having to have my own way all the time. I am respectful of what hurts you and what heals you. I am willing to forego some of my needs if they collide with yours in a way that is harmful to you.

Boundaries, when intact and healthy, allow two unique people with differing needs to come together and connect. With a healthy sense of our differences as well as our similarities, we are able to be *interdependent* rather than *dependent*. With interdependence, we need each other in lots of little ways, but our survival does not depend on having the other person. We both know that we would grieve over the loss of our relationship, but that we would go on living and would thrive again, even finding a new love down the road. This is in contrast to dependence, in which there is the erroneous belief that a loss of the partner would mean the loss of the one and only right person, our last chance for "true love." Unhealthy relationships are almost always characterized by this belief, held by one or both partners.

Good Boundaries from the First Date.   Our dating relationships provide the perfect opportunity to practice establishing boundaries, without which a healthy romance is simply not possible. Unfortunately, our culture and myths about romantic love do not encourage us to do this. We're taught that lovers should have no boundaries, that "true love" is all it takes to have a great relationship. Hollywood romanticizes the "instant relationship": Take a boy, a girl, a generous dose of chemistry, stir, and *voila!* A fabulous romance. Consider the following instant relationship.

One month after Sheila and Don started dating, they found themselves expecting a child. Surprised but happy, they made plans to marry right away. After all, they were in love and the future looked nothing but rosy. Four months later they were married, their son was born four months after that, and the problems in their marriage had only just begun. By the time their son was a year old, Sheila and Don were almost ready to divorce. "A good day is when we don't get in a really bad fight," Don said, "and that's the best it gets." In therapy they discovered that they both had problems with boundaries: They didn't know how to voice their feelings, ask for what they wanted, negotiate, compromise, and so on. Both had erroneously believed that because they "loved each other," this was enough on which to build a family and a lifetime relationship. They might have taken the time to date for a number of months, building a relationship slowly through the process of discovering each other's separateness and sameness, experiencing growing trust through the process of negotiation and respect for each other's feelings, needs, and wants. Instead, they had gone from being strangers to building a family virtually overnight! Lost to them forever was the opportunity to explore boundary issues without the pressures of parenting, a mortgage, and other bills.

Sheila and Don's relationship isn't a lost cause. At the time of this writing they are both in counseling. With a lot of work they certainly have the possibility of salvaging their marriage. But it didn't have to happen this way.

The early stages of dating and courtship are the best opportunity for boundary setting. *Good boundaries allow for healthy relationships.* It's much easier to set up strong boundaries at first and then relax them later than it is to have weak boundaries and later try to shore them up.

Good boundaries also allow us to screen out unhealthy partners. Individuals who have low self-esteem or a poor sense of identity are usually not able to respect others' boundaries. If I say "No, I'm not comfortable with that," a healthy partner will respect my answer. An unhealthy partner will feel rejected by my no and will take it as a challenge, attempting to persuade me to change my mind. An abusive partner will try to force me to comply with his needs. Obviously, it is wise to be able to spot unhealthy and/or abusive partners as early as possible.

Having healthy boundaries and setting them as we meet and date others also creates positive dating experiences. If I can take care of myself, then I will enjoy my time with you just that much more. I will enjoy dating more if I know how to avoid potentially hurtful situations. Having positive dating experiences keeps me on the playing field, moving forward in my search for the right partner.

Setting limits and boundaries also allows the possibility for a potentially good relationship to grow. John, who was beginning to venture out and date after several months since his last relationship, shared with the group about his "blind date" set for the upcoming weekend. The plan was for his friends to arrange for a meeting between John and their female friend, *without telling her;* he was simply going to be there. His friends were not giving her the full story. The group pointed out that this might really anger her when she found out (secrecy being a boundary violation), and I said it was a shame that this opportunity to meet someone who sounded really neat might be ruined by the way in which it was being set up. John quickly resolved to speak to his friends and have them make straightforward arrangements with the woman.

First Dates: Safety and Discovery

We've all been there: It's the first date. Maybe it's a blind date, maybe it's a first date after meeting a person once, briefly. Dressing up, getting ready for the date, anticipating a fun time. The doorbell rings. You open the door, face each other, and within five minutes *you know that you don't want to be with this person*. And what do you have planned for this first date? Well, there's dinner, the theater, dancing, drinks afterward, and on and on. You've got five hours of entertainment planned with someone you don't want to be with! Of course, the date usually goes downhill from there, not to mention the emotional aftermath ("Why do I bother? Dating is such a waste of my time. There just aren't any really good people out there. I give up—I'll never find anyone right for me." And so on . . .) My clients call this the "Date from Hell."

Making Good Investments. The incredibly long and uncomfortable first date happens as a result of our "instant relationship" culture. Men think they have to "wine and dine" a woman from the first date; women think they have to accept dates like this if they're offered. Both men and women have unrealistically high expectations about these first dates.

Think of it this way. Candlelight and roses, champagne and strawberries, seven-course meals, starlight dancing: This is the stuff of courtship and romance. How do you know you want to romance someone you've only just met? Why make such a significant investment with a virtual stranger? Furthermore, if you do it all in the beginning, what is there to look forward to as the relationship progresses?

If someone makes an investment like this with me on the first date, I am likely, as a woman, to feel obligated for sex, another date, or a relationship. This doesn't mean I'll deliver (or even that his intentions are bad), but those feelings can be very uncomfortable and aren't conducive to developing trust.

Jill related the story of meeting a man at a bar recently. The next day he sent her a dozen roses with a romantic message on the card. I asked Jill what unspoken message that sending the roses might be conveying. "Well, I guess it's his way of saying 'I want to impress you.' It's rather an extravagant gesture if he just wants to say 'I like you.' There's also something about wanting to sweep me off my feet, sort of like those fairy tales we all read as children. It's flattering, that's for sure. But I just don't feel comfortable with it."

Romance is a very real investment of our time, energy, emotions, and finances. Why not be discerning about who we choose to make that investment with? Why not have your first dates be more like an interview and save the romance for those people you choose to make that investment with?

Having your first dates be more about checking each other out rather than instant romance sends a couple of messages. First, it says that I respect myself enough to take my time to find out more about you. I'm not willing to make an emotional investment unless I have a pretty good sense that things could work out for us. Second, it says that I respect you enough to allow you the same opportunity. I don't have to impress you or sweep you off your feet. I want you to take your time in getting to know me and feeling comfortable with me.

First dates should never, ever have to be agonizing, and they should never last beyond the time that you feel comfortable being with your companion. Obviously, a first date should never be unsafe for either person in any way. You can ensure that this doesn't happen by using the recommendations that follow.

The Three-Date Interview Process

First dates should, first of all, feel safe, and second of all, allow for discovery. This means setting certain boundaries right from the start.

What Is a Date?   Many people are confused about what constitutes a date. If Stan says to Laura, whom he's just met, "How about if I come over Friday evening sometime after seven?", is that an appropriate scenario for a date? Not in my book it isn't! Remember that we're working on healthy boundaries in the beginning. A *structured date* is one way to do that.

A date request that communicates respect includes a day of the week and date, an exact time, an event, a suggestion of attire (if not during business hours), and an approximate ending time. So, a request for a date might look something like this:

"How about dinner Friday evening the twenty-third at Pepi's Italian Grill? We could meet at eight, if that's convenient for you, and plan on finishing up around ten. It's a relaxed place, so we can dress casually."

Not terribly romantic, huh? But remember that you don't know yet if you want to *be* romantic with this person. That brings us to your next consideration.

What Is the Purpose of a Date?   According to television and the movies, the purpose is to kindle some romantic sparks (instant romance), to impress our date with how sexy and savvy we are (the package), and to create desire in our date, regardless of whether we're interested in a relationship or not (manipulation, exploitation). Yuck! This may sound exaggerated, but these are the messages that our culture sends to us.

On the other hand, if your purpose is discovery about the other person (is there a possibility for a relationship?), then you might take a different approach. The key words here are *discovery,* meaning that you may be strongly attracted to the person but don't know yet whether he or she is good relationship material, and *possibility,* meaning that you can look for red flags that will tell you whether or not this could be a good relationship.

Yes, No, or Maybe.   In the beginning every new relationship is a No or a Maybe. Sometimes it's definitely a No: There's not enough attraction or there are too many red flags or impossible differences. A new relationship can very quickly turn from a Maybe to a No in the first few dates.

Often I hear people saying, "I knew on the first date that this was the person I would marry." There's the idea that the relationship was a Yes from the very beginning.

This is actually a romantic illusion. What is really happening is that the chemistry is so high that our brains malfunction. We think we've found "the one" because it feels so good to be with them. The truth is that there's no way we could have any inkling as to whether or not this person is right for us after only one date! Sometimes it turns out that they are, so we look back and remember how good we felt at the start, telling ourselves that we *knew* right away that this was "the one."

Then there are the Maybes. Maybe we could have a relationship: there's potential, no obvious insurmountable issues, and there's definitely attraction. But it's too soon to tell. Viewing a relationship in the beginning as a Maybe is realistic and allows the time to discover true potential rather than getting caught up in the romantic illusion of an instant Yes.

A Word About Safety.   In our fast-paced, highly mobile culture, the risk is great for abuse in the dating process. Most singles today don't have the luxury of a small community of people who know each other from which to draw dating partners. We are often taking a chance on someone who is a virtual stranger at the first encounter. This means that, especially for women, the need for safe first dates is essential.

Some Basic Guidelines.   For first, and usually second, dates, try the following suggestions:

- Have lunch, coffee, or brunch rather than dinner
- Plan to stay no longer than one to one and a half hours
- Meet at the restaurant or coffee shop
- Avoid alcohol
- Avoid setting up another meeting at the end of the date

Making your first date lunch, coffee, or brunch and of short duration sets the stage for a *mutual interview*. The message is clear and straightforward: We're meeting in order to discover if 1) we like each other and 2) there is any possibility of a friendship or dating relationship between us. Because you're meeting there and it's a public place, you both have the ability to escape if the encounter is unpleasant or not to your liking (less risk of a "bad date"). Obviously, it's not safe for women to invite men whom they don't know to their homes. Not having alcohol on the first date enables you to have clearer judgment.

Setting up your first dates this way establishes good boundaries that allow you to explore the possibility of a new relationship. Instead of plunging headlong into an instant romance, you can take the time to get to know your potential partners. If the encounter becomes unpleasant, you can cut it short and thereby prevent the Date from Hell from ever happening to you again.

Handling the End of the Date. There's a sort of custom or ritual that often takes place at the end of first dates. This is the awkward moment when the date is drawing to a close and it's difficult to know what to say. Most people have difficulty with closure, so we feel uncomfortable just saying, "Thanks for meeting me, good-bye." Therefore, the ritual goes something like this:

> JOHN: (feeling awkward and not knowing what to say) "I had a good time. It was really nice meeting you." (At this point he could just say good-bye, but that seems too abrupt, so he says nothing.)

MARY: (feeling awkward also) "Me, too. Thanks for inviting me to lunch. Maybe we could do this again sometime." (Mary's not sure she really wants another date with John, but she doesn't want him to feel rejected either.)

JOHN: (not wanting to hurt Mary's feelings) "Sure. That would be great. I'll call you." (He has no intention of calling her, but he doesn't want to reject her.)

MARY: "That sounds great. I'll look forward to hearing from you." (She plans to leave her answering machine on and screen her calls for the next couple of weeks to avoid having to talk to him and turn him down.)

This end-of-the-date ritual sets up both men and women for several uncomfortable scenarios. Men often say they'll call in order to avoid hurting feelings or being rejecting, with no intention of following through, or perhaps some intention, but on later reflection they decide not to. Women often accept another date for the same reasons, then either stand the guy up or cancel the date later.

Sometimes there's just too much pressure at the end of the date while this ritual is going on. In order to sound polite and accepting, we say things we don't mean. We misunderstand or misread each other's communications. What might have been the beginning of a friendship or a dating relationship can fall completely flat now. The way to keep this from happening is simple: Avoid making any promises of future behavior (i.e., calling or going out again) at the end of the date.

The one exception to this guideline is the rare occasion on which you feel a very strong and mutual attraction, there are no immediate red flags, and it's obvious that you both want another date. Obviously, in this case it would be very appropriate to go ahead and set another date.

The way to avoid committing yourself to a second date is simply to say something like, "I'm not sure, but if you'll call me in a couple of days we can talk about it." You could even say something like, "I don't have my calendar with me. If you could call me in a couple of days, we could discuss it then." If you're a man and the woman has asked about a second date, you can say that you don't know but that you'll call her later and talk about it, or (to avoid committing to a phone call) you can say something like, "I'm not sure, but I'll let you know if I decide that's appropriate." There are lots of ways to say "I don't want to commit to anything more now," and these are just a few.

You can also be creative and think of how you might convey the same message. The point is to plan ahead, having something to say in the event that this happens. And, of course, to be honest without being hurtful. You don't have to tell someone that you had an awful time and have nothing in common with them in order to avoid another date.

Time to Reflect.   Often, one short lunch date is simply not sufficient to have a good enough sense of another person to be able to make a clear choice for another date. There may not have been time to find out enough personal information. Perhaps there was the sense that "I like you but feel no real romantic sparks." For whatever reason, the end of the date leaves feelings of ambivalence or doubt. This is the time to avoid committing to another date. Later, you can reflect on the first date, asking yourself questions such as:

• What, if any, were the "red flags" I saw? (See the discussion later in this chapter.)
• Could I see myself dating this person? Were there *any* romantic sparks at all?
• What, if anything, made me uncomfortable? Is it something worth addressing or should I just pass on this person?
• What does my gut tell me? Do I have generally positive or negative feelings about being with this person?
• Finally, do I *want* another date with this person?

If your answer to the last question is no, you can then plan how you'll respond when the person calls. Remember the Too Nice Syndrome in the last chapter? Now that you know that being too nice leaves both people feeling bad, you can prepare yourself for the uncomfortable but freeing task of just being honest. Picture the following scenario.

After one date with John, Mary realizes that she's not sure how she feels about a second date with him. In response to his request for another date (at the end of the first one), she asks him to call her in a couple of days to discuss it. Reflecting on her own later, she remembers that John lit a cigarette after the meal. Mary knows that a partner who doesn't smoke is one of her Non-Negotiables. However, that was the only obvious red flag. She definitely felt romantic sparks. Their conversation was lively and they seemed to connect in many areas of their lives. What, she asked herself, should I do?

Reflecting more deeply, Mary acknowledges to herself that yes, she is definitely attracted to John. And she's lonely, not having had a real relationship for over two years. But, dating him would be a violation of one of her Non-Negotiables. She pictures the two of them together in restaurants, in her home and in his home, and she envisions how uncomfortable she'd be, both physically and emotionally, with his smoking. She knows herself well enough to admit that she'd probably try to get him to stop, and very soon.

On a deeper level, Mary realizes that John's smoking represents a fundamental value difference. Mary is very health conscious and committed to her well-being, doing everything she knows how to maintain her good health. She would never consider jeopardizing her health by smoking or doing anything that is so damaging to her body. She wants a partner who feels the same way.

This means, she realizes, that going out with John could be done, for her, only with a condition: that he change. And the change wouldn't be minor; nicotine addiction is one of the most difficult to overcome. Mary knows that she can't accept John just the way he is, even this early in the game. After much soul searching, Mary comes to the conclusion that dating John would be a mistake.

When John calls for a second date, Mary says, "Thanks, John, for calling and asking me out again. Since our first date, though, I've thought about it and decided that this just isn't right for me. I really appreciate your invitation, though. And thanks for going to lunch."

How is Mary able to pass up a man she is strongly attracted to? First of all, she is absolutely committed to her own well-being. She has made a decision that no relationship is worth compromising her own psychological and emotional health. Second, she knows herself well enough to be aware of what she wants and doesn't want in a relationship, and, again, she has made a conscious choice to not settle for anything less than what she wants. Third, she chooses to believe that there are lots of potentially right men out there for her. Fourth, she has a full and fulfilling life already; finding the right man would be the icing on the cake, not a dire necessity. In short, Mary can afford to pass up this relationship and wait for one that is better for her. She chooses not to believe that she must grab the first good prospect who comes along.

Second and Third Dates. Suppose Mary hasn't seen any insurmountable red flags about John and therefore accepts an invitation for a second date. At this point, the interviewing process is still taking place, and will continue at least through the third date. The guidelines for second dates are the same as first dates, except that you may want to spend a little more time, and may feel it's okay to have a single drink. Again, though, you want to keep your perceptions very sharp since you're not yet ready to make a romantic investment. If your feeling by the third date is still Maybe, it's okay to make it a dinner date.

Making these first three dates lunch, coffee, or dinner is very important, as that allows plenty of time to talk and interact. Often singles will center these early dates around an event, such as a concert or play, and while fun, this kind of date doesn't allow much opportunity to interact. *You need the information that's available from talking with your partner and paying attention to eye contact and body language in these early dates.*

If you're paying attention, you're learning a great deal about the potential for a relationship with this person. Later in this chapter and in the book we'll explore what to look for in these first dates. Women: By the third date, if you have a strong sense that this man is safe, it's okay to have him pick you up at your home. If you're not sure, set another "meet there" date and be firm about it. Men: If a woman seems hesitant when you ask to pick her up at home, offer to meet her somewhere. Obviously, it's never okay to pressure your date into doing anything that makes her uncomfortable.

Discovering Relationship Potential

Now that you've set some good boundaries by following the guidelines for first dates, what do you do on the date?

Since the purpose is *discovery* not instant romance, the focus should be on determining, as much as possible, the following:

- Do I feel any spark of attraction for this person?
- What red flags (if any) are telling me that this relationship may not be right for me?

Attraction: Just a Spark. Remember that attraction is the fuel that runs the engine of a relationship. Without attraction, which leads to romantic love, there is a likelihood that one or both partners will be unable to make a commitment later on, or to maintain that commitment in the face of problems. Consider Tad and Donna's story.

After six months of marriage, Tad and Donna were in counseling to begin to resolve a series of misunderstandings that threatened their marriage. Donna, whose childhood neglect had left her feeling unloved, tended to interpret most of Tad's behavior (e.g., he didn't hold her hand in the restaurant tonight) as evidence that he didn't want her. Tad was having trouble listening to Donna's feelings without becoming defensive. As therapy progressed, Tad professed his strong commitment to their marriage. He compared his feelings for Donna to the way he had felt dating other women before her. "The reason my other relationships never went anywhere was because I never fell in love with anyone before you, Donna. Without this feeling, I just got bored and so did they, and we just stopped seeing each other. With you, I really feel love for the first time." Fortunately, Donna felt as strongly about Tad and resolved to work out her feelings of neglect. The romantic love this couple experienced, sparked by an initial attraction, was providing the incentive for them to work on the problems in their marriage and continue trying. The fact that their feelings were mutual gave them a healthy basis for a relationship.

Contrary to popular belief, attraction doesn't have to be bells and whistles and Roman candles from the first encounter. In fact, most healthy relationships begin with *just a spark* of attraction, which steadily grows over time. This spark of attraction may feel like "What an interesting person; I'd like to get to know him better" or even "I feel so comfortable with this person; I'd like to spend more time with her." Sometimes it's more like "What a cute guy; I'm definitely going to go on another date with this person." Obviously, there are many ways you might experience the beginnings of attraction to someone. It's important to be realistic and not expect too much too soon.

Attraction: Not Enough Spark.   Sometimes attraction just doesn't happen, even when you want it to. David's story shows how frustrating that can be. "I had a date with the most gorgeous woman I've ever seen," he said. "She was, no kidding, Miss America, sitting right there across the table from me. I just kept looking at her and thinking how beautiful she was. But I was so frustrated because no matter how hard I tried, I just couldn't find any real feelings of attraction to her. We just didn't click, I just didn't feel any sparks at all."

Most singles have had this type of experience. It's tempting to try to force the feelings to be there, to rationalize them into being. But this usually leads to lots of frustration and confusion. David chose to move on and keep looking. One month later, he met someone who was much more right for him.

How can you be sure that your lack of attraction to someone isn't just a fluke or something that will change over time? You can't ever be absolutely certain because nothing is when it comes to relationships. As a general rule, however, if there isn't a pretty good spark by the third date, the odds are that there will never be. That doesn't mean, though, that feelings won't develop. In fact, two people can become very *attached* who never really felt attraction in the beginning. (Later we'll examine the nature of attachment in more detail.) Let's look at what happened to Joseph.

Joseph met April at a meeting of their charity organization. April was instantly and strongly attracted to Joseph, who didn't return the feeling. Joseph liked April as a person but felt no sparks toward her. She was persistent, however, and eventually he began dating her against his own best judgment. For the next two years, Joseph struggled with his lack of attraction to April. By this time he was quite emotionally attached to her, and, in fact, loved her, but did not feel sexual toward her and couldn't imagine marrying her. In therapy, they kept bumping up against the same obstacle: Joseph just didn't have romantic feelings for April and couldn't make himself have them. Because of their attachment, however, they were unwilling to just let go. The last time I saw them they were attempting, with a great deal of pain, to break up.

Joseph second-guessed himself about his initial feelings for April. He said things to himself like "Why wouldn't I want to date her? She's a lovely woman. I'd be a fool to not want her." He rationalized himself into a romance rather than trusting his own feelings. The result was a dysfunctional relationship and a great deal of heartache for him and her.

Ignoring your own gut feeling in a dating situation doesn't work. Some things to ask yourself about the spark of attraction:

• Do I feel any kind of tingle of excitement about being with this person? Can I trust that feeling rather than looking for it to be more or different?

• If I didn't feel a spark, am I trying to talk myself into it? Am I trying to convince myself that I *should* feel a certain way rather than accepting the way I do feel?

• Am I relying on what other people think I should feel?

• Have I given myself sufficient time and opportunity with this person to know how I feel?

Remember, there are no right or wrong answers, only *your* answers. You should listen to them.

Attraction: Too Much?   There are those who say that there is a level of attraction that is too high, that is so intoxicating it can only lead to trouble. This kind of attraction, they say, automatically leads to unhealthy love.

I certainly agree that in many dysfunctional relationships a powerful attraction may keep two people together who are not right for each other. Often these romances are characterized by a great deal of chemistry but very little compatibility. Sometimes the chemistry itself is so strong that, just like a drug, individuals find it impossible to use restraint. In chapter fourteen we'll examine these kinds of relationships in greater detail.

I think it's important not to throw the baby out with the bath water, however. A strong and powerful attraction, in and of itself, is hardly ever the problem in a bad relationship. The problem is usually when one person feels significantly more attracted than the other. Or when both are equally attracted but their values don't mesh or there is emotional unavailability on the part of one or both partners. Beware of a powerful attraction to a partner who feels ambivalent or apathetic about you, or who is emotionally unavailable.

Red Flags: Looking Out for Trouble.   The other thing to be focused on in the first three dates (the interview process) is red flags: indicators of future barriers or problems. Some examples of red flags are:

• Indications that your partner is emotionally unavailable. (We'll examine this in more detail in chapter thirteen.)
• Indications that your values do not blend
• Violations of your Non-Negotiables
• Abusive or insensitive behavior: Remember that people are on their best behavior on the first date; if their best is offensive to you, it will only get worse as time goes on.

What do you do when you see red flags on the first couple of dates? First of all, it doesn't always mean you should dump the person and forget about a relationship. Red flags are actually a *strong caution signal:* They tell you that there's a problem or potential problem that you need to address before you proceed. Bill's story illustrates how this works.

When Bill met Marilyn she told him right away that she was recovering from a divorce and was not interested in a relationship. At the same time, she accepted invitations from Bill and went out with him, even showing affection in a romantic way. This was a mixed signal that left Bill confused. In therapy he realized that Marilyn's emotional unavailability was a red flag that he needed to check out, that it wouldn't be wise to assume that because she was dating him that everything would just work out. He decided to bring this up with her. First, he told her that he was interested in a relationship with her and that he wasn't sure from their previous conversations if she was or wasn't returning the feelings. Then he asked her if she just wanted a platonic friendship or if, in fact, she was ready to enter into a dating relationship with him. After some discussion, Marilyn stated that she did want what he wanted. This red flag had now been handled (assuming, of course, that Marilyn had given herself adequate time to deal honestly with the aftermath of her divorce).

This situation could have gone the other way, too. Marilyn might have said that she didn't want to date Bill. In that case, he would have saved himself a lot of heartache pursuing a nowhere relationship. By addressing the red flag (his concern over her emotional availability), a couple of things happened. First, they were able to have a significant conversation about their feelings and intentions toward one another, which promoted more emotional intimacy in the relationship. Second, they cleared up any misunderstandings that might have kept them from progressing. Third, Bill got to practice being assertive and addressing an issue, something that strengthened his confidence that he could gently confront a woman he cares about when necessary.

Red flags can also be seen as opportunities for intervention, discovery, boundary setting, and intimacy promotion: *intervention* to handle a potential problem or save oneself the pain of continuing in a dead-end relationship; *discovery* about a partner, about one's own strengths and communication skills, and about relationships; *boundary setting* when an issue holds the potential to do damage to one's emotional well-being; and *intimacy promotion* by virtue of the level of communication that it takes to confront a red flag.

Possibilities Versus Guarantees.   What if you get through the first three dates and there are no red flags? Does that mean you can now breathe a deep sigh of relief and sail into the sunset knowing that your relationship is set for life? Certainly not. Relationships, like anything else that holds the potential for great fulfillment in life, require constant vigilance on our parts: to notice and address issues, resolve differences, nurture intimacy, and promote the welfare of both people.

The fact that a potential relationship holds great possibility doesn't in any way mean that you have a guarantee of success. Even after a successful courtship and the wedding day have passed, it's dangerous to rest on the assumption that everything will be okay.

The purpose of the first three dates is to do the best you can to spot *insurmountable* red flags: problems that, even if addressed, can't be resolved; issues that undermine the very foundation of a potential relationship and which indicate that it's best to move on. If you can successfully do this, you will save yourself agonies by the score, and you will move yourself more quickly along the path to the right relationship.

In chapter thirteen we'll look at emotional availability and how to spot that very early.

Using These Guidelines

To review, remember that your first date should be short in duration, you should meet the person there, it should be lunch or brunch, you should avoid alcohol, and you should try to not set another date at the end of that date. Some other guidelines that will help you use your first three dates to explore the possibility of a relationship are:

- Wait several days between the first and second date.

This gives you time to reflect on the first date, it conveys a message of non-desperation, and it can allow you to get back down to earth at those times when you feel swept away by romantic feelings.

We've all had the experience of a first date in which the chemistry was so thick you could cut it with a knife. Long, meaningful looks, holding hands, the seeming ability to talk about anything; before you know it, you're picturing the rest of your life with this person and you've had only one date! While these are delicious feelings to have and there's nothing inherently wrong with them, they are not very conducive to level-headed thinking, which we must have in order to be most likely to choose healthy relationships. So, the several days between the first and the second date (and even between second and third) can be a cooling-off period, allowing you to collect your sanity again, which you're going to need even more when the chemistry is this high!

- Group and double dates can be fun early on, but make sure that at least one of those first three dates is just the two of you in an atmosphere conducive to talking.

- Keep your second and third dates relatively short, allowing several days between them.

Remember that you're trying to have a healthy relationship grow, and that means going slowly. You have all the time in the world later for longer dates. Shorter dates, spaced with several days in between, help you avoid the "instant relationship" trap, help you stay level-headed, and convey respect for both of you. It says "I don't expect you to drop your life and give it all to me right away, and I don't expect that of myself."

- Trust your own instincts.

Intuition is often an overlooked commodity when it comes to dating. Your very best source of information is the feeling you have on a gut level. Does being with this person twist you up in a knot or make you unwind and feel relaxed? Are there any danger signals or warning lights going off or do you feel safe? These are important messages to pay attention to.

Making Dating Around Work for You

In chapter five we looked at two typical dating strategies that we've all tried but that didn't work: going to bars and playing the waiting game. These often lead to a dating pattern that looks something like this: After six months of meeting nobody new, you finally meet someone charming and attractive who seems interested in you. You begin dating this new person, which rapidly turns into a relationship.

Because of a lack of meshing values or emotional unavailability or lack of compatibility, the relationship crumbles after a few months or a couple of years. You find yourself alone and single again, and weeks or months or even years go by before you meet anyone else interesting, at which point you latch onto this new person and a new relationship begins, and so on.

Serial Monogamy.   This pattern has been called "serial monogamy," and what makes it so frustrating is the lack of an abundance of choices. Only finding one or two relationship possibilities per year is just not enough to make good choices.

Having More Choices.   The Dating Around stage of relationships becomes much more effective when your social world is expanded and you have the opportunity for lots of potential dating partners. This way, you may have two dates in the same week with two new people. You follow up with one or both or neither of them, depending on how the dates go. Maybe you meet someone else before you even have a second date with either of the first two people. The idea is to have as many one-, two-, or three-date relationships as you feel comfortable with. This is the essence of dating around.

Rather than concentrating from the beginning on just one person exclusively, why not have several potential partners whom you're checking out? This gives you a sense of abundance and removes the desperation factor. You make better choices because you *have* more choices.

Typically, this only works up to a point. Most people, by the end of three dates, are beginning to get emotionally attached. To continue more than one relationship at the same time beyond three or four dates means someone's likely to get hurt. (We'll take a deeper look at attachment later so that this will be clearer.) Therefore, I recommend that you stick with the formula: lots of one-, two-, or three-date nonsexual relationships, leading to better choices for a more involved relationship.

Your Dating Game Plan

Let's now look at your complete Dating Game Plan:

- Expand your world: participate in activities you enjoy
- Network for new friendships and dates
- Play the Meeting Game
- Maintain a balance of good judgment and choice
- Know what to look for
- Practice healthy relating
- Practice assertiveness
- Read and send signals
- Say no to those you're not interested in
- Know when to ask for a date and when to accept one
- Have first dates that offer safety and discovery
  Meet for lunch or coffee, short duration, no alcohol, don't automatically set another date
  Use as interviews
  Notice "red flags" and "sparks"
- Structure second and third dates so you can progress slowly
  Continue the interview process
  Pay attention to your gut responses
- Experiment with lots of one-, two-, and three-date relationships

Your Dating Game Plan for meeting more people, having more choices, and establishing healthy relating patterns early is now basically complete. In the next chapter we'll look at some of the basic do's and don'ts of dating for men and women, and in the next section of the book we'll explore the dynamics of love relationships and how you can build a romance that is more likely to last a lifetime and be emotionally healthy for both people.

10

♥　　♥　　♥

Changing Roles, Changing Rules

They're in every dating class I teach. She sits at the back of the room looking tentative and unsure. He fidgets and looks at the door as if he's ready to bolt. Who are they? The "Newly Single"! After ten, fifteen, twenty, or more years of marriage, they find themselves unexpectedly single once again. Divorced or widowed, the Newly Single never expected to have to deal with having to date again. And, of course, they're scared.

"I'm astonished at how the rules for dating have changed," Fran said. "In fact, I can't tell if there really are any rules anymore!" Heads nodded affirmatively all around Fran.

The truth is, there really aren't any hard and fast rules for dating in the nineties. If you're just getting back in the singles game after a few or many years out of it, then you've no doubt discovered that everything's different.

A New Look at Relationships

In order to make the most of your new Dating Game Plan, whether you're newly single or you've been trying to get it right for years, it helps to take a fresh look at relationships. Our old ideas about men and women and their roles together don't fit as well with modern romance. For example, men are no longer expected to make all the moves, and it's much more acceptable for women to be assertive in the dating game.

Unlike our parents and grandparents, we expect a lot more from a spouse than simply a helpmate and procreation partner. We want and even expect our marriages to provide us with love, romance, nurturing, partnership in every sense, and fulfillment, just to name a few needs. We want honesty, trust, and open communication. We want to be able to express our feelings and have our partners listen and understand.

Equality is the name of the game in modern love. Most men actively seek out women who are well-educated with successful careers, as well as having charm and attractiveness. Women want men who are sensitive and understanding, as well as being good providers.

Just like the dating game of the nineties, marriage no longer has any predetermined rules or formulas for success. The *way* we pair is often as individual as our personalities. This simply means that we must work harder to define our relationship, no longer taking for granted that what worked for Mom and Dad will work for us.

Flexibility of Roles. Egalitarian marriages are becoming more and more prevalent. The women's liberation movement has heightened our awareness that in marriage, as in our society as a whole, individuals have the right to be treated with dignity and respect. Additionally, many women have gained their economic independence, giving them the choice to leave bad marriages. We now know that neither gender is superior. Both men and women are unique human beings, each with their own thoughts, feelings, and needs. Both have a right to the pursuit of happiness in marriage, to be able to voice their feelings and wants, to be listened to and respected.

With these new understandings it is only natural that the standard for modern marriage is now one of equality. Both men and women have the right to pursue the kind of work that's most fulfilling. So, if

Sally truly wants a career outside the home and John truly wants to be a full-time dad, they may find their roles reversed from the traditional ones we grew up with. Meg and Kevin, on the other hand, both want careers outside the home, so the question is: Who does the dishes, the dusting, the vacuuming? In their case, roles must be blended, with both partners sharing responsibilities inside and outside the home.

Paula and Dave had been married for less than a year when Dave decided to make a career change, starting his own consulting business. Suddenly, Paula was working ten-hour days and paying all of the bills. She saw Dave staying at home to do his work and generating very little income. Even though intellectually she supported his choice to work at home and to make the transition into something new, the old role models provided by her parents were causing interference. She became resentful, and the friction between them escalated.

In couples' counseling, Paula realized that she was expecting Dave to make the majority of the money in the family (just like her father had), even though her career was far more likely to generate the most income (a very different circumstance than her parents'). She finally adjusted her thinking and expectations to fit the reality of her marriage, becoming more flexible. When they finished counseling, they were planning for Dave to care for their expected baby and their home while Paula continued her career. Both were happy with their newly defined, nontraditional roles.

One of the keys to successful modern marriage, then, is to have *flexibility*. Rather than blindly trying to follow in our parents' footsteps, we must discuss our individual wants and needs and create a blending of roles that is right for *our* relationship.

Beginning with Dating.   Remember that how we date determines the kinds of relationships we will have, which determines the kind of marriage we will ultimately find ourselves in. If we want a marriage that has a good chance of lasting, we must be able to adapt to the reality of today's changing roles in relationships.

Dating offers a world of opportunity to explore these new roles until we discover what fits. This is the time to experiment with new ways of approaching the standard dating rituals, reversing roles, blending roles, breaking old rules and creating some new ones. In the rest of this chapter, we'll discuss some basics of dating from both men's and women's perspectives. The goal is to expand our thinking about traditional approaches to dating, just as we must eventually do in marriage.

What Women Need to Know About Dating

Welcome to modern dating, ladies! Dating, like relationships and marriage, will never be the same. Now that equality is the standard for love in the latter twentieth and early twenty-first centuries, it's time to look at how that affects dating and courtship. As the old saying goes, there's good news and there's bad news.

The good news is that it's now acceptable for women to be assertive, to make the first (and other) moves, and to actively seek out and choose partners.

The bad news is that, because making the first move entails the risk of rejection, women now get a taste of what men have always had to face. It also means that women are now expected to assume some of the economic responsibility in dating.

But how do we know when to take charge and when not to? How do we pursue relationships and interact with men in a way that establishes an equal relationship but that doesn't throw romance and courtship completely out the window? Let's look at some typical dating questions that demand new answers.

Who Makes the First Move?   The answer is simple: whoever thinks of it first! No longer bound by the old standard that it's the man's responsibility to make the first move, women as well as men are free to initiate introductions, make telephone contact, and ask for dates. If Belinda notices Philip across the room, she has several choices. She can approach him directly and introduce herself. Or she can decide to do nothing, knowing that she'll probably see him again at the next similar function.

Let's say Belinda chooses to approach Philip directly and introduces herself to him. They talk, and Belinda becomes aware that she is attracted to this man and that he seems interested in her. She now has other choices to make. She can ask him out. Or she can continue talking, hoping that he'll take the initiative and ask her out. She can offer her phone number, letting him know that she would welcome more contact such as a lunch date, if he's interested. Or she can ask for his phone number, offering to call and set up a date at a later time.

Let's say she takes the initiative, asks for Philip's phone number (which he gives), and calls him up later for a date. Now she has more choices! She can ask him to dinner, a play, a movie, or whatever else she wants the invitation to include. As we discussed previously, it's probably safest for her to ask him to lunch or coffee for the first date, especially if she didn't know him prior to their recent meeting. Now comes another big question.

Who Pays? With today's relationship equality, it's no longer safe to assume that he'll pay just because he's the man. To be in step with the times, you should assume that you'll pay at least half on the first date. *And, if you asked him out, be prepared to pay for the entire date.* Matt's perspective on this issue is typical of the times.

"I met Teresa through a dating service. She picked me, and we talked and set up a dinner date. When the check came, she left it sitting there, so I picked it up and paid for the meal. A few days later, she called me back and invited me out again. This time when the check came I let it sit for a long time, ten or fifteen minutes. Again, she made no move to pay, so I did. But I really resent her assumption that I was supposed to pay for the entire date when she invited me out, not once, but twice!"

I think Matt had a right to be indignant. If women are going to exercise the right to be assertive, we must be ready to follow through. Teresa sent a very mixed signal: "I'm assertive and strong enough to choose you, initiate contact, and ask you out, but not assertive enough to pay." A consistent signal for women, then, is to simply follow the rules of good etiquette: *Whoever asks for the date pays for the date!*

Sometimes the issue of who pays carries important symbolic meaning. If a first date equals instant romance and he's pursuing me, then I might expect him to pay. After all, I want to establish this as a courtship as soon as possible. On the other hand, if a first date is an *interview* in which I'm primarily interested in discovering who he is, whether or not he's truly available, and if there's any relationship potential, then I'm probably going to pay for at least my half. (The latter is a healthier way of approaching potential partners.)

Money and Power. Who pays can also be a power issue. Since money often equals power in our society, it has traditionally been the male role to possess the most money and to wield that power in the form of paying for dates. Sometimes the automatic assumption that men should pay for the date can inadvertently lead to subtle feelings of obligation on the woman's part. Since he paid for that expensive dinner, I should at least invite him in for a nightcap, shouldn't I? Or, I guess I owe him a good-night kiss (even if I'm not really comfortable with that) since he spent so much for the entertainment. Or, since he bought lunch, I should accept another date with him.

To avoid the subtle feelings of obligation that can sometimes creep in, make it your practice to go "dutch treat," at least for the first couple of dates, or if you ask him for the date, to pay the entire tab. When the check comes and you begin to pay, if he protests and wants to pay, offer to let him pay half but don't feel that you have to turn the check over to him. Remember that sometimes men are offering to pay because they feel obligated, but in reality would feel relieved if you shared the burden.

Jeanie, age sixty-two and widowed, didn't want any part of sharing the tab on dates with men. "In my day, men always paid for dates, and I like it that way!" she declared. Jeanie also maintained that this incurred absolutely no feelings of obligation on her part. For her, sharing the cost of dates just wasn't an option. Since she planned on dating men in her age group, she didn't anticipate this being a problem and she's probably correct. Most likely the men she'll be dating will share her values and will willingly assume the job of paying.

Generally speaking, though, singles who are baby-boom age (born between 1946 and 1962, roughly) and younger are not going to view this issue in such a black-and-white manner. Women must face the reality that they'll be paying at least some of the time.

Talking About Money.   How do we discuss who pays? Probably even more difficult than the issue itself is how we should talk about it. Money, along with sex, is one of the most contentious issues that couples face. And the biggest problem with both issues is the inability to talk about them! As a therapist, I am often called upon to help couples develop some comfort in talking about these two emotionally sensitive issues.

What makes money such a sensitive issue? As we discussed earlier, money is associated with power in our culture in a very real way. The old saying "he who has the gold makes the rules" still holds true. In a traditional marriage, the man earns the money and usually decides how it will be spent. The woman in this kind of marriage sometimes expresses anger or rebellion by spending too much. The husband attempts control by limiting how much she can spend. And when these marriages fail, what is all the fighting about? Who gets what and how much!

Many a contemporary marriage has run into trouble when the woman earns considerably more than her husband. In a world in which men are socialized to feel that they should be more powerful, his smaller income can make him feel inadequate as a man. On the other side of the coin, successful women often feel guilty about earning more than their mates.

And what about our family of origin issues regarding money? Maybe your parents fought about money. Maybe there was never enough to go around, or maybe you had a parent who tried to buy your love with excessive gift giving. Like sex education, discussion about money was noticeably absent in most of our families. Thus, we all bring a certain amount of emotional baggage, misinformation, and lack of information about money matters into our adult lives.

No wonder that we find it difficult to talk about money! With all of our baggage, and the unconscious issues about power hanging over us, it's not surprising that we tend to just keep quiet about it and hope for the best.

The alternative, though, is to dare to approach this touchy subject early in a relationship. Remember that the goal is to establish a pattern of open and honest communication early on, even about sensitive matters. So, how do we get started?

Know What You Want. First of all, know what your own personal policy is going to be. Jeanie knew hers, so it was simple for her. When the check came, she just ignored it. (However, I did advise her to always have enough money, just in case she was out with a progressive man who expected her to share the tab.) That old advice for women to always have enough money for carfare on a date should be amended: Always have enough money to pay for the date *and* to get yourself home!

My personal policy is that I want to pay for at least half on the first date (depending on who asked whom out). If I ask him out, I'm prepared to pay the entire tab, but I'm willing to share it if he insists. If he asks me out, I want "dutch treat," and will almost always insist on this on the first date. This helps me to feel no sense of obligation and to have total freedom to decline another date if that is warranted. It's easiest to address the issue while we're setting up the date. I'll say something like, "By the way, on the first date, I insist on paying for my portion."

Most men respect my wishes, but one protested strongly. "Oh, no, I'll pay," he said. "I would really be more comfortable paying my half," I responded. He continued to protest in spite of my assertions and I ended by saying that this wasn't going to work out and declining the invitation. Sound harsh? Perhaps. But I'd learned by that time to pay attention to my own internal monitors, and they were letting me know that I felt very uncomfortable with the interaction, and thus it was unlikely that the date would be any better.

Raise the Issue.   There's nothing wrong with discussing finances with your date in advance. In fact, I believe that this is an excellent opportunity to uncover and reveal some important attitudes about money and men's and women's roles. Like it or not, money is a major issue in today's relationships. Deciding who pays can actually help you develop some familiarity with discussing a topic that we tend to avoid honestly discussing.

What Happens Next?   What about payment after the first date? Again, this depends on how you feel about the date. If you're still in the interviewing mode, you may want another "dutch treat" lunch or coffee date. If there are some definite sparks and you feel a progression toward a romance, who pays may be a less significant issue.

When you see a budding relationship, however, it's a good idea to bring up the subject of who pays. What are your expectations? What are his? A little honest disclosure about financial situations may be warranted. If one of you has a smaller entertainment budget, you may want to discuss alternatives such as preparing meals at home. Getting these issues out in the open allows you to relax and enjoy your dates together instead of worrying about money matters.

After the First Move.   Now that we've gotten Belinda past the first date (which she paid for!), what happens next? Certainly there's nothing stopping her from taking further initiative and asking Philip out again. She can call him and ask for another date if she chooses. But there are some factors she may want to consider first.

If Belinda feels attracted to Philip and senses that he's feeling the same, she may want to wait a few days and give him the chance to make the next move. The purpose of this is to allow Philip a chance to assess his feelings. If he wants another date with Belinda, he will almost certainly call and ask her out at this point.

Because most men have been so heavily trained to be polite to women and not hurt their feelings, there's a chance that if Belinda initiates the second date, Philip will accept even though he's not strongly attracted to her. She may still be wondering what his feelings are for her after their second date.

Letting him take the initiative for the second date allows him to communicate a powerful message: "I'm attracted to you, too! This is not a one-sided deal." This can establish mutuality for the relationship. From this point on, dating is a reciprocal process, with each taking turns initiating and asking for dates.

Why Men Say They'll Call and Then Don't.   Remember the Too Nice Syndrome covered in chapter eight? TNS makes men say they'll call when they have no intention of doing so, and makes women say they'd welcome another date when they don't.

Mostly, people simply want to avoid the discomfort of confrontations that hold the potential for hurt feelings. (If, however, you've been dating someone for a period of time and they don't call when they say they will, you should confront them.)

Dealing with Potential Abuse.   It's never too early in a relationship for a person to be on the outlook for abusive behavior in a dating partner. Remember that abuse can take many forms, so we're not talking about only physical abuse but verbal abuse as well as behavior such as neglect, infidelity, alcohol and drug abuse, and monetary or sexual exploitation. While men are responsible for most physical abuse in relationships, women are also responsible for some types of potentially abusive behaviors that can spring from addictions, the need for control, etc.

There are almost always signs in the first few dates that can give a warning about a person's potential abusiveness. The most important warning signal, however, is your own gut response. Pay attention if you get a knot in your stomach while on a date with someone!

Warning signals in the *first few dates* to notice include:

• Excessive questioning, with jealous overtones, about your past or other current relationships (which may be a sign of possessiveness, always a trait of an abuser)
• Time commitments not honored, e.g., being chronically late, changing plans at the last minute, not showing up for dates, being

excessively late without calling, defensiveness about any of these when confronted

- Excessive need to be in control of dates, interactions; hurt feelings or anger when you assert your own preferences
- Abusive treatment of women in his past (this may seem obvious, but lots of women have continued to develop relationships with men who have disclosed their history of abuse, naively believing his statements that he's "changed" or that he would "never do that to me")
- Alcohol abuse: If he drinks to excess on your first three dates, be forewarned—this is a significant indicator that the drinking will only be worse later
- Lack of respect for your boundaries: if you tell him you'd prefer lunch for the first date and he insists on an evening date; you state your preferences and he belittles them or overrides them with his own; and so on
- Demeaning references to women in his past or to women in general
- Any kind of belittling behavior or verbalization of it
- Pressure for sex if you've communicated reluctance

Again, the kinds of behaviors listed here are warnings of more and worse to come. It's crucial to not pass them off as unimportant.

What to Do.   If you see red flags like the above early in a relationship, should you just refuse to see the person again? The answer is: probably. If you aren't in the market for a guy who needs a major overhaul (i.e., years of therapy), if you're committed to finding a partner whose level of personal awareness and growth is somewhat equal to your own, if you've given up fixing men and loving too much, then your answer is going to be an unqualified *yes*. On the other hand, if you still believe that "love conquers all" and that if you love him enough he'll change or be different with you, then your answer will be no. (In which case I'd recommend you reread the first part of this book.)

The other possibility is to confront him in a direct and straightforward manner, asking for behavior change and being willing to end the budding relationship if he refuses. The problem with this approach is that the odds are against its working. Most of the time, people don't change destructive or abusive behavior until they've lost something really big, and even then they often don't. Men who are abusive to women require extensive treatment in order to change their attitudes and behavior. You could easily spin your wheels for months, years, or a lifetime waiting for this kind of change. Even worse, the longer a woman stays with an abusive man the lower her self-esteem tends to fall and the less empowered she feels to get out. This vicious cycle is not worth the risk of falling into.

What if you're not sure the behavior is abusive? Maybe you're having trouble trusting your own judgment. When in doubt, talk to a trusted friend. Ask if he or she would tolerate the behavior. Often, after an abusive relationship ends, friends will tell a woman that they never had a good feeling about her ex-boyfriend. Women who have been through this cycle once or twice often decide that the barometer of their friends' feelings toward a man should be sought out and listened to in future relationships.

If you've put your Dating Game Plan into effect and if your self-esteem is good, you should be able to easily move on from the temptation to continue a relationship with a potentially abusive partner. Meeting lots of new people and having lots of dates has given you the perspective of abundance. You know that you'll meet someone new who will be right for you and who won't be abusive.

If you find yourself dating someone abusive, yet feel unable to break it off, *seek professional help immediately!* Abusive relationships can drain your emotional and psychological energy, leading to stress-induced illness, injury, and even death (in the case of physical abuse). This is nothing to be casual about. These relationships begin with red flags and warnings in the early stages, so be aware, listen to your own gut responses, and act on them.

What Men Need to Know About Dating

Well, guys, if you just read the previous section, you know that the rules have all changed. Yes, today's woman is very likely to initiate the first contact and ask for the first date. She's likely to be assertive in lots of ways, and as I said to the women, I'll say to you also: There's good news and bad. The good news is that some of the initial pressures of possible rejection and bruised egos are lessened. It's also now okay for you to expect a woman to share the financial burden of dating. The bad news is that you may have to give up some of the control in dating and relationships. But how do you know whether a woman wants to play by the old rules or the new ones? Let's look at some of the potential trouble areas and some possibilities for dealing with them.

Handling Payment for Dates.   You now know that women are likely to want to pay their share or even the whole tab on dates. For men who are accustomed to calling all the shots, this may be hard to handle. For most men, however, this is nothing short of a relief! We live in a time in which all of us struggle to some extent to survive and thrive financially. Single-income families are on the decline. Why should dating be any different? Since so many of us share the financial burden after marriage, it makes sense that we would do the same in dating. But how do you handle this in an actual dating situation?

The first thing you have to examine is your own policy for who should pay for which dates. As a general rule, if you ask for the date, you should be prepared to pay. At the same time, remember that a woman may be trying to avoid feelings of obligation and would therefore prefer paying for her half. If so, respect her wishes and split the tab.

What about when women ask you out? You may prefer to simply assume that you're paying. Or you may feel strongly that if a woman asks, she should pay! In this case, don't assume that she's read this book and knows to pay. Remember that there's still some confusion about our changing roles. Therefore, you may need to address the issue directly.

If it's difficult for women to bring up money issues with men, it's doubly difficult for the reverse scenario. In the past, men have been trained to be the financial caretakers of women, and even if you can see past those old roles, it may still feel uncomfortable to break them.

If you really want a more equal relationship, though, it may be worth it to you to feel the discomfort and address the issue anyway.

One way to do this is to talk about it when you're setting up the date. You might say something like, "May I assume that since you're asking me out, you'll pick up the tab?" Her reaction will be revealing. If she says no, or seems offended, then you know you have a difference of perception on this issue. You have a choice to make. You can continue the conversation and explain how you feel about it and ask how she feels. This could open the door for a lot of honest disclosure from both of you about role expectations. If she doesn't seem willing to compromise (paying at least half), you have a decision to make. You might want to go ahead and go out (and be willing to pay the whole tab) or you might decide that this issue is too important for you to make a compromise.

Dealing with the Pressure to Do It All.   Men have traditionally been the initiators of romantic relationships. They did the calling, the arranging, the pursuing, the paying, everything. Women were the passive recipients of all this wooing and courtship. But no more! Pursuit and courtship can be a two-way street, but it isn't always.

Even though times have changed, old attitudes and feelings die hard. A man may realize intellectually that dating is now a two-way street, but emotionally he may still feel as though he's responsible for the whole ball of wax. He may feel guilty about expecting women to share the initiative and the financial responsibility.

Thus, it's easy to fall into the trap of shouldering the entire responsibility for initiating and maintaining the relationship. Stan's story shows how this can become problematic.

Stan, in his early thirties, was always the initiator. When he met an attractive woman, he asked her out. After the first date, if he still liked her, he called and asked her out again. He initiated the third, fourth, and fifth dates. It never occurred to him to wonder if the current woman he was pursuing returned his feelings. He assumed that if she accepted his invitations, her feelings were the same as his, and rightly so. With several of his recent relationships, however, eventually the woman would begin canceling dates, and ultimately the day would come when she would end the relationship. Through all this time, Stan was still the initiator.

When he looked back, after three women ended their relationships with him after two to six months each of dating, he realized that he needed to change this pattern. His past relationships were one-sided because he had believed that it was his job—and his job only—to initiate contact. He had never given a woman the opportunity to really reciprocate, and therefore had failed to allow for a mutual relationship. He resolved to initiate for two or three dates, then sit back and see if she picked up the ball and initiated. Also, he learned to disclose his feelings about wanting reciprocity from a woman, so that his partners knew what he was expecting. This way, he would be able to see whether the feelings were shared or one-sided.

Carrie's story shows what women may do when men are willing to be the sole initiators. After a three-year relationship ended (not by her choice), Carrie was depressed and despondent for several months. Finally, when she began to feel better, she became more open to overtures from men. She began accepting invitations for dates, but she knew she wasn't ready for a relationship. Like so many who have been rejected by a lover, she wanted to feel attractive again. When a man asked her out, she felt special again and desirable. The fact that she had absolutely nothing to offer to a man except the pleasure of her company over dinner didn't enter into her decision making. If they asked, she accepted. And she did this for as long as the man would ask her out, until he realized that there was no relationship developing with her. Amazingly, most of them didn't realize this for weeks and even months.

Both men and women, from time to time, ask for and accept dates for reasons other than to explore the possibility of a committed relationship. If you're in the market for a romance with a future, you may want to initiate only the first couple of dates, then wait and see if she takes the initiative for the next date. This especially applies if you want an egalitarian relationship with a woman who sees herself as your equal.

Avoiding Getting Stood Up.   Just like the men who say they'll call and then don't, there are women who accept dates that they don't really want. Sometimes women do this because they have Too Nice Syndrome. If he asks, she reasons, I can't hurt his feelings and say no. So, I'll accept and figure out how to handle it later. This woman will often cancel the date before it happens or, in the case of the person who will do anything rather than have to say no, she will stand him up. How can you tell when this is likely to happen?

Taking the time to assess a woman's interest level helps. When you first met her, did she smile at you a lot? Did she make lots of eye contact and seem really interested in what you were saying? Was her body language open (i.e., uncrossed arms, body turned toward you rather than away)? Did she seem genuinely interested when you asked her out, or did she seem hesitant? Was it difficult for her to find time to see you, or did she quickly make room in her calendar for you?

If her interest level is low, if she makes little eye contact and her body language is closed, if she hesitates to set a date, you have a good probability of getting stood up. Another sign of low interest is when a woman makes flimsy excuses for not getting together. *The truth is that when someone is really interested in you, they make the time to see you.* If time is really an issue, the interested person will make sure you know that they really want to see you and to please not give up on them.

Some men feel that even if a woman's interest level is low, it's still worth the pursuit. They believe that if they wine and dine her enough, send enough flowers and romantic notes, entertain her lavishly enough and inundate her with gifts, that she can be "won over." The hesitant woman is seen as a challenge, and the chase is exciting indeed.

The problem is that this kind of one-sided pursuit is not the basis for a healthy relationship. For love to work in the long run, it must be felt by both partners. Remember the pyramid in chapter three? Equal desire for the relationship forms half of the foundation, without which the romance will eventually crumble. Even if she accepts and keeps dates, if the feelings aren't mutual, you will spin your wheels and wind up frustrated and empty-handed.

Dealing with Potential Abuse.   Yes, men can be abused by women. Men are by nature physically stronger and more powerful, making the probability lower of men being victimized than vice versa. This doesn't mean, however, that it can't happen or that men don't hurt just as much as women when it does.

Men have been emotionally and physically abused by women, and it can begin in the early stages of the dating relationship. The same list of warning signs earlier in the chapter applies to men as well as to women.

What makes this task harder for men than for women is that there is little belief in our culture that men can be hurt by women emotionally, sexually, or physically. Men who are sexually harassed or abused face an uphill battle in convincing anyone of the truth of their story.

Men are not usually on their guards for signs of abuse from women. It's easy to believe that women are incapable of this kind of behavior because our culture emphasizes the physical prowess of men. Male heroes smash cars and carry big guns, and the vast majority of Hollywood villains are male. But sociopathic and insensitive women exist also, even though not in the same numbers as men.

Men and Women and the Dating Game

The old rules are out; the new ones are up for grabs. This chapter doesn't begin to cover all the issues that you'll encounter in the singles dating scene. Challenges abound in the search for a lasting relationship, and no book can totally prepare you for what lies ahead.

The most important thing you can do is pay attention to your own feelings and responses as you meet, mingle, and date. This means being aware of your own values, preferences, and inner experience. Awareness like this enables you to set the boundaries that you need in order to protect yourself and help you create the most positive and rewarding dating experiences possible.

Part II

The Relationship

11

♥ ♥ ♥

Communication:
The Fertilizer for Relationships

At this point you may ask, "What about love? We've created a Dating Game Plan, we've outlined what the first three dates should look like, we've talked about boundaries, and we've created Relationship Shopping Lists. When does love enter the picture? After all, isn't this what we're looking for?"

The answer is an unqualified yes. Love is the energy that fuels relationships. When eyes meet, hands touch, and we feel a tingle of delight, the sparks of love are ignited. When warm words soothe away the worries of the outside world, when we feel totally listened to, love flourishes. Being drawn to a special person, giving our hearts, feeling totally accepted and loved: This is potent magic.

This energy, this force that occurs between two people, is incredibly powerful. Love puts a sparkle in the eye and a dance in the step of even the most jaded. Love puts individuals in a state of euphoria that is more energizing than any drug and that can last for days, weeks, and even months. Loving and being loved by one special person can heal the deepest wounds in life. No wonder we seek it so tenaciously.

With love, all things are *not* necessarily possible, but many things are. Fueled by these powerful feelings, we are motivated to work at a relationship. We talk and express feelings, we listen to each other's concerns, we strive to meet each other's needs, and we do the things that maintain our connection.

Without love, a relationship would have to be sustained by duty alone, and that would be small comfort in a world full of problems and worries. Lacking in sufficient love, a relationship becomes empty and meaningless. Without this fuel, we flounder in our efforts to resolve differences. There is no doubt that modern relationships require a tremendous amount of energy, and love is the primary source of that energy.

But what exactly is love? How do we know when we've found it? What is real love versus something less than real?

What Is Love?

Social scientists, psychologists, theologians, philosophers, and every-day people by the millions have struggled with the meanings and definitions of love. Because it is a subjective experience that's different for each of us, and because we can't look inside one another's heads and hearts to really see what it's like for the other person, we are left with the struggle to put together the right words to give love some kind of universal meaning.

Even though love is different for each person and a unique experience in every relationship, there are some distinctions that help us have a greater understanding of this mysterious force. There are four basic kinds of love that are possible:

1. Familial love. This includes the love between a parent and a child, or between siblings, or between a niece and an aunt, or between grandparent and grandchild, and so on.
2. Friendship love. This is the kind of love that occurs between both same-sex and opposite-sex friends, and that has no romantic

or sexual energy. Sometimes friendship love can turn into romantic love.

3. Altruistic love. This is the kind of love that is expansive and includes humankind in general, such as the feelings we have when we do something with no expected reward that is a benefit to others. Some have said that this is the truest kind of love in that it is completely a gift, with nothing expected in return.

4. Romantic love. This is love that has sexual energy, and often includes the desire to form a family and have children together.

Concerning this fourth type, there are many kinds of romantic love, some of which are:

• Instant love. Known as the "love at first sight" syndrome (and a favorite of Hollywood), this is when two people meet and feel a powerful attraction that seems undeniable. This kind of love may be the beginning of a lasting love or it may be a flash in the pan that fades as quickly as it began. Couples who experience this and marry quickly are truly gambling with their lives and their hearts due to the high degree of risk that it will not be the long-lasting kind.

• Lust connection. This kind of romantic love is primarily sexual and can exist even when the two people involved do not like or respect each other, making it a very dangerous kind of attraction. If there are no common values or mutual commitment, this kind of connection is doomed to failure, whether it takes weeks, months, or years. The lust connection often leads to addictive love, which we'll explore further in chapter fourteen.

• Friendship first. This is the kind of romantic love that begins with a strong friendship connection and grows into a sexual connection as well. With shared values, this kind of romance becomes even stronger. If paced out and allowed to develop, this kind of romantic love has the greatest possibility of turning into a lasting love.

There is no doubt that romantic love is one of the most powerful kinds of love, at least in the beginning of a relationship. It is also very fragile in that it can be killed rather easily if the right conditions aren't met. One of the things that kills romantic love is clinging to myths and fantasies about what love *could* be rather than experiencing and nurturing the very real love that you have. Let's look at some of these myths and how to counteract them.

Myth: The Only Successful Love Is Permanent Love

Donald, forty-six and divorced once, had been dating Connie for about four months. "Things are going really well. In fact, sometimes I can't believe how well they're going. I get afraid that I'll fail somehow and screw it up. I really want this to work out," he said.

Asked how he was defining success for this relationship, he answered, "Well, it means that you stay together no matter what and you communicate and you work things out together, even when times are bad. Sometimes I'm so scared that we won't make it I just want to get some crazy glue and stick us together so we'll have to make it work!"

"If the definition of success is staying together forever, then have you ever had a successful relationship?" I asked him. "No," he answered, looking kind of sad and defeated.

"What if you had a different definition of success?" I asked. For instance: being committed to being the best possible partner in your relationship; expressing yourself fully, communicating openly and honestly; giving your partner the emotional safety to express him/herself as well; being committed to your own and your partner's well-being; doing everything in your power to nurture the relationship to the best of your ability. I asked how that kind of definition might feel and whether his current and all future relationships might be successful regardless of whether they lasted forever or not. "That feels totally different," Donald said, his face considerably lighter. "That definition makes me feel successful already. And, I think I could relax more with Connie instead of worrying about whether or not we stay together forever at this point."

Donald's definition of success is not unique. After all, a successful marriage has always been thought of as one that lasts throughout a lifetime. Until the last thirty-five years or so, that definition was adequate for most people. Now, though, we live in a time in which the reality is that half of all first marriages fail, and an even greater percentage of second and third marriages as well. Many of the people reading this book may be divorced, and if staying married is the only definition of success we have, then there's a lot of failure out there!

Most singles over the age of twenty-five have had more than one relationship that didn't last, and the older the age group the more likely it is that there was a marriage or two as well. That can be a lot of failure to drag around, which doesn't inspire feelings of confidence in your attempts to enter new relationships.

Reality: Successful Relationships Are More Than the End Result

A more empowering definition of success might be much more about the process of relating in the best possible way rather than having to make it last forever. We've all met couples who have managed to stay together for a lifetime but are miserable with each other. It's difficult to see that as a success.

Why not focus on being the best possible partner, communicating and expressing yourself openly and honestly, allowing the other person the safety to communicate, taking care of your needs, and caring about the well-being of your partner? This kind of focus allows:

- a sense of mastery and control (I am in charge of myself and my own behavior)
- a more relaxed approach to the relationship (I realize and allow for the fact that we may not be together forever)

- personal growth and development (I'm becoming a better person as I become a better partner)
- empowerment and self-esteem (I'm a success already, regardless of how this ultimately turns out)

Does this mean that we give up on the concept of lasting love? That we take wedding vows and not mean them? That we become cynical about the possibility of a lifetime relationship? I hope not!

Lucy, in her late thirties and divorced once, was telling the story of a long-distance relationship she'd had that lasted just a couple of months. "We connected so well and I felt so good with him. I really wanted the relationship to last, but we both had to eventually face the reality that neither one of us was willing to move." Lucy still felt sad about the relationship because it hadn't lasted.

Asked what was good about the relationship, she had much to say. "We were very honest with each other, no game playing. When we ended it we did it with a lot of respect for each other. We were both genuinely sad, but we didn't try to force it to work. Neither one of us sacrificed ourselves just to keep us together. That felt really good." Lucy came to realize that this relationship had been an unqualified success even though it hadn't lasted. She had stayed in touch with her feelings, needs, and wants. She had communicated them honestly and clearly, and she had let go of the relationship when she saw that she could no longer get her needs met.

It's one thing to *believe* in the possibility of lasting love relationships and to *endeavor* to have them. It's quite different to feel that the only way to experience a successful romance is through permanence.

Successful Love Is Healthful Love.   In healthy relationships there is a strong sense of commitment, though not a strong investment in happily-ever-after. There is the strong desire for the relationship to last but the willingness to let it go if it doesn't work. Open communication is more important than sparing feelings (i.e., "If I tell you how I really feel, I might lose you"). Keeping personal integrity intact while having a genuine respect for your partner's wants and needs is more important than just getting one's needs met through others.

Healthy love relationships begin with successful dating, which begins with an attitude of being the best possible you. By this definition, a successful dating relationship could last for only three dates.

Lois, thirty-four and divorced twice, had been dating Randy for about four weeks. Strongly attracted to him, she was beginning to see a future with him. At the same time, she was certain she didn't want to waste her time if he wasn't ready for a committed relationship at this point in his life. After several conversations, they realized they were on two different tracks. They decided to end the relationship and did so with honesty and respect. Even though Lucy was sad about the loss, she counted the relationship a success.

Whether one date or a lifetime of dates, there's no way to completely control the outcome of a relationship. What you *can* control is how *you* communicate and respond in a relationship. How you do that has a direct impact on the success of your romances, regardless of how long they last. And remember, it begins with the very first encounter.

Myth: Love Is Mostly a Feeling

This myth says that love is primarily that tingly feeling you get when your lover calls, those chills you feel when he kisses you, and the way your heart pounds when you see him. Add all that up and you have love, and somehow it is supposed to be enough to sustain a relationship over a lifetime.

Unfortunately, the excitement and thrills of a new relationship simply cannot be sustained over years of daily living, paying bills, changing diapers, and working from dawn to dusk. Passionate kisses eventually give way to warm embraces. Romantic gestures go by the wayside as the pressures of other concerns take priority. Steamy sex can devolve into routine and even boring sex. What about love then?

Once the initial thrill has subsided, feelings of love must make the transition from passionate to deeply caring if a relationship is going to last. Mutual commitment, with both parties wanting the relationship and placing it in a position of high priority, becomes the main fuel for the romance. Once this happens, feelings of love become less important than the *behavior of love*.

Reality: Love Is a Behavior That Starts with a Feeling

The true meaning of lasting romantic love is the performance of loving behaviors over and over again, even when you don't always want to do this. The beginning of a romantic love, with all the energy and good feelings, provides the incentive to begin the process of a loving relationship. Later, when those feelings fade and more deeply caring ones take their place, *loving behavior* is what fuels and sustains the relationship.

This means taking the time to talk at the end of the day; really listening to each other and sharing feelings; giving each other massages; bringing your partner a cup of coffee in the morning; initiating sex even when you're not particularly in the mood; providing comfort for hurt feelings; giving flowers and writing love notes; taking care of each other when there's illness—all these and countless other little behaviors add up to real and lasting love.

Unreal love means counting on the feelings to last forever all by themselves; being addicted to the high of romantic love; deciding that because you're a little bored you should end it; caring much more about getting your own needs met than about your partner's well-being; failing to do loving things just because your partner hasn't done anything good for you lately; all these and many more. *Unreal love is all about feelings and very little about loving behavior.*

Love is much more than feelings, and the ability to *be loving* as well as to receive love is essential. Probably the most important of all loving behaviors is the ability to communicate effectively.

Communication: Creating Real Love

Making sure that you're both available for a commitment sets the stage for half of the foundation for a healthy relationship. Remember that one half is shared values and the other half is equal desire for the relationship, which allows commitment to occur. In addition to this all-important foundation, a couple needs to feel strongly connected at the intellectual, emotional, and sexual levels.

Even with the foundation and the chemistry in place, even with all the love your heart can hold, a relationship can flounder at any point if the communication isn't there or doesn't work. The number-one issue that marriage counselors address in therapy is nonexistent or ineffective communication. *All the ingredients for a great relationship can be present, but if we can't talk to or listen to each other effectively, it amounts to nothing.*

A relationship is like a garden. It is either growing and flourishing or it is shrinking and dying, depending on how you nurture it. If you water it, fertilize it, and keep the weeds out, it will grow and flourish. If you neglect it, the weeds will choke out the plants, which will gradually die from lack of water and nourishment.

If loving behavior is the water for a relationship, then communication is the fertilizer. And this fertilizer is needed from the *very beginning of a dating relationship*. It doesn't work to wait until you're married and *then* try to start communicating, or to assume that just because you love each other you'll always be able to work things out.

Not all communication is equal. There are different levels of communication that we all engage in throughout our daily living and in all kinds of relationships.

In Figure 11-1, the bottom part of the pyramid is wider to indicate the frequency of occurrence of this type of communication, while the smaller size of the top indicates the rarity of that kind of communication. As you move up the pyramid from bottom to top, the level of emotional risk increases as well.

At the bottom of the pyramid is *social chitchat,* the kind of talk that goes on the most in everyday life, such as "How's the weather?" or

LEVELS OF COMMUNICATION

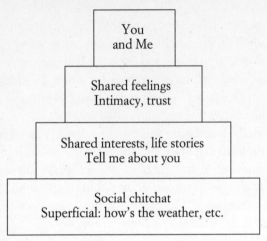

You
and Me

Shared feelings
Intimacy, trust

Shared interests, life stories
Tell me about you

Social chitchat
Superficial: how's the weather, etc.

Figure 11-1

"Did you catch the game last night?" or even "How are you?" when it's meant superficially.

We all engage in social chitchat to pass the time, to establish rapport with someone we don't yet know well, to connect on a very emotionally safe level. We need this level of communication for those purposes. In the process of engaging in social chitchat we can test the waters with someone new. If you respond to me positively, then I'll begin to trust you. If not, I may back away, or I may choose to keep our future encounters on a strictly impersonal level.

Some relationships, such as in the business world, call for social chitchat as a rule. In a business meeting the conversation is usually on the topic to be handled and interaction is otherwise kept at a very superficial level.

On first dates, social chitchat is a way to break the ice and to test the waters. But as the relationship progresses, so does the level of communication.

The next level is *shared interests and life stories*. At this level we begin to talk about ourselves on a more personal level. I tell you about me and you tell me about you. We disclose information about our family, where and how we grew up, career paths, past relationships, and so much more. This is a way of testing the waters with a higher level of risk. If I tell you about my alcoholic father and you still accept me, then I trust you at a deeper level than before. If you reject me (through criticism, a disgusted look on your face, or an abrupt departure), I instinctively know that I can't really trust you in matters of the heart.

This second level of communication carries more risk because it hurts to open up and then be rejected. At the same time, the risk really pays off when a connection is made. If we share our personal stories and feel a sense of mutual positive regard, then trust is deepened and with it, intimacy. And deeper intimacy and connection with another human is inherently rewarding.

This second level of communication doesn't happen as often in our daily living because of the increased emotional risk. We tend to carefully choose whom we will open up to and not everyone we meet gets to hear our life story. Those who do, and who win our trust, may eventually move up another level in the communication pyramid.

The third level is *shared feelings*. At this level a statement such as "I'm really upset. I just found out I didn't get the raise I asked for and I'm angry and hurt" might be made. At this level of communication, we are very vulnerable as we open up about the most intimate parts of our selves: our emotional world. Again, the risk is even higher because of the increased vulnerability. If I tell you I'm hurt because you haven't called me in two weeks and you tell me to grow up and stop being a baby, the chances are that I won't risk my feelings with you again! A rejection of innermost feelings feels like a rejection of oneself, and that can be very painful. So we are generally very careful about whom we open up to at this level.

Some people are so afraid of emotional risk that they *never* open up about their innermost feelings. Sharing feelings is an act of great trust and can deepen and bind a relationship in a very powerful way. Those who don't do so may save themselves potential hurt, but they completely miss out on one of life's greatest rewards: emotional intimacy with a special person.

The You and Me Conversation

At the top of the pyramid is *You and Me,* the level of communication that carries the greatest emotional risk and also the one that occurs least often between people. This is the kind of conversation that asks questions such as: Who are we to each other? What is our relationship? Where are we going with this? How do we feel about each other, about our relationship? and so on.

The potential risk at this level of communication is very high because we put the relationship itself at risk when we do this. If we begin asking and answering these kinds of questions, we may discover, to our horror and pain, that we are on two entirely different tracks! Maybe I've thought that ours is a serious romance heading for commitment while you've assumed that we're only here for fun and games or until something better comes along. The next question is obviously: What now? Many times this means that the relationship is over or that we continue in emotional pain, knowing that our needs won't be met.

Communication and Love. Relationship experts agree that constant nagging or criticism can dampen even the most passionate love. Withholding negative feelings or expressing them in a hurtful way can kill the most promising romance. Neglecting to share positive and warm feelings, not taking the time to talk—these are like withholding water from a growing plant.

Without a strong commitment to regular, effective communication, all the passion and love in the world is worth nothing. In fact, the very essence of love is good communication.

One of the most loving things you can do is to consciously open the gates of communication, starting from the earliest dates and in particular with the You and Me conversation. By placing your relationship at risk in this way, you accomplish one of two things: 1) you strengthen the bond between you by revealing where you are with each other, or 2) you face the reality of your differing levels of commitment, allowing you both to move on in the search for a right partner. Either way, you can't lose!

Remember Lois and Lucy from earlier in this chapter? Both took the risk of having the You and Me conversation, knowing that the relationship might end. Both discovered that success isn't in trying to force a romance to last forever, but in the practice of honest, open communication.

This doesn't mean, however, that you won't feel some pain in the process. In romance, expectations can soar after only a couple of dates. Time after time, clients sit in my office and rave about the new person in their lives after only two or three dates. "He's so wonderful. He's nice and he likes the same things I do and we communicate so well! He's everything I've been looking for," they'll say. All this after only a couple of dates, as if it's possible to know a person's entire personality with only a few brief encounters. How does this happen?

Powerful Needs, High Expectations.   The desire and need to connect with and to love and be loved by a special person is very strong. We all want, on a very basic level, to find that one special person with whom to have a relationship.

Lots of dates don't lead to romance, and it's easy to feel discouraged by that. So when someone comes along that you feel lots of sparks with, there's the sense that wow, this person's different! This one has possibilities! If you feel a connection beginning to happen in the first couple of dates, it's easy to begin projecting into the future.

Singles who will admit it say that even after *one date* they sometimes begin fantasizing about a future, and it goes something like this: "Wow! What a great date. We talked so easily, we shared so much! I feel so connected to this person, we have so much in common. I can really tell the feeling is mutual. I can't wait for our next date! And since it's summer, we'll go out every Friday and Saturday night, and probably spend a couple of nights a week together. Maybe by August we can meet each other's families and spend Labor Day weekend together in September. Then there's the holidays: We'll have to figure out whose family to spend Thanksgiving with and whose to spend Christmas with. In the spring we can get engaged and by next summer, who knows? Maybe we'll have a June wedding!" Sound far-fetched? Not considering how high the need may be and how quickly expectations can rise.

Once the fantasy takes on a life of its own, the crash can be devastating. The pain of losing a wished-for relationship can sometimes be greater than losing an actual one. This is because losing the wished-for romance is like losing hope. Once again, I got my hopes up and thought that maybe I had really found someone special, only to have them dashed again.

Because losing a wished-for relationship hurts so much, you may be tempted to avoid the You and Me conversation in order to sustain the fantasy. This can have disastrous consequences as you spin your wheels, investing months and years plus lots of emotional energy. Later, when you discover that your dream relationship was mostly fantasy, that your dream partner was just a dream, it can hurt like hell.

Postponing the Pain.   Putting off or avoiding the You and Me conversation only postpones the pain. Even if you are both in the same place, you've overlooked an important opportunity to practice your communication skills, to deepen your relationship by revealing innermost thoughts and feelings, and to forge a powerful bond of honesty and self-disclosure.

I like to think of communication skills in the same way I think of muscle strength and endurance. The first time I ever worked out was a real challenge. My muscles were weak and flabby and I had to really strain to lift the weights. I felt uncomfortable and awkward, not sure of exactly how to use the equipment. Afterward, I felt exhausted and sore.

But as I continued to work out, my muscles became stronger. I got used to the equipment and my awkwardness disappeared. Eventually, I looked forward to my workouts, enjoying the feel of strengthening my body.

Communication in relationships is much like this. At first you feel awkward, not sure what to say or how to say it. If you work at it, though, you begin to develop a certain strength and confidence in yourself and in your relationships. Eventually, even the most difficult conversations, such as the You and Me, feel natural. You've developed emotional and communicational muscle strength.

Dating relationships that focus mainly on having fun together, enjoying the romance but neglecting the work of communication, can lead to marriages with weak foundations. Not having practiced difficult conversations, disclosing risky thoughts and feelings, leaves you with a low level of skill. When painful issues arise, as they always do in marriage, you're both stuck, not knowing how to express feelings to each other or how to confront each other. The issues don't get resolved and get bigger and bigger, eventually driving you to a therapist and possibly even divorce.

Building Emotional Muscle

Why not use your dating relationships to build and strengthen your emotional and communicational skills? Rather than assuming that just because you enjoy each other it will all work out, take the risk of opening up to your partner and expressing feelings. Share both positive and negative feelings. Practice self-disclosure in all aspects of your life and your relationships, building the emotional muscle you need to sustain the lasting love you will eventually find.

Dare to bring up the You and Me conversation, inviting disclosure on both your parts about where you stand in your relationship. Be willing to put the relationship at risk rather than sustain a fantasy. Be more committed to your own emotional health and well-being than you are to keeping a particular person in your life.

The rest of this book is about increasing your awareness of the dynamics of romantic love and developing healthy relationships that are more rewarding and more likely to lead to commitment. The key to making all this happen is communication, the fertilizer for relationships. Being able to make it work means being able to take some risks and build your emotional muscle.

Yes, romantic love is the goal and it feels really good. But that's only the beginning of healthy, nurturing relationships. *To create and sustain a lasting love is much more challenging and infinitely more rewarding than any other pursuit in life.* How you go about dating, especially how you communicate with potential partners, lays the foundation for this kind of love.

12

♥   ♥   ♥

Courtship Versus the "Settle-for" Relationship

Human beings are by nature social creatures. We seek companionship and a sense of community. From the time we're born we need other people: first, a nurturing caretaker; later, friends and companions; eventually, a mate with whom to share life.

Biologically speaking, we are wired to seek the proximity of other human beings. Infants need more than just food and protection from the elements. They need nurturing and physical contact as well. In one famous study with primates, orphaned baby monkeys were given the choice of a surrogate mother made of wire or of a second one made of cloth (both surrogates had bottles attached). The babies invariably chose the cloth mother, thus showing the powerful need of infants to have soft, nurturing contact. When the researchers removed the bottles from the cloth mothers and left them on the wire mothers, the babies still chose the cloth surrogate mothers.

The need for care and nurturing follows us into adult life, setting the stage for friendships and romantic love. We unconsciously long to feel close and loving like we did with our early caretakers. Because this need is so great, human beings will often choose a bad relationship over nothing at all. In dating, we are sometimes

tempted to settle for less than what we want because it seems prefer-
able to being alone.

Two Kinds of Dating Relationships

The innate, biological drive to seek companionship with other human
beings fuels our search for friendships and social contact. Only in a
romantic relationship, however, can we hope to receive both love
(unconditional, positive regard) and nurturing (touching, holding,
caressing), the combination of which satisfies our deepest needs.

In the context of a committed relationship, nothing is more satisfying than giving and receiving the love and nurturing to which we
feel entitled as human beings. Commitment provides an emotional
"safety net," meaning that there's less chance of being abandoned;
therefore, we are more able to open up and be fully emotionally available to a partner. Without this openness and emotional availability, a
relationship soon stalls or runs into other troubled waters.

In a committed relationship between two people who both want
the relationship, the opportunity exists for a great deal of healing
from the pain of living an imperfect life. Lovers can listen to, touch,
and hold each other. They can offer empathy and compassion. They
can be each other's champion, cheering from the sidelines. They can
explore the joys of being sexual and sensual together. They can provide a safe haven in times of stress.

Being without a romantic relationship means that this kind of love
and nurturing just isn't available. Friends may offer empathy and
compassion. They may be our cheerleaders. But friends aren't there
on a daily basis, waking up beside us, holding and touching us in intimate ways. Friends just can't be what lovers can be, no matter how
hard they may try. Thus, most singles are continually looking for
someone to share a romantic relationship with.

The "Settle-for" Relationship.   This type of relationship is not
exactly a romance for life. It usually lacks any kind of commitment,
yet it offers some of the goodies of romantic love. There's compan-

ionship, touching, sex, and the sense that you're not completely alone. Sometimes there's genuine positive regard and caring. What there isn't is a sense that this is something lasting, something worth fighting for when the going gets rough. Sometimes one person, or even both, in this kind of relationship is actually hoping something better will eventually come along.

When two people agree that this is the kind of relationship they want, and they keep it fairly short (a couple of weeks to a couple of months), there's actually a good chance that they will come out of it relatively unscathed emotionally. Sometimes we call this the "transitional relationship," meaning the one between the last significant one and the next significant one. Sometimes this kind of relationship helps with the healing after a particularly painful breakup. There's nothing wrong with getting some needs met this way, as long as both people involved are extremely honest about their feelings and motives.

Most often, however, this ends up being what I call the "Settle-for" Relationship, meaning that one person, or both, is settling for less than what they really want. This happens when the pain of being alone exceeds the commitment to having the best possible relationship. The drive to meet those needs for nurturing may cloud judgment, driving people to pursue or stay in romances that just aren't right. Karen's story shows how this happens.

"I was a junior in college and I had just moved out on my own. For the first time in my life, I had no family around, and I hadn't yet made very many friends at my new college. The loneliness at night in my little apartment seemed almost unbearable at times. I met Joe and we were instantly involved. He came over every night, and I didn't have to feel lonely anymore. After a few months I knew he wasn't 'the one,' but I kept seeing him anyway. Even though he wasn't right for me, he was better than nothing. I felt guilty for continuing to see him this way, but I was convinced that breaking up would devastate him. I stayed with him for four years, and the last two were sheer agony."

Karen, like many singles, got caught in a nowhere, Settle-for relationship in order to get some of her needs met and avoid feeling alone. Because she wasn't honest with her partner, both ended up being hurt. Meanwhile, she was emotionally unavailable to other men, one of whom might have been right for her.

Courtship. Contrast the Settle-for relationship with another kind. In the second kind, two people meet, feel sparks, spend time getting to know each other, and eventually realize they want a relationship with each other. They find that they share most of the same cherished values. Through mutual self-disclosure, setting boundaries, and open, honest communication, they build a foundation of intimacy and trust. They find that they connect on an intellectual, emotional, and sexual level. After a few weeks of dating, they commit to concentrating on their relationship to the exclusion of all others. Both partners feel an equally strong attraction to each other and a desire for their relationship to continue and flourish. Each strives to treat the other with kindness and respect, wanting to please and to meet the other's needs. When conflict arises, they talk it out together, both being willing to make concessions for the sake of the relationship. Both have a strong sense that they've met the person they want to spend their lives with. They talk in terms of a future together, and they arrange their lives so that their relationship is a top priority. This is what I call "Courtship."

Getting the Kind of Love You Want

In the dating world, we are constantly faced with choices: whom to go out with, whether to continue dating, whom to make a commitment to, and so on. These choices become stalemates when we don't know what we want. Some say, "Just go out and have a good time. Don't worry about where the relationship is headed." On the surface this sounds like good advice. After all, we do tend to overanalyze our relationships these days. Why not just enjoy being with someone?

The problem is that we're human beings and that means that we need to attach to other human beings. Regardless of whether we plan on it or not, we find ourselves becoming involved with people whom we spend romantic time with. Even if the intention is just to get some needs met and then move on, attachment can interrupt the plan. Without meaning to, we become romantically attached, often to people we don't really like or respect, or whom we don't share values with, or whom we're not really in love with. This leads to the Settle-for Relationship, which ultimately results in heartbreak and pain. Remember that the goal is to build positive relationship experiences, not collect more negative ones. Thus, it's wise to consider with whom and to what degree we'll become romantic, *before attachment occurs.* But first, we have to consider what we're looking for as we date.

What We Really Want.   Ask a hundred singles what kind of relationship they want and you'll get several responses, depending on where they are in their lives. Someone who's recently divorced, whose spouse left them for someone else, might say, "Nothing. I don't ever want to fall in love again! I'll just live the rest of my life alone, thank you very much!" Someone who's never been married but wants to be might say, "A committed relationship with marriage as the goal." Someone who recently lost a long-term dating relationship might say, "Just fun and good times. Nothing serious, not for a long, long time!"

When relationships fail, it's not unusual to feel a certain amount of skepticism or even cynicism about love. Sometimes those feelings fade in a couple of months, sometimes it takes years. Feelings of cynicism about love are often equal to the amount of pain associated with the last relationship. Thus, when we say we don't want a relationship, what we're really saying is, "I don't want another one like the one I just had!"

Bobby, forty-one and divorced, had been single for several years. After his failed marriage and two or three relationships that didn't go anywhere, he was resolved that a good relationship and a happy marriage just weren't in the stars for him. He worked and socialized with his buddies and occasionally had a date or two, but he was sure he didn't ever want to be married again. Then he met Sandy. They were attracted to each other and their values meshed. They let their relationship grow slowly over time, experiencing a few bumps along the way, but both were willing to talk and work out the issues. After a year and a half, Bobby marveled at his own transformation. "For the first time in many years, I can see myself married—to this lady," he said. "I never thought it would happen, but the quality of our relationship has given me hope once again that marriage can be a good thing."

Part of what Bobby needed to recover was the *hope* that good relationships are possible and that there really was someone out there with whom he could have a real and lasting love. With enough time and healing, this hope almost always returns. In fact, one of the most astonishing things about romantic love is our capacity to try again and again, in spite of what we see as multiple failures.

After enough time has passed since the last disastrous relationship, most people are once again able to say that what they want is a committed relationship that has a strong possibility of marriage. (If you don't want that right now, give yourself a few months. The chances are that you'll once again find yourself looking for love!) If this is what you want, it is now time to decide that you will settle for nothing less. Having decided that, you have now taken the first step toward getting it!

Asking for What We Want.   One of the crucial factors in getting what you want is actively, regularly, assertively asking for it. This sounds so simple, yet in the dating game it is often left out. Because we are exposed to a flood of love propaganda every day (via the movies, television, romance novels, etc.), it's easy to conclude that the best way to romance is a crooked path. Being coy, indirect, and even downright manipulative is the way to capture your true love's heart.

Imagine that you are an alien sent to our planet to study human habits of courtship and marriage. You turn on the television and observe lovers saying one thing to each other and something entirely different to their friends. You see ads extolling the surefire remedies for loneliness that the right aftershave and toothpaste provide. You eavesdrop on conversations between single friends asking for relationship advice, where you hear everything but the obvious: "Tell her what you just told me." What would you conclude? From the outside looking in, it would seem that the way to true love for Earthlings lies in never, ever telling the full truth, no matter what!

If we want to have genuinely loving, trusting, healthy relationships, we must leave this myth behind forever. Honesty and openness don't magically start when we exchange vows. They begin from the very first encounter and are strengthened with each interaction, if you truly make them your goal.

The Honesty Double Standard

Often, I ask groups of singles what they're looking for in a relationship. Honesty is always at the top of the list. We all want to know that we can trust our dating partners to be truthful and open with us. Why? Because without honesty, we are in the position of making important, life-altering decisions without having a full picture. Later, when the truth comes out, we feel betrayed and trust is sacrificed.

Yet how many times have we evaded or covered up the truth of our situations in order to look good to a potential partner? Or masked our real feelings in order to not risk scaring them off? We all want honesty, but most of us are reluctant to belly up to the bar and be honest ourselves. Yet this is exactly what we must do if we are to expect it in return. And without being honest about what we want in a relationship we run the risk of sending out mixed messages and getting something we don't want. It just doesn't work to operate under this kind of double standard: "I expect the full truth from you but I, on the other hand, maintain the right to hedge, cover up, and avoid the full truth if it makes me too uncomfortable to be totally straight with you." The cost of this double standard is lack of trust, which keeps a relationship from being truly intimate or healthy.

It's important when establishing trust in a relationship to express early on (first or second date) what you're looking for. This does two things: First, it establishes a pattern of honesty and trust on your part, which encourages your partner to do the same, and second, it allows you to address the courtship question early, instead of finding out months or years later that you're in a dead-end relationship. By being honest about what kind of relationship is wanted, the groundwork is laid from the very beginning for Courtship.

Establishing Courtship

In the beginning, Bill pursued Nora until she gave in and became involved with him. Once their involvement was established, Bill let Nora know that he wasn't ready for marriage and that was that. Nora, having by now fallen in love with Bill, was sure that he was "the one." So, she resolved to be patient and wait for him to change his mind and mature enough to also want marriage. They had numerous discussions about marriage in which they each took positions that were polar opposites. This led to fighting and threats by Bill to end the relationship. Nora always backed down, retreating into the hoping game once again. After two and a half years, she discovered that he was dating someone else. Devastated, she realized too late that her relationship with Bill was a Courtship only in her eyes. In his, it was a transitional, Settle-for Relationship.

What Are You Shopping For?   Nora might have avoided the heartache she experienced had she had a very simple and straightforward conversation early in her relationship with Bill. I call this the "Shopping Conversation," and it goes like this:

> NORA: Bill, I want you to know that even though this is only our second date, it's very important to me to be straight with you about where I am in my life. I've reached a point where I know I want to be married someday. In fact, I'm looking for someone with whom to have a committed relationship in which there's a strong possibility of marriage. *I don't know if that's you or not,* but I want you to know that that's what I'm looking for. What about you?

The part in italics is for clarification: It's important that you let this person know that you have not made up your mind that they're "the one," as you obviously haven't gotten to know them well enough yet, but that you're interested in getting to know them better, and you want to know that you're both looking for the same kind of relationship.

Nora has now let Bill know what she's shopping for. Certainly she doesn't know at this point if Bill's "the one," but she probably wouldn't have this conversation if she weren't interested in him and foreseeing future dates.

When to Have the Shopping Conversation.   Once it has been established that there's definite attraction on the part of both parties (usually by the second or third date), now is the time to have the Shopping Conversation. Why? Because attachment happens very quickly and the idea is to intervene in the developing relationship as soon as possible to be sure that you're on a course of mutual fulfillment and satisfaction.

Now that Nora has disclosed her feelings, the ball is in Bill's court. He will do one of several things: 1) become very uncomfortable and start to hedge about where he is (which would be a red flag); 2) state that he's not in the same place, that he's more interested in just having fun (which would tell Nora that this is probably a dead-end relationship); 3) say he feels the same way but cancel their next date (actions speak louder than words in this case); 4) say he feels the same way and express gratitude for her honesty and for bringing it up so soon; or other scenarios that you can imagine.

Does bringing up this conversation early in a relationship guarantee a good outcome? Certainly not! Remember that the goal isn't to *always* get what you want, but rather to *eventually* get what you want. And that happens by practicing healthy relating skills, like being honest and straightforward and asking for what you want.

But I'll Scare Them Away.   Jeannie spoke for the whole class when she said, "But that sounds so intense. I'm afraid that if I say that, it'll scare men away."

"First of all, are you looking for a committed relationship with the possibility of marriage?" I asked her.

"Yes, of course I am," she answered, still looking skeptical.

"Well, then, if you were to say that to a guy and he couldn't deal with it, what would that tell you?" I queried.

"It would tell me he's not ready for the kind of relationship I want," she said, laughing at how obvious the answer is.

The person who is ready for Courtship, the person who wants a committed relationship with the possibility of marriage, will welcome this conversation. That person will be grateful that you had the guts to bring it up first! The truly emotionally available person who's interested in you will be glad.

The person who might have dated you in order to get some relationship goodies without a commitment will be uncomfortable. The person who's still recovering from a broken heart and not ready for an involvement will not be receptive to this conversation. And you will discover the roadblocks to getting the kind of love you want *before* you become attached. At this point you can make an informed decision. If you choose to go ahead with a partner who doesn't want what you want, you know that you have a high probability of spinning your wheels and ending up with a broken heart yourself. But at least you're choosing consciously rather than feeling deceived and ripped off later.

So I say: Scare a few people off! I'd rather you do that than spend months and years in relationships that have a built-in dead end.

Remember that operating with a sense that there's an abundance of good people out there means less desperation. This person is not the last opportunity to find love but merely *one of many opportunities*. Therefore, I can afford to take some risk, to rock the boat a little, to ask for what I want and let the chips fall where they will. If this person's not ready for the kind of relationship I want, someone else will be.

Conversations like the Shopping Conversation lay the groundwork for Courtship. Rather than just hanging out together, you are engaged in a mutual exploration of the *possibility* of spending your lives together.

Slowing Down Without Stopping

One vitally important aspect of healthy relating is the pace of a relationship. Healthy love is a mutual exploration of the possibility of spending a lifetime together. This takes place over time and at a reasonable pace. It is *not* the assumption that we're meant for each other just because we had a few dates that felt really, really good.

Healthy individuals can afford to take their time to get to know one another, realizing that good relationships have a strong foundation that is built over time. Through the process of interacting openly and honestly about feelings, discovering differences as well as sameness, and resolving conflict with a minimum of damage, a relationship foundation is established and strengthened. This simply cannot happen overnight or in the blush of early love.

In the beginning of a relationship we all tend to put our best foot forward. Unconsciously, we attract our mates by revealing only the most positive aspects of our personalities. As we're falling in love we feel a heightened sense of well-being, which makes us all the more prone to presenting only our good sides.

As relationships progress, we begin to see those aspects of our partners that are not so positive. Those feelings of glorious well-being begin to fade and we both return to reality. All the problems that were there before we fell in love return for us to face. We feel slightly disenchanted with our partners, and we have our first fight. Now we are beginning to discover our true potential as a couple. *A relationship is only as good as our ability to experience negative feelings toward each other and to resolve conflict in a way that's positive for both individuals.* And these things don't come out until months and sometimes years into the romance.

To decide that a relationship is "the one" while still in the earliest stage, the falling-in-love stage, is a gamble. It may turn out to be so or it may not, but the truth is that you just don't know what you're getting. This would be like buying a house based only on photographs of the exterior. You have some idea of what you're getting, but your knowledge is far from complete.

To gamble with the most important aspect of life, your primary relationship, is a high-stakes game. When couples marry after only a few days or weeks of courting, they are assuming a very large risk. The odds are not in their favor. And, let's face it: Love is risky enough without throwing the odds against us! Letting a relationship grow over time is essential, laying a strong foundation from which to weather the inevitable storms ahead.

The Skyrocket Relationship. When Debbie and Luke met, the sparks were instantaneous. By their third date they were talking for hours, sharing past histories and planning their future. Within a month, Luke told Sherry that he was sure he would marry her, and they were already discussing the number of children they would have. Fortunately, they planned to date for a few more months before becoming engaged. By their second month, Luke began having strong doubts about his feelings for Debbie. Just after their third-month dating anniversary, Luke broke up with Debbie, saying that he realized she wasn't right for him. What happened?

This couple had what I call the "Skyrocket Relationship." Instant fireworks, lots of flash and dazzle, but no real substance. Once the sizzle faded, Luke was gone.

Romance Junkies. Some people are very good at falling in love but not so good at sustaining it. These people tend to rush headlong into new relationships with very little caution. They fall madly in love, delighting in the heady excitement of a new romance. When those feelings fade, they are terribly disappointed, more so than the average person. The "Romance Junkie" takes it very personally when the good times are accompanied by some bad ones. They interpret the end of the falling-in-love stage as a sign that they just haven't found the right person yet. Once the relationship has ended, the Romance Junkie is off and running with a new love as soon as possible.

The Marathon Date. Patty and Michael met at a nightclub on Friday night and decided to go for coffee. Coffee turned into a midnight meal that progressed into a late-night talk session at her apartment.

By 6:00 A.M. they were exhausted but convinced that they had found their true love in each other. Their second date was Saturday night. That date lasted until Monday morning, when they reluctantly parted to go to their respective jobs. Patty and Michael's expectations soared in direct proportion to the romantic illusions that these extra-long, intense dates had inspired. Their disappointment and hurt was immense when conflict erupted and the relationship broke apart within six short weeks.

The "Marathon Date" sets the stage for expectations that usually cannot be met. They often lead to Skyrocket Relationships that soar very high and fizzle quickly.

How to Let a Relationship Grow.   One way to avoid the Sky-rocket Relationship is to pace your relationships. Set some boundaries with your time in the beginning. Using the guidelines in chapter nine, have your first two dates be short, one to one and a half hours. Have four or five days or even a week go by between dates. By the third date, maybe spend two to three hours together. Let a few more days go by before another date. Let several months go by before becoming physically intimate. Gradually build the amount of time you spend together rather than having Marathon Dates right away. Romance Junkies will be very impatient with this pace and will probably give up or divert their attention elsewhere (saving *you* a lot of pain!).

Pacing your relationships will accomplish several things. First, it will give you a more realistic perspective as you allow yourself time to come down from the emotional high you feel from being in love. Second, it conveys a message of respect, namely, that we care enough about ourselves to take our time getting to know each other. Third, it allows you to move beyond the falling-in-love stage and discover what your true compatibility potential is. Fourth, it is good practice at behaving in a less desperate manner, which builds your confidence. Fifth, it sets the stage for Courtship and commitment. Last of all, and sometimes most important, it gives you something to look forward to!

In our instant gratification culture, we are often too hasty in doing all the most wonderfully romantic things immediately. Later, we've already exhausted our repertoire of romantic interludes.

Why not start out with just dating, letting the feelings and the romance build momentum over time? There's something very romantic about pacing a relationship, savoring each encounter and looking forward to the next one. If you are presented with a gourmet meal, you can gulp it all down hastily or you can eat it one slow forkful at a time, delighting in the aromas and flavors. Why not delight in the slow building of a romance? Remember that a well-paced Courtship full of good memories can provide an anchor for a relationship, helping you weather the stormy seas that are to come.

Slowing the pace of dating relationships also helps you establish something very crucial: friendship. So often singles fall in love with people they would never choose as friends. What does this say about the relationship?

All couples who enjoy satisfying, nurturing lifetime relationships say the same thing: We were good friends first and foremost, and we are each other's best friend today.

Setting the Stage for Commitment

The things we've discussed so far in this chapter (the Shopping Conversation, pacing a relationship) set the stage for Commitment. But what is this thing we call Commitment?

Often jokingly referred to as "the C word," the term commitment carries many connotations and has a unique meaning for each of us. This is what is known as a concept word, meaning that it isn't something solid that we can all agree upon, such as the meaning of the word *chair*. We all pretty much agree that a chair is an object used for sitting. If we asked a hundred people to define commitment, we would get a hundred different responses, with some overlapping themes.

Because we need some common ground for our discussions, I'll present my idea of what commitment is, as it applies to *romantic relationships*:

Commitment Is Both a Feeling and a Behavior.   The feeling is one of desire, love, and a sense of bonding with another person. This feeling includes a sense of *relationship* as an entity outside ourselves that we both work toward growing and maintaining. The behavior is of actively placing the relationship in a position of top priority in our lives. This includes initiating contact, both verbal and physical, even when there are problems between us. This initiation of contact and the performance of loving behaviors *especially* during those times when we don't feel positive toward one another is one of the most distinguishing features of commitment.

Commitment comes from the heart and is followed through via behavior. Certain behavior may indicate commitment (e.g., I call and we go on dates) but is not enough to sustain a loving, healthy relationship if it isn't from the heart. Love may be present (I want to be with you), but without commitment (I'll stand by you even in bad times) it is doomed to wither and die. Genuine commitment cannot be faked, and only when it comes from the heart does it have a chance of lasting.

Courtship sets the stage for commitment, which sets the stage for a lifetime relationship. Going on dates together, talking in an open and honest way about our thoughts, feelings, hopes, and dreams; sharing early on about the kind of relationship we're looking for and really paying attention to whether that matches our partner's desires; making conscious choices based on what we learn about those we date; pacing our relationships, letting them grow over time; making a conscious choice to be committed to a certain relationship and discussing this openly: This is the stuff of which Courtship is made. And Courtship creates the opportunity for a lifetime relationship.

Not Just Fun and Games.   This kind of dating, as you may have noticed, is not just fun and games. A lasting, loving relationship, while it offers laughter, fun, and joy, includes a lot of work. And that work begins from the very first encounter.

Lifelong loving relationships are not for the faint at heart or for those who don't like to face the pain of dealing with issues and problems. The joy that comes with a marriage for life is *earned,* it is not a freebie. It comes as a result of lots of difficult communication, effort, and sometimes tears and anguish. Your reward is the fulfilling sense that you've created something wonderful together. Commitment and love provide the incentive to do all this hard work, and it must be mutual. One person simply can't carry the entire weight of the relationship.

When we make a conscious effort to set the stage for Courtship, we are saying that we will settle for nothing less than a complete relationship. By being committed to having what we really want—a mutually loving and satisfying relationship—we invite other potential committed partners into our lives and we leave no room for those who are not. This is serious dating, but I promise it gets serious results!

Creating Intimacy Versus Strategizing.   The bookstores are full of how-to manuals that tell you the secrets of successful dating: dress this way, walk that way, use this line, and so on. If you do this, then you will entice another person to go out with you, have sex with you, fall in love with you. This approach is fine, as long as your only goal is to win over another person. With enough of the right techniques and social exposure, anyone can eventually get another person for a relationship.

If your goal is a lifelong, healthy relationship, then your methods will be quite different, and infinitely more challenging! *Creating intimacy, not strategizing, will get you the love you want.* Being open and honest, and being willing to say what you want and challenge your partner to be equally forthcoming is one way to begin. Finding someone to be truly committed to, and taking the time to let a relationship grow, are the secrets of lasting love. These things require us to examine ourselves, make changes, and grow. The reward is a loving relationship with ourselves first, and eventually with a significant other.

13

♥　　♥　　♥

The Northbound Train

Darlene and Mark met while their respective divorces were in process. Hungry for validation and healing from their past hurts, they latched onto each other like survivors to a life raft. At first it looked like they had found in each other the answer to previous disappointments. They became very attached and spent all their available time together. The intimacy was wonderful, especially after the rejection they had both gotten from their previous mates. It never occurred to either that they might need time to heal from their divorces or that this might be a "transitional relationship" rather than "true love." Thus, they both invested heavily in the relationship in an emotional sense. At the same time, both being very gun-shy about commitment, they each waited for the other to make the commitment first.

As the relationship progressed, disenchantment set in. Darlene debated with herself about whether Mark was right for her. Mark maintained a certain distance. They began struggling to get their needs met, but without a commitment in place they were unsuccessful in resolving their issues. Two years later, they broke up and both found themselves back in the same painful place they were in when just divorced. They recognized that they had both Settled For less than what they ultimately wanted in a relationship out of the fear of facing the inevitable loneliness that follows a divorce. Both realized that they had bypassed some important steps at the time of their divorces, steps that would have enabled them to be more emotionally available for a partner later on.

Emotional Availability: A Must.   If you consider yourself to be emotionally available, then it's vital that you know how to spot availability in your dating partners. Otherwise, you will find yourself spinning your wheels with people who can't or won't commit.

But how do you tell if someone else is available? While you can never fully know another person's mind and heart, there are signs and indications that provide a wealth of information. In order to distinguish the different kinds of availability, I've borrowed an analogy that I picked up at a sales seminar.

Looking for an Available Partner

People aren't trains, but they do seem to be headed in certain directions when we cross paths with them. Depending on the time of life, past experiences, current situations, and so much more, I may or may not be focused on finding a committed relationship. Then there's whether or not I want a commitment with a particular person. I may be available for a commitment but not want it with you.

Let's look at the different levels of availability in relationships. We'll talk in terms of looking at your partners; however, it's essential that you examine yourself as we go, asking, "How available am I at this time in my life to be in a committed relationship?"

The Southbound Train.   Relationally speaking, the "Southbound Train" is someone who is *not available* for a relationship and who has *no desire* for one with you. This is the person you may admire from afar but who doesn't even know you exist, or who doesn't think of you in that way. Your boss's husband seems like the kind of guy you could be happy with. You feel some attraction to him and consider him a model of the kind of man you're looking for, but he barely knows you or is merely friendly when you see him. He's a Southbound Train. Movie stars are Southbound Trains. We idealize them, but *there's no possibility of a relationship.*

The Eastbound Train. A person who *is available* for a relationship, but who has *no desire* for one with you is the "Eastbound Train." Ouch. This is the woman you work with, who you know is unattached and unmarried, but who won't give you the time of day.

The Eastbound Train is looking for a relationship, too, but just doesn't feel the sparks with you. Attraction to someone like this can really hurt, because it feels like a personal rejection. Remember that chemistry and attraction are a fluke and, therefore, the lack of them is not your fault! Learn to pass up these people quickly and not let them damage your self-esteem.

Sometimes singles say that everyone they meet is Eastbound. Sam, in his late twenties, had never had a date. A very shy person, he had only approached women for dates a handful of times in his adult life. Each and every time he was turned down. As we examined his way of approaching women, we discovered that he was leaving out some very important rapport-building steps. He learned to remedy this very quickly, and within a few weeks he was dating. If everyone you meet is Eastbound, you may want to go back to the rapport-building skills covered in chapter seven.

If you put your Dating Game Plan into action, you will undoubtedly encounter a few Eastbound Trains. However, you can avoid some of them by paying attention to body language. Remember that lots of eye contact, open body posture, and engagement in conversation are indications of interest, while the lack of these tells you that this person is probably still looking for someone else.

The Westbound Train. The "Westbound Train" is the most important individual to be wary of. This is the person who is *not available* for a commitment but who *has the desire* to be with you. He or she is emotionally unavailable in some way.

Westbound Trains pursue, send flowers, ask for dates, accept dates, are romantic, fall in love, and will even be monogamous. But they always hold back a large part of themselves and are unable or unwilling to commit. This happens for a variety of reasons, which we'll explore later in this chapter.

The Westbound Train is hard to spot. This is the person who may be technically single, although still involved in another relationship. He or she may be uninvolved with anyone else but hasn't had sufficient healing time since the last relationship. Seeking connection and love, the Westbound Train is genuine about the desire to be with you but can't deal with long-term commitments.

A romance with this type of person is an exercise in heartache and frustration. It's easy to misinterpret their attentions as a bid for a committed relationship. But just when you think you've finally found "the one," the Westbound Train will slip through your fingers, leaving you hurt and confused. There are several ways in which a person can be Westbound:

- The Quick Fizzle. This is the person who starts out hot and heavy, then fades out suddenly. They may wine you, dine you, and send flowers, or accept romantic dates and give you passionate kisses, but their hearts aren't in it. They send mixed signals with their behavior. One minute you're "it" for them, the next minute you find yourself out in the cold.

- Still Hurting. This is the person who hasn't had sufficient time since a divorce or the breakup of a long-term relationship. Seeking validation that they're still desirable, this person will appear to be available, but in reality you'll find yourself their "transitional relationship." After months or even years of dating you, they will announce that they need to "play the field," something they never got to do after their divorce or breakup. Not knowing what he or she really wants, this person will settle for you, silently waiting and watching for "something better" to come along.

- Too Tanked. This is the person whose interest in alcohol and/or drugs is more than passing. The addict's first love is always his or her substance of choice, so you'll always be second in this person's life. Because of the frequent distortion of mood, you never know who you're trying to interact with, the substance or the person. Beware the trap of trying to fix or change this train's direction.

• I Love You, *But* . . . This person is the one who is too busy evaluating the package to appreciate the person who you are. Desiring a perfect partner, this Westbound Train will constantly try to change you, asking you to lose weight, go back to school, change your hair, change your wardrobe, and so on. This is the person who has difficulty making a commitment on an emotional level, and you will spin your wheels until you're dizzy trying to satisfy them. And no matter what you do, they will leave you for someone younger, thinner, or richer.

• I've Got a Secret. This is the person who is involved with or married to someone else and keeping it from you. This person is probably the worst kind because of the deliberate deception. You will surely end up with a broken heart if you get run over by this train. Keep reading, though. Later we'll look at some of the signs to warn you about this kind of person.

• Now You See Me, Now You Don't. This person is involved in an on-again, off-again relationship. Smarting from the most recent breakup, they are looking for validation and a way to fill the time until the old lover comes back. Possibly this person needs you to spark feelings of jealousy in their lover. Either way, you'll be the unsuspecting person who thinks you've found someone wonderful, only to look up and discover yourself empty-handed.

• What, Me Commit? This is the person who is truly emotionally incapable of commitment. Perhaps he or she is a Romance Addict: always seeking the new and different, perpetually disdainful of the loyal and true. This person only wants a relationship as long as it's easy, fun, and romantic. Any emotional demands placed on them cause them to scurry for the hills.

• Let's Be Friends . . . Between the Sheets. This person wants all the goodies of a romance in the guise of a friendship. That way there's no possibility of commitment and the work that comes with it. In this context, "let's be friends" means "let's have sex with no commitment." It may be tempting to comply, but in most cases you will end up with nothing and feeling used, to boot.

• I Need You To ... Make my life worthwhile; make up for someone else's mistreatment; give me a purpose in life; medicate my pain; rescue me from someone or something else. This person isn't looking for a relationship but rather a way to solve the major problems of their life. He or she can't truly commit to another person because their focus is strictly on getting their own needs met; they truly have very little to offer a partner.

Spotting the Westbound Train.   Westbound Trains never announce their unavailability. Remember that we all date for a variety of reasons, only one of which might be the desire for a committed relationship. Sometimes Westbound Trains don't even realize they're emotionally unavailable. Therefore, the responsibility for determining your own and someone else's availability lies with *you*. This means being aware of (and on the lookout for) attitudes and life circumstances that may keep someone from being available. For the Westbound Train, some of these include:

• *Not having enough time since the last significant relationship or divorce.* Without sufficient healing time, the newly divorced or broken-up person simply can't give you their all. There will be grief and ambivalence, feelings that can interfere with a developing relationship. The ability to make a commitment is often weak at this point.

• *Little or no awareness of personal responsibility in the failure of past relationships.* This Westbound Train has had no therapy or personal growth work to understand or resolve past mistakes. Without that understanding, and especially if there have been multiple marriages, there is no capacity to assume responsibility for the well-being of future relationships. This person will simply expect everything to go smoothly, and when it doesn't, you will be blamed or they will end the relationship.

- *Anger or bitterness toward ex-partner.* Feelings of resentment or bitterness toward an ex-spouse severely diminish the joy of a new relationship. What seems like love may in reality be the comfort of a good sounding board. And when the bitterness fades, you may find yourself, once again, out in the cold.

- *Ongoing conflict with ex-partner or spouse.* This person is constantly in a stew about the latest thing their ex did. Instead of gazing into each other's eyes and whispering sweet nothings, you're listening to the most recent rehash of the same old song in its umpteenth verse. Again, you're the sounding board, and your usefulness isn't likely to last.

- *Lack of basic respect and positive regard for the other gender.* This is the person who generalizes about the entire opposite gender, concluding that "all men are jerks" or "all women want is a meal ticket" or something else negative. This Westbound Train may exhibit a fundamental lack of respect for the opposite gender via off-color jokes, sarcasm, or cynicism. Beware the person who tells you, "You're so different from all those others out there!" Eventually, when the glow fades, you'll discover that you're just like the rest in their eyes.

- *Likes being with you but doesn't want a permanent relationship or commitment.* This Westbound train has already decided that you're not the right partner. "Let's just enjoy our time together," they'll say. With no real commitment in place, you have no basis from which to resolve issues or to experience safety and trust.

- *Incomplete or nonexistent identity.* This person has little personal insight or direction and will look to you to define them and the relationship, taking a passive stance in every aspect of your life together. Without a well-defined identity, it's almost impossible to make a genuine commitment in a relationship.

- *Unresolved family trauma.* This person carries enough emotional baggage to fill the carousel at your local airport. Without therapy, this Westbound Train cannot make a real commitment because all their energy is spent reacting from pain and fear. Rather than planning a future together, you'll spend all your time helping this person just survive another day.

What to Do If You're Westbound.   If you're reading this last section and seeing yourself, don't despair. Awareness that you're not truly available at this point isn't the end of the world. It simply means that you have some things to consider as you venture back into the dating scene.

Being Westbound because you haven't had enough time since the last relationship means that it may be appropriate for you to focus on socializing and making new friendships rather than getting romantic with someone. You may also want to be honest with anyone you do go out with, letting them know that you're in a healing phase and not really available for a commitment.

This raises certain issues about honesty, and opinions are divided. Some say, "Don't tell the full truth about your situation right off the bat. You might scare someone off, and you never know, that could be the right person for you. In the long run you might sabotage what turns out to be a perfectly good relationship." There's more than one grain of truth in this advice. It is true that in the long run even the most ill-fated relationships can turn out well. It's also true that telling someone on the first date that you've only been divorced two weeks might scare them away.

The problem, in my view, is that a decision to withhold important information (that might affect someone's desire to enter a relationship with you) in the beginning is like holding all the cards. This puts you in a position of power over the other person, without their consent. Eventually, when the truth comes out—and it always does—you may find that you have a very angry partner and that you've damaged the relationship beyond repair. The other person may feel, rightly, that they weren't given all the relevant information that they needed in order to evaluate whether or not this relationship was a good risk for them. They will have lost forever the opportunity to make an *informed choice.* Furthermore, there's the risk of doing damage to the trust that person may have had in you. Barry's story illustrates the disastrous effects this can have on a dating relationship.

Barry was strongly drawn to Donna from their first meeting. Both had been divorced once and were close to the same age. They shared interests and felt a growing positive chemistry. One of the things they were in agreement about was that neither one wanted children, and this they had established very early on. But Donna had a secret. After three months of dating she finally disclosed to Barry that she had lied. The truth was that she had joint custody of her four-year-old daughter from her first marriage. She confessed that she'd initially hidden the information because of Barry's feelings about not wanting children. Somehow she'd hoped that he would fall in love with her and then not care that she had a child.

Barry was devastated, not by the fact that Donna had a child, but by the fact that she'd lied about something so important. His budding feelings of trust and emotional closeness were shattered. "The sad thing is that I would have still dated her if she'd told me up front that she was a mom," he said. "Now, I can never be sure that she'll be honest with me about difficult things." Barry decided to end the relationship.

When counseling singles about whether or not to disclose important information (it's potentially embarrassing or likely to scare the other person away) to a prospective partner, I like to ask my client to stand in the other person's shoes for a few minutes. "If the situation were reversed, what would you want? Would you want your partner to be honest with you or would you want them to withhold this information?" In almost every case, my client has voiced the desire for honesty.

What to Look For.   If you're wondering how to judge whether or not someone is Westbound, pay attention to the signs or "red flags" that may indicate a lack of emotional availability, such as:

- canceling dates at the last minute
- waiting until the last minute to ask for dates
- consistently showing up late or not at all
- never inviting you to their home or giving you their home phone number (a huge red flag!)
- conversations always seem to turn back to their ex-spouse or partner

- the ex seems to have their first loyalty (e.g., "Jill and I have lunch every Tuesday, so I'll have to see you another day of the week. Of course we're just friends!" or the phone rings, it's her ex, and she goes into the other room with the door shut to talk to him)
- lots of time or money given to the ex with no legal obligation to do so
- defensiveness about past relationships
- blaming statements toward the ex or toward the opposite gender
- lack of courting behavior, e.g., wants to just come over and hang out versus going to dinner, sending flowers, etc.
- finding excuses not to spend time with you
- reluctance to have a monogamous relationship (e.g., "I want to keep my options open")
- voicing uncertainty about and fear of commitment
- you're putting all the energy into the relationship
- avoiding the "You and Me" discussion (refer to chapter eleven and later in this chapter)

What to Do If They're Westbound.   If you're seeing some or all of these red flags, it doesn't mean you should automatically write off the person. It does mean that it's time to confront the issue and find out what's behind it.

For example, say that your partner is late a lot or cancels dates at the last minute. You might sit down with them and say something like, "I've noticed that you're late a lot and you've canceled two of our last three dates, and I'm wondering if there's something going on with you. Are you so busy that you're having trouble keeping up, or is there something else?"

How you address it is important, but the main thing is that you *do address it.* Letting these things go on and on establishes a pattern in a relationship that may be very hard to break later. Plus, it sends a message that you expect something less than the best of treatment. And, of course, what we expect is generally what we get.

Knowing a potential partner is Westbound means that if you continue to date them you've chosen a more difficult path than you would have with an emotionally available person. You need to *take responsibility* for that choice, knowing that the odds are against you. While all relationships are inherently risky, a relationship with a Westbound Train is riskier than most. Make sure that you're willing to pay the price if you choose such a partner.

The Northbound Train

The Northbound Train is the kind of partner you want to *be* and to *find:* someone who is available for a relationship and who has the desire for one with you. This is the person who knows what she wants and isn't afraid to go for it. The Northbound Train is emotionally available for a committed relationship and knows that he wants one.

If you are a Northbound Train, you've reached the point in your life in which you are aware that your only shot at a healthy relationship is to be able to make a commitment and open your heart to love. You are aware that you've missed the mark in the past and that you're in a process of growth and discovery about what it takes to have a good relationship. You're by no means a perfect person, and you possess a certain level of awareness about your shortcomings and flaws. You're not looking for a perfect person but rather for someone with whom you can connect intellectually, emotionally, and sexually, with whom you share common values, and who is equally emotionally available; someone who's ready to be a partner in *creating* a healthy relationship.

When you find a Northbound Train, you'll know it. This will be the person who is ready for a relationship, able to love and be loved, ready for a commitment, and, most important, who wants that with you!

You'll recognize the Northbound Train as the person who:

• has had sufficient healing time since the last long-term relationship or divorce (as a general rule, this is at least one year after a divorce and six months after a dating relationship ends; depending on the amount of trauma, it can be much longer in both cases)

- takes responsibility for their past failures in relationships
- if divorced, has had therapy or personal growth work to resolve their part in the failure of the relationship
- sees most men or women as inherently good and worthy
- gets self-esteem from within rather than relying on partners to provide it
- is willing to pass up an unhealthy relationship no matter how strong the attraction
- is aware of personal shortcomings and strives to do better
- exhibits responsibility and integrity
- is self-supporting and self-nurturing
- is in touch with and able to express his own thoughts, feelings, needs, and wants
- is not indulging in any addictions
- wants a committed relationship with you!

Turning from Westbound to Northbound.   If you recognize yourself as a Westbound Train, you can begin to take steps to eventually become a Northbound Train. Think of the above list as checkpoints for determining your own emotional availability and use the following tips as guidelines:

- Use the first months after your divorce or breakup for healing, taking time to get in touch with yourself; to reevaluate your life and where you want it to go; and to take a new look at what you want in future relationships.
- If you have anger or bitterness toward an ex or toward the opposite gender in general, get therapy to resolve these issues. Do the same if you have unresolved guilt.
- Get your life in order if it isn't already: Get your career on track, know what you want and go for it, be responsible, and develop your sense of integrity.
- Do whatever it takes to make sure that you feel good about yourself from the inside out; not just your accomplishments, but that

who you are is someone good and worthy that you would choose for a relationship.

• If you aren't already in recovery for any addictions you have, run to your nearest twelve-step group for help.

• If you have childhood or other traumas that affect your ability to function in relationships (e.g., fear of intimacy, rage, lack of trust, sexual dysfunction, etc.), get help.

• Take a stand in your life for healthy relationships. Resolve once and for all, to *never again* settle for less than what you really want in a relationship or in a partner. Make absolutely certain that you're able to pass up a relationship that's not right for you, no matter how strong the attraction.

Availability: Talking About It

We've all done it—gone on dates with people we're attracted to and *assumed* that because we're both having a good time we must be on the same track. This is understandable because of the susceptibility we all have to seeing what we want rather than what may really be there. And nowhere does this occur more often than in dating relationships.

Be wary of falling in love with a person's imagined potential. You may feel that, if you give your partner more time, space, leeway, or ignore certain problems, he will wake up one day and love you for it.

The Shopping Conversation. Remember the Shopping Conversation from chapter twelve? This is one way you can weed out the Westbound Trains *before* you get emotionally involved. Mary's went something like this:

> MARY: John, I want you to know that I've really enjoyed spending time with you these past couple of weeks. I feel like we have a lot in common and I like your company. What about you?

JOHN: I feel the same way. I think we have a lot of good potential, too.

MARY: Before we go any further, I need to let you know something. I've been single for a long time, and I'm really not just looking for a fling or a just-for-fun relationship. I'm ready for a long-term commitment, possibly leading to marriage.

Before you get too scared, what I mean is that I don't know yet if you're that person for me. We've just barely begun to get to know each other. However, I do feel that you *could* be, and I just need to know if you're looking for that kind of relationship also or if you're more interested in having a good time without much possibility of commitment. So, I guess I'm asking this: Are you looking for a committed relationship at this time in your life? And am I someone who's a *possibility* of that for you?

John, if he's a Westbound Train, may respond in any one of these ways:

"Boy, this is really strange for someone to ask something like this so soon. I don't think I'm ready for this kind of talk. How about another drink?"

"Well, I think I'm just interested in having a good time right now. I don't know what I want in the long run. I might want a commitment someday, I just can't be sure today about what tomorrow will bring. I think you're nice and I'd sure like to go out again, but that's all I can commit to."

"Actually, I'm not sure I ever want another serious relationship again. But I think you're really attractive and I hope you'll want to see me again."

He may hedge, hem and haw, beat around the bush, and otherwise communicate that this conversation makes him really uncomfortable. This is Mary's signal that she may be with a Westbound Train or someone who doesn't see her as a *possibility* for a long-term relationship. She can now choose whether to continue the conversation to try to understand more, drop it for now, or even to conclude that John's just not emotionally available and that she's better off moving on.

If John's Northbound, however, chances are he'll respond something like this:

"I'm really impressed that you brought that up, Mary. I've wondered the same thing about you, but I couldn't quite get up my nerve. I've had a couple of relationships where I wanted a commitment and I thought they did, too. I guess I just assumed they did because we went out and had a good time together. But later, when I wanted to talk about commitment, they backed out in a hurry. I felt like I'd wasted months and years of my life in nowhere relationships. I sure don't ever want to do that again.

"I'm looking for a strong relationship, too, and I'd like to explore that possibility with you."

Don't expect these conversations to go as smoothly as the ones I've outlined. You have to do this in your own words, and of course your partner isn't going to have a script handy! The important thing is to get the message across:

"I'm looking for a commitment. I don't know if you're 'the one' for me, but you're a good *possibility* at this point. What are you looking for, and am I a good possibility for you?"

I stress the word *possibility* because it's the most important word in this communication. We're talking about the first three dates and there's no way you could know at this point that this person is right for you. Remember that every potential relationship is a Maybe in the beginning, and only the passage of time and repeated interactions can turn that into a Yes. So when you bring up the Shopping Conversation, be sure to stress the idea of possibility. Otherwise you'll come across as if you've already made up your mind that this person is "the one," and that you're targeting them for an instant relationship and commitment. That would be scary!

However you resolve it, the Shopping Conversation opens the door for mutual self-disclosure about your intentions *going into* the relationship. Instead of assuming, seeing only what you want to see, and hoping for the best, you can take charge of your relationships by communicating in an honest and open fashion. Other Northbound Trains will respect your guts and integrity and will respond positively.

How to Interview for Availability. In addition to the Shopping Conversation, it's important to know what questions to ask to help you see how available a potential partner really is. Remember that Westbound Trains don't announce their unavailability, so you have to learn to listen to what people *don't* say as well as to what they *do* say.

I've outlined the following questions in a direct fashion. This doesn't mean that you should go on dates with your list of questions and fire them at the other person. That would probably close down communication. Instead, you should approach these topics slowly and with discretion, sharing about your own history first, then gently inquiring about your partner's. This is a give-and-receive process that develops over the course of your first several dates as your comfort levels with each other increase.

How the person responds to the questions will reveal a wealth of information. Obviously, defensiveness or evasiveness should send up a red flag. Be sure to hang in there, even though the other person may be uncomfortable. Remember that a potential partner's emotional availability has a direct effect on you and your life if you become involved with them.

Some important things to ask include:

• How long has it been since your last relationship and how did it end?

This question accomplishes several things. First, it tells you how much time the person has had to heal since their divorce or breakup. Second, asking how it ended lets you get a sense of the degree of trauma involved in the breakup. If the answer is "last week, and she threw all my clothes on the lawn and burned them up!" you should run, not walk, away from this obvious Westbound Train!

If it's been a very short time since the last relationship, it's fair to ask how long it's been since they last saw their ex-partner. If the answer is "recently," this is a big clue that the relationship may not be over.

If it's been less than a year since a divorce or less than six months since a breakup, or you sense that there are still strong feelings about it, it's fair to ask the next question:

• What kind of therapy or personal growth work have you done to get help with that? and,

• What have you learned about yourself and about relationships in general as a result of going through all that you've been through?

Again, listen carefully not just to what the person says but to how they answer you. Are they making eye contact? Do they seem open about sharing their experiences in past relationships with you? Are their comments heavily charged with emotion?

The next most important area to ask questions about is family. Some things you might ask are:

• Tell me about your family, how you got along with your siblings and your parents.

• What is your relationship with your mom and dad like today?

• Are your parents still together? If not, why? Are they both still alive? If not, how and when did they die? How did that affect you?

Of course, as time goes on, the sharing about family and past relationships will progress to a deeper level. But initially, you should be able to get some idea of how much emotional baggage the person may be carrying.

What to Listen For.   Everyone has emotional baggage. It's impossible to go through life without collecting some, and most of us aren't equipped to resolve each and every painful moment in our lives as it happens.

If you're looking for someone who has no unresolved issues from their past, you'll be alone forever. There's no such person out there, any more than the person reading this has no unresolved issues.

Sometimes singles take this reasoning a step too far: "Since everyone has 'stuff,' I'll just stay with this person rather than looking for something better." This is just a way to rationalize settling, and ultimately it won't work.

What's important is to find someone who's baggage isn't too extensive (carry-on luggage versus steamer trunks) and is stuff you can live with.

Once you've gathered all the information you can about past relationship history, including nonverbal clues from listening to them talk, you must listen closely to your gut. If you are not desperate and not swayed by intense attraction, you'll get your answer. You'll either conclude that this relationship is still a Maybe or you'll realize it's a No, that this person is clearly Westbound. (In chapter seventeen we'll explore how to end dating relationships powerfully.)

There's also the possibility that you'll conclude Maybe and discover later that this person is less available than you originally thought. So it's wise to keep your mind open and continue to talk and listen with an ear to discovering who the real person is in front of you, rather than carving your initial impression in stone.

If you find that you can't tear yourself away from the wrong person, continue with the next chapter, as we explore the nature of attachment and how it can turn into addictive love.

Being able to say no to partners who aren't right for you is essential to paving the way to healthy relationships. Being a Northbound Train means keeping yourself emotionally available for the right partner, something you can't do if you're involved with a Westbound Train. If you can learn to wave the wrong trains on, you will be ready and available for the right one!

14

♥   ♥   ♥

Attachment:
The Most Powerful Force in Love

Frank, thirty-six years old and divorced, had a real dilemma. He'd been dating Elaine for three and a half years but still didn't want to even consider marriage. Asked about how they first got together, his answer sounded like a lot of Settle-for Relationships: They met, he liked her, he couldn't find anything wrong with her, no one else was in the picture, he was healing from his divorce, and so on. So, he just kept seeing her, thinking that he could always break it off if he met someone better. Now, years later, he can't break off the relationship because he's *attached* to Elaine. Neither can he go forward with a real commitment because his heart's not fully in it.

Attachment, an invisible energy that binds two people together, is by far the most powerful force in love. When it happens between two people who are compatible, who both want a relationship with each other, and who are both emotionally available for a commitment, it acts like a sort of glue that holds a relationship together even when there are problems. When it happens without one or more of the above, the result is emotional pain and suffering.

Attachment can bind together two people who: a) aren't really in love, b) don't even like each other, c) have nothing in common, d) really make each other crazy, e) feel differently about each other (one's in love and the other's not), and many other scenarios. Attachment is such a powerful force in relationships that not understanding it fully can cause you to end up in long-term romances that will never go anywhere or even marriages that are doomed to failure.

Attachment has its roots in the earliest of human relationships. Thousands of years ago, humans needed to band together in order to survive, the environment being far too hostile for individuals to live on their own. Attachment held these people together, enabling them to form families and work groups. Between mother and child, it enabled infants to get the care and nurturing they needed. This force had great evolutionary significance in that it allowed procreation to occur and permitted the survival of our species. Thus, we are biologically wired to seek and form attachments with other human beings.

Attachment and Romantic Love.   In the context of a relationship between two compatible partners who are ready for a commitment, attachment works beautifully as a binding agent for the relationship. Over time, partners grow closer and more intimate, they strive to spend time together and to nurture each other, they fall in love, and they grow in that love.

In earlier times, prior to our modern, complex, technology-based society, the rules of relationships were simpler. People lived in communities in which they encountered others who shared their basic values. It was understood that dating was for the purpose of choosing a marriage partner. So when couples met and courted and became attached, they naturally moved into the marriage mode. Given the simpler expectations of marriage, most of the time things worked out well enough.

Now, however, relationships are much more complex and the same old understandings can no longer be counted on. Nowadays, dating isn't necessarily a prelude to marriage. Thus, there's always the possibility that we'll get attached to the wrong dating partner if we're not careful.

Because the drive to attach is biological and innate, we don't have conscious control over it. In dating, the power of attachment pulls two people together and keeps them together, *even when the relationship is clearly not right for one or both of them.* We can see how this happens when we take a closer look at Frank's story.

After eight years of marriage, Frank was devastated when his wife left and filed for divorce. At first the pain was almost unbearable. Then, after a few months, the worst seemed over and he began to think about dating. His self-esteem had taken a beating and although he didn't think about it consciously, Frank was seeking validation that he was an attractive and worthy man. He told himself that he wasn't looking for a relationship yet, just for the fun of going out with different women.

When Frank met Elaine and asked her out, he felt a pleasant surge of interest. She was pretty and seemed very nice, intelligent, and self-sufficient. After a couple of dates, they kissed, and within a month they were sleeping together. It was nice to have a sexual partner again, and Elaine was very warm and loving. Things could be a lot worse, he told himself. What he said to her was that he wasn't interested in a commitment, but that he wasn't seeing anyone else, either.

Meanwhile, Elaine was falling madly in love with Frank. He was everything she was looking for, and she resolved to be patient and give him time to build the same feelings for her. They fell into the routine of dating.

The first time Elaine brought up the subject of commitment, Frank was jolted out of his state of contentment. Just the thought of pledging himself at this time to one woman was too scary, so he resisted her efforts. Soon, though, the subject began to be the source of all their conflict, with Elaine pushing for a commitment and Frank resisting. Finally, he asked himself why he was staying with someone he didn't want a future with, someone he just couldn't make himself be in love with, and he realized that the thought of breaking up with this woman was very uncomfortable. Frank had become attached to Elaine even though he wasn't in love with her and didn't see a future with her.

Many times singles try to rationalize their way into Settle-for relationships. Because of loneliness, the need for validation, or the drive to be close to another human being, we tell ourselves that it's okay to date and be intimate with someone who isn't really what we're looking for. We say that this is just short-term, that we can leave whenever we feel like it, that as long as we're honest and tell them that we don't want a commitment, no one will get hurt. We fail to take into account the power of attachment.

The truth is that spending lots of time with someone, talking, doing things together, holding hands, kissing, and making love—all these things eventually lead to attachment, even if it's with someone who doesn't seem right for the long term. *Intimate behavior repeated over and over with the same person leads to attachment, regardless of the suitability of the partner.* That's how attachment works, like it or not. Therefore, we need to carefully choose whom we will spend intimate time with in order to avoid Settle-for relationships and other nonworkable patterns.

Making Healthy Choices

If you want to avoid the trap of unhealthy, Settle-for relationships, there are several steps you can take:

1.   Realize that spending romantic time with the wrong partner may set you up for heartache and frustration.

2.   Make a commitment to yourself to never date someone for any extended period (more than three or four dates) who you know is not an appropriate choice for a partner.

3.   Resolve to be fully conscious and avoid rationalizing in your dating process.

4.   Respect your intuition and remember that *you don't need a good excuse to not become involved with a particular person.*

Love Addiction: Attachment Gone Wrong

• Linda, thirty-three years old and divorced once, has been seeing Tom, thirty-eight and also divorced, for more than three years. He's a compulsive gambler and an alcoholic, and avoids emotional intimacy and commitment. She's insecure and seeks validation. Their power struggles have led to verbal and physical abuse. Linda knows the relationship is destructive and has tried to end it at least half a dozen times. Each time she grieves heavily, begins to feel better, misses him, he calls, and they end up back together.

• Stanley, fifty-six and divorced twice, met Melissa, forty-nine, while she was still married to her husband of thirty years. Against his better judgment, he began dating her, and even though she quickly separated from her husband, she spent the next two years trying to decide about divorce. Stanley wanted a commitment from her, she wanted space to work through her divorce. Their power struggles led to shouting matches and many, many dramatic breakups. Stanley resolved over and over to end the relationship but always ended up back with Melissa.

• Bill, forty-six, fell in love with his secretary, Carol, and separated from his wife to pursue the relationship. Although deeply in love, his and Carol's romance quickly became unhealthy as each struggled unsuccessfully to get their needs met. She wanted Bill to make her life okay but resisted showing him affection in the little ways, while he wanted her to return the loving behavior that he showed her. Their power struggles led to many breakups and reattachments.

What these stories have in common is attachment gone really wrong, or what some have called "Love Addiction." This occurs when a relationship contains unhealthy dynamics (an intense power struggle, or emotional, verbal, or physical abuse) and neither partner is able to change the dynamics or leave.

Love addiction is characterized by some or all of the following behaviors and characteristics:

• mood swings; intense emotional highs and lows, which are dependent on how the relationship is going
• obsessive thinking about the lover

- focus on winning over the partner despite warning signals in the beginning that there are built-in barriers
- disagreement on the direction of the relationship (one partner desiring a commitment, the other resisting it)
- abandonment of other aspects of life, including involvement with other loved ones
- attempts which become increasingly desperate as they fail to control the partner
- escalating feelings of loss of control and desperation
- loss of self-esteem, leading to increased need for the relationship as a bolster
- an intense and growing need for contact with the partner, with symptoms of withdrawal when separated
- denial of the reality of the relationship, with a preference for maintaining false hope and illusion
- blaming oneself or one's partner for the problems rather than perceiving the shared responsibility

All of these behaviors can ultimately lead to ill health, self-destructive behavior in other areas, and even suicide if there is no intervention. How does this dynamic begin?

Individuals who are prone to love addiction often haven't developed a sense of self earlier in life. Not knowing who they are or being solid within themselves, they are ill-equipped to handle love relationships. This lack of a healthy identity prevents them from being able to stand up for themselves in a relationship, or even from choosing partners who won't mistreat them.

Love addicts carry the false belief that love can be lost by being yourself and that it can be won by being someone whom you are not. This leads to even lower self-esteem and sets them up for mistreatment. It also requires their partner to be overly responsible for their well-being.

Love addicts can be either male or female, and may be highly successful in their chosen careers. To the world, they may appear very self-confident, but in romance, they become obsessive, compulsive, and driven to seek the most destructive relationships. The beginnings of the problem lie in their true self-image, not the one they project. Dale's story illustrates how this happens.

Dale, forty and divorced once, fell for Jill the moment he met her. Their courtship was rapid and intense, and they married after only five months of dating. But highly disparate values, lifestyles, and goals left them floundering to maintain their connection. Their relationship soon deteriorated as she revealed her highly volatile style of relating and he tried to caretake and control. Their power struggles intensified, and even marital therapy didn't help. Within a year and a half, they were divorced, but Dale couldn't let go of Jill emotionally.

As a highly successful architect, Dale's personal dynamics paralleled his professional ones. "I'm a romantic. I imagine things. I can invent a relationship: imagine what it can be and then work to fulfill it," Dale said. Even two years after their divorce, Dale was still trying to find ways to repair things with Jill and get her back into his life. In the process, he was sacrificing his self-respect, his health and well-being, and even his finances. Finally, he sought therapy.

Dale found the root of his love addiction in his relationship with his mother, who was aloof and very difficult for him to connect with. Consequently, Dale time and again chose women who could not be emotionally available for him or who needed fixing in some way (e.g., women with financial troubles or various addictions, etc.). Dale turned his life around when he shifted his focus from trying to repair his relationships with women to healing his relationship with himself. Four years later, he talked about the changes he had made.

"I learned that the key to relationships is finding your own peace and sense of who you are. I spent my whole life trying to take care of everyone else but me. In my business I was constantly worrying about whether or not I would generate enough to cover the payroll for all my employees. With women, I was obsessed with meeting their needs and making their lives okay. Finally, I decided to concentrate on my own life. For the first time, I considered life without a partner. It wasn't that I gave up on wanting that, but more like I gave up on the notion that life couldn't be okay without that.

"I asked myself: If I could design the ideal life, what would it look like? And I began taking steps to create the kind of life I envisioned for myself, regardless of whether or not there was a woman to share it.

"I gave up caretaking in all areas of my life, both business and personal. I changed my view of being selfish from something bad to something okay and even desirable in a way. I became willing to listen to my own feelings and trust myself above all. I became more aware of what really *is,* rather than what could be or might be. Focusing on these things, plus just the passage of time and geographical distance, enabled me to relinquish my attachment to Jill and move on."

Love Addiction and Dating.   The primary way that love addiction shows up in dating is in the *loss of choice.* This means that as you meet new people and make discoveries about who they are (values, emotional availability, etc.), your attraction to a new person completely chooses the relationship for you. Even if you discover a major incompatibility very early on, if there's a lot of chemistry you feel powerless to pass the person up. *In fact, you find that the people who are least likely to meet your emotional needs are the ones you are most attracted to.* There's no sense of choice about it: You feel compelled to go forward with the wrong partner.

Identifying Love Addiction.   How do you know if you're vulnerable to the dynamics of love addiction? The following are indicators that you might be:

- One or more parents were alcoholic and/or violent.
- You were abused either verbally, physically, or sexually.
- Your primary caregiver was emotionally aloof, distant, or neglectful.
- You felt abandoned by one or more parents early in life, either through divorce, illness, or death.
- You were belittled or put down in some way on a regular basis while growing up.

• One or both of your parents was highly intrusive emotionally, or you felt obligated to take care of them (parenting your parent).

Recovering from Love Addiction. If you recognize your own behavior in the list of addictive behaviors, plant your feet squarely on the path to recovery and try the following steps:

• Like Dale, shift your focus from trying to fix your relationships with others *to healing your relationship with yourself:*
    1. Practice acknowledging your true feelings and validating them daily, no matter how irrelevant they may seem.
    2. Practice acknowledging that which is fulfilling and joyful for you (e.g., flowers, music, art, conversation with friends, etc.) and actively bring those things into your life on a regular basis.
    3. Notice any negative self-talk and practice changing it to something positive each time you see it.
• Discover and use all your natural talents. It's very difficult to find time for obsessing when you're busy being creative and accomplishing goals.
• Pursue and develop friendships through activities you enjoy; choose people with values you share and who are affirming and positive about themselves and you.
• Get therapy to help you make these things happen!
• Most important: Take a stand in your life to never, ever again allow yourself to stay in a relationship that's destructive or abusive.

These steps may sound simple, but practicing them adds up to a fulfilling life filled with people and activities you enjoy, a sense of accomplishment, and good self-esteem. With these things in place, you will easily resist falling into destructive relationships, and you will draw people into your life who are also committed to having a healthy romance.

If you are currently in an addictive love relationship, the next step is to admit to yourself that you have a problem and that your usual ways of trying to fix it haven't worked. Ask yourself the following questions:

1. Is it possible to change the patterns in this relationship so that it is healthy for me and my partner, and am I willing to take the steps to make that happen?
2. Is my partner willing to also take those steps?

If your answers to the above questions are yes, then your next step is to find a competent therapist who is well-versed in the dynamics of love addiction and who can do both individual and couples' therapy. Make sure you find one who does not take the rigid stance that the only way to cure love addiction is to end the relationship. The truth is, you can recover from love addiction whether or not you stay in the current relationship.

There are many books that deal with love addiction. Some of the ones I recommend are:

Women Who Love Too Much by Robin Norwood
*Escape from Intimacy: Untangling the "Love" Addictions—
   Sex, Romance, Relationships* by Anne Wilson-Schaef
Is It Love or Is It Addiction? by Brenda Schaeffer
Obsessive Love by Susan Forward
Facing Love Addiction by Pia Mellody

15

❤   ❤   ❤

Sex, Love, and Communication

The 1960s and 1970s gave us the sexual revolution, the birth control pill, women's liberation, free love, and rock and roll—all the old values were turned upside down. Then came the 1980s and 1990s, with herpes, AIDS, widespread abortion, skyrocketing divorce rates, and unprecedented numbers of babies born to unwed teenagers. The way men and women relate, the very fabric of families, was forever altered. Today, we still struggle to understand all the mixed messages and come to terms with them. In dating, this means there has never been more confusion about sex and love.

For those who came of age during this turbulent era, the messages were many and unclear. The only certainty is that we added to our store of myths about relationships, especially with regard to sexuality.

Sex and Love: Myth and Reality

Therapists' offices today are filled with singles who have been casualties of the clash between the myths and the realities about sex and love. The sexual revolution may have freed us to some degree of the old taboos against enjoying a full and rewarding sex life, but unfortunately we didn't get the complete picture. Unspoken and spoken, we received messages about sex via movies, television, and books, most of which were inaccurate and as misleading as our romantic love myths.

Myth: Sex and Love Are Two Completely Different Phenomena Which Have Nothing to Do with Each Other and Are Easily Separated. This myth says that sex is a function of biology: hormones, sex drive, instinct, and so on; that it's natural for human beings to seek and enjoy sex with one or many partners, depending on lifestyle, and that it's easy to have sex outside the context of a loving relationship as long as you're honest with your partner. Love, on the other hand, is strictly a function of emotion and intellect, and is totally separate from sex.

Reality: Sex and Love Are *Both* Functions of Biology, Instinct, Psychology, Emotion, and Many Other Factors, All of Which Are Very Intertwined and Extremely Difficult to Separate. One of the most famous experiments of the 1960s was the commune, in which a number of men and women lived together with the idea that they would all be lovers and that there would be no pairing of couples (there were actually rules against this). What happened every time was that certain pairs would begin to fall in love, and would sneak around in order to spend more time with each other and develop a relationship. This is a testament to the powers of attraction and attachment.

The truth is that trying to have an ongoing sexual relationship with a particular partner without either falling in love or getting attached is like trying to swim with sharks without getting bitten: It goes against the nature of the beast. Human beings by nature seek attachment and love, even when not consciously aware of it. Shared physical intimacy with the same partner creates a bond between two people even if they don't really like each other or have common values.

With the acceptance of premarital sex, men and women began getting sexual as soon as an attractive partner came along. This led to lots of promiscuity, brought on by a faulty rationalization that it was, after all, just sex. What happened was that other factors began complicating the picture: guilt from going against personal morals, attachment to wrong partners, anger and jealousy, and a deep sense of emptiness at the conclusion of each affair. Many of my and other therapists' clients have experimented with their sexuality via lots and lots of partners, and have discovered that there's no reward at the end of that tunnel. The truth is that human beings seek a loving connection; there's something profoundly unfulfilling for most people about being sexual with a partner without that emotional bond.

Myth: Because Sex Is Biological, It's All Right to Meet That Need with Whomever You Want in Whatever Way You Want As Long As Both Are Consenting Adults. This myth says that the only thing to consider prior to having sex is your own preferences and those of your partner; that there are no consequences for this other than pleasure.

Reality: Sex Is Intricately Tied to the Psyche and Emotions, and There Are Many Potential Consequences, Some of Them Quite Negative, Which Need to Be Considered Prior to Having Sex. Sexually transmitted diseases, unwanted pregnancy, emotional and psychological damage: These are some of the consequences of irresponsible sex.

Because sex and emotion are tied together, becoming sexual partners triggers psychological and emotional dynamics that are very powerful. Despite intentions to be only physical (i.e., rationalizing that this is "only a fling"), one or both may fall in love, become attached, or develop expectations of a more committed relationship. Shelly's story is a good example of what happens when these expectations are thwarted.

"I had always been a 'good girl,' only sleeping with men I had a commitment with. I was lonely, and Kurt was a very attractive man in my computer class whom I'd known for months. I asked him out intending to sleep with him, and he was very responsive. I expected it to be a one-night stand, but to my surprise he asked me out the following week. We had a couple of more dates, spending the night together each time, and never talked about love or commitment. I realized that I didn't want to continue to see him because I was beginning to get emotionally involved and I didn't think he was a good candidate for a relationship, so I broke off with him on our fourth date. He seemed surprised but okay. Two weeks later he called me up, furious, and accused me of using him just to get sex! Obviously, he was really hurt. I felt confused and guilty. I thought a guy would jump at the chance to have a sexual relationship with no strings and that there couldn't possibly be any emotional consequences."

Shelly bumped into the reality of sex and love: that spending intimate time together can lead to attachment, love, and high expectations, *and this is true for both men and women.* Disappointment and pain can be very intense when these relationships flounder.

There's much more to sex than just making sure two adults are consensual. Having sex carries emotional and psychological meaning for both partners, and it's important to know what that is for each of them. For one person it may be the beginning of a grand and passionate romance. For another it may be a way to get some needs met for a period of time. For someone else it may imply a commitment, whether spoken or not. Sometimes sex feels like love, even when partners don't love each other. Not knowing these hidden meanings prior to having sex is like striking matches in a dark room full of dynamite: You never know where or when the bomb will go off or how big the explosion will be. From mere disappointment to outright devastation, the emotional fallout of hastily entered, unthought-out affairs is considerable.

Myth: Promiscuity Doesn't Hurt Anyone, As Long As You Practice Birth Control and Protect Yourself Against Diseases. Another legacy of the sexual revolution, this myth says that having sex with multiple partners carries no emotional consequence; that all you need to do is be honest with your partners so that they have no illusions of exclusivity with you.

Reality: Promiscuity Hurts Everyone, Even If You Practice Birth Control, Protect Yourself Against Diseases, and Are Honest with Partners. Because sexuality is so connected with emotionality and psychology, a large part of our identity is also a part of how we feel about ourselves sexually. Being sexual with another person means that we, in a very real sense, *give ourselves* to that person. If we value ourselves, then we want to be treated with respect and dignity. It's difficult to feel dignified waking up in the morning, after a night of sexual abandon, with a complete stranger.

Promiscuity, or giving ourselves indiscriminately, has a way of diminishing our self-esteem as we allow ourselves to be used for sexual gratification by others. With no emotional connection or sense of relationship in these encounters, we are sending a message to ourselves that we aren't valuable enough to have a caring partner. Desiring love and attachment and not getting it, we begin to feel undeserving of the real experience of love. This can lead to a self-defeating, vicious cycle: trying to get love through indiscriminate sex, not getting it, feeling empty, losing self-esteem, trying harder to get love, etc.; it's like that old song lyric, "looking for love in all the wrong places."

Individuals engaged in promiscuous behavior often try to disconnect themselves emotionally from their experiences in order to not feel the pain and emptiness. This process creates more problems: psychic numbness, addiction to sex, loss of ability to feel love and intimacy, and even loss of self.

Psychotherapists know the reality of the consequences of promiscuity, as they treat people who have lost their self-respect and dignity, or who are burdened by guilt, or who have lost the ability to connect in a meaningful way in a relationship. Twelve-step groups such as Sex and Love Addicts Anonymous are filled with people whose lives have become unmanageable due to acting out sexually in a compulsive way.

Myth: The Best Sex Is Spontaneous.   This myth is largely a result of romance novels and movies and conveys the notion that being "swept away" on a tidal wave of desire is the way to begin a sexual relationship. Further, that to think out the consequences ahead of time and to carefully consider them ruins the passion and desire.

Reality: Spontaneous Sex Is Usually Unsafe Sex, with Serious Health Consequences, Both Mental and Physical.   Getting swept away by desire, not thinking about the consequences, and just acting on the passion can have grave consequences. This is, after all, how babies get conceived by teenagers. This is also how sexually transmitted diseases are spread.

The truth is that being totally spontaneous about sex may feel exciting, but the consequences aren't worth the high. Also, taking the time to consider the ramifications of becoming sexual with a particular person doesn't ruin the passion. On the contrary, knowing where you stand and taking care of yourself physically and emotionally opens the door for healthy intimacy and vibrant sexuality that is free of negative consequences.

Myth: Talking About Sex Beforehand Takes the Passion and Fun Out of It. Again, due to the programming we've received via the movies and romance novels, we erroneously believe that the best way to begin a sexual relationship is by just going with the feelings. According to this myth, a discussion about the ramifications of what we're about to do together sexually would take away all the fun. After all, how often do we see our romantic role models in the movies stop and discuss sexually transmitted diseases or birth control prior to going to the bedroom? Let's face it: Straightforward communication doesn't sell theater tickets. Intense passion and steamy sex do.

Reality: Not Talking About Sex Beforehand Is Literally Life-Threatening; Talking About It Creates Safety and Therefore a Much Greater Level of Freedom to Enjoy the Experience and to Be Intimate. The reality is that sex is a significant part of human experience that affects every area of our lives. Psychological and emotional well-being, physical health, and the birth of our children: all are affected by and bear the consequences of our sexuality. To not discuss these things prior to the act of being sexual is the height of irresponsibility.

Considering the importance of a discussion like this, why, as a general rule, don't we do it? First, because we're afraid of destroying the passion. Even more important, though, is the general taboo in our culture against an open discussion about sexuality. Even though the sexual revolution supposedly made us all savvy about sex, it didn't erase all the programming that went before. All it did was add some new ideas to the mix, and the result is even more confusion.

Attitudes today about sex are more divergent than ever. On the one hand, we have those who believe that the less we talk about sex the less we will be tempted to do it. So let's not educate our children about sex, the thinking goes; what they don't know won't hurt them. And as adults, let's not talk about sex, either—let's just abstain until marriage and then it's okay.

On the other hand, we have the advertising industry bombarding us daily with erotic and suggestive images. Whether they're trying to sell peanut butter or blue jeans, the agent is the same: sex, sex, sex, and the more of it, the better. How do we reconcile these vastly different messages? Which is right and which is wrong?

The truth is probably not in either stance but is somewhere in between. The reality is that selling anything through the use of sexual images diminishes and demeans this all-important area of human experience. Furthermore, it perpetuates erroneous messages that feed our mythology and fantasy and that block us from the joy of a responsible, adult sexual connection with an intimate partner.

Not educating our children about sex or talking about it as adults doesn't work, either. Ignorance leaves a vacuum, and nature abhors an empty space. So, we fill it with myth, superstition, and fantasy, and out of these come behaviors that are self-destructive and that tear apart the fabric of relationships. Teenagers make babies because they don't really understand how conception occurs and because they're seeking love through sex. Adults set themselves up for heartache because they don't understand the connection between love and sex. Because of the spread of the AIDS virus, having sex without discussing sexual history and taking precautions is literally risking your life.

Sex and Communication.   Marital therapists know that one of the biggest challenges in marriage is sustaining a healthy sexual relationship over the years. Usually one of the first things a marital therapist addresses with a couple whose sex life is suffering is the lack of communication about it. Often these are people who have been married for years and have children together, yet who have never had an open discussion about the most intimate area of their relationship. Without a healthy dialogue, misunderstandings abound. He thinks she's not interested in sex anymore, she thinks he's no longer attracted to her, they're both hurt and withdrawn, and their sex life diminishes.

In dating, the opportunity is there to build a foundation for a healthy, lasting relationship. One of the most important areas is sexuality. By bringing up this topic and initiating an open dialogue during dating, we are setting the stage for being able to deal with it later in marriage. Passion is easy: A good dose of chemistry and you're off and running. Sustaining healthy emotional and sexual intimacy over years and years is a challenge, and the key is communication.

Myth: Abstaining from Sex Isn't a Reasonable Alternative. This myth, a legacy of the sexual revolution, says that because humans have a sex drive, it is unreasonable to expect them to not act on it. Therefore, when sexual attraction occurs we act on it, regardless of whether or not that's healthy, because we *need* sex.

Reality: Everyone Is Capable of Abstaining from Sex Until the Right Circumstances Make It Safe Physically, Psychologically, Emotionally, and Morally. Yes, the human sex drive is biological in nature, and thus not something we can merely turn off and on like a light switch. But the sex drive is not a physical need in the same sense as the need for food and water. Humans cannot physically survive without nourishment, but they can survive just fine without sex.

Wanting sex is one thing. It's human, it's natural, and there's nothing inherently wrong with the feelings. Desiring a particular person is also natural. Remember that chemistry is a fluke: You can't make it happen and you can't help it when it does. *Feelings of sexual desire and sexual attraction are not a choice.* Like all feelings, they come and go, and we have little conscious control over them.

Having sex is entirely different. Acting on sexual feelings is a choice, one over which we have complete control. It is an abdication of responsibility when adults say, "I couldn't help myself. The feelings were just too strong." No matter how strong the desire or the passion, the act of sex can always be put off until the circumstances are right for both people.[1]

The message from the 1960s and 1970s was: "If it feels good, do it." This is an incomplete message. A more complete message might be: "Enjoy your sexual *feelings,* and when it comes to *acting on them,* make wise choices and wait for circumstances that are morally, emotionally, and healthfully right for both you and your partner."

Talking About Sex

The topic of sex is one of the most difficult to bring up in a dating relationship, but avoiding it is a setup for future failure. A frank discussion sets the stage for healthy relating and opens up a dialogue that, in an ongoing relationship, lasts a lifetime. But how do we get started on this kind of communication?

One place to begin is to take a personal inventory prior to talking with your partner or potential partner. Some questions to consider are:

- What is my moral stance with regard to premarital sex?

If premarital sex is not acceptable to you, consider the following:

- Most likely, you will need to find a partner whose moral stance is the same as yours. Otherwise, this will become the source of major conflict in your dating relationship, as one of you argues for sex before marriage and the other resists. Or, you may find yourself getting married too quickly in order to move into a sexual relationship.

---

[1]Individuals who truly feel that they cannot control their sexual impulses should immediately get professional guidance, as this is a serious disorder that can have grave consequences.

• Beware of compromising your beliefs in order to please a partner. You could end up with guilt and anger toward yourself and resentment toward your partner. Remember that sharing your deepest values creates a powerful connection that just isn't available with someone whose values are radically different.

If premarital sex is acceptable to you, then other questions to consider are:

• At what point am I most likely to be emotionally ready to have sex with my partner? Do I need a commitment of some sort? What kind of commitment? (e.g., monogamy, engagement, living together)
• Do I need emotional and sexual exclusivity with my partner prior to having sex?

Timing.   When do you bring up these kinds of issues with someone you're dating? While there's no right or wrong way to look at this, generally you should begin discussing your beliefs about sexuality as soon as you've moved past the interview stage (the first three or four dates) and it's clear that you both want to explore a relationship with each other. Most important, *be prepared to talk about sex before you actually sleep together!*

Engaging in a mature sexual relationship means having an adult discussion beforehand. What to discuss:

• beliefs and values about sexuality, including your moral stance about premarital sex
• sexual history, including any sexually transmitted diseases both past and present
• what becoming sexually involved means to each of you
• expectations of how the relationship might change once you become sexual
• exclusivity and what that means to each of you (see chapter sixteen)

- protection that you will use against disease, including having AIDS tests before becoming sexual
- protection against unwanted pregnancy
- the level of commitment that you each want or expect once you become sexual
- anything else that you feel might have a bearing on your relationship and your sexuality together

Straight Talk.   Clearly, this level of communication demands that you be honest and straightforward with your partner and expect the same in return. When I teach seminars and recommend this kind of communication, I almost always get some objections, such as:

- "Bringing up sex might offend my potential partner."
- "But I might scare them off—that's so serious."
- "He seems like such a nice person, I don't think I have to worry about diseases or conflicting values."

My response to the first two is: "So what?" So, someone gets offended or frightened off. What does that tell me? That tells me that they weren't ready for the level of honest communication that I'm ready for. Anyone who can't discuss sex in an adult way is, in my opinion, a bad risk for a relationship.

Remember that dating is the time when we're setting the stage for our relationships, practicing communication skills that will help us create healthy romance and a lasting marriage. Bringing up sex and discussing it openly creates an opportunity for dating partners to strengthen their growing bond, to deepen their respect for one another, and to build trust.

The last objection is a good example of how AIDS and other sexually transmitted diseases continue to spread. This is truly being the ostrich and sticking your head in the ground, fearful of what you might see but willing to die rather than take that risk. The truth about sexually transmitted diseases, including AIDS, is that nice people get them, too. There's no way to discern how much risk you're taking by trying to judge how nice someone is. The only way to begin protecting yourself is through honest, open dialogue.

Putting Off Sex.   Because of the sexual revolution and the loss of inhibitions about premarital sex, we have perhaps gone a little too far in the other direction. The typical dating scenario goes something like this: Man and woman meet, go out together five or six times (sometimes less), find out enough about each other to feel like there's a good relationship possibility, feel enough chemistry, and go to bed together, never having had any discussion of the ramifications that this will have. We're both looking for a relationship and neither of us wishes to be viewed as promiscuous, so at that point we consider ourselves to be "involved" with each other.

Then, the "Great Experiment" begins: Can we now build an emotional bridge to each other? Are we indeed compatible? Can we fall in love or learn to love each other and create a committed relationship? All this, *after* having become physically intimate. This is like putting the cart before the horse. The natural order of a relationship has been reversed: Sex has come before love, instead of vice versa. There are several difficulties with this:

- With physical intimacy we sometimes try to create something that isn't really there: If we believe we aren't promiscuous people, we conclude that we must be in a "relationship" if we're having sex.
- An unspoken commitment is created but without having had the sense of consciously choosing it; this commitment may be mutual or it may be one-sided, leading to confusion and emotional pain.
- Emotionally, it can be uncomfortable to be in this "instant relationship" with someone we barely know.
- We lose the opportunity to get to know each other without the pressure of commitment.
- Again, because we don't see ourselves as being the kind of people who have meaningless sex, we feel obligated to "love" each other, even if those feelings aren't really there.

• Having sex too soon can lead to Settle-for relationships, due to feelings of obligation or due to the natural emotional bonding that occurs.

Having sex first and then experimenting to see if the emotional part will follow does work at times. We all know of couples who have started their relationship with sex and love naturally followed. It is a gamble, however, and a high-stakes one at that. The danger is in taking this risk with each new partner, getting hurt or causing hurt, and accumulating a lot of emotional damage over time.

The best advice I can give singles is to *put off sex for a while,* for at least three or four months of dating, if at all possible. This allows the emotional side of your relationship to develop *first,* without any sense of obligation. Once your feelings for each other have developed and you've moved into a monogamous, committed relationship, sex can be a natural expression of the romance and intimacy that you feel for each other. With a foundation of genuine love and caring, sex is deeply meaningful and fulfilling, becoming a powerful bond in your relationship.

Author's Note: It would be possible, by taking parts of this chapter out of context, to assume that I am advocating premarital sex. Actually, I am not advocating any particular moral code. This chapter is written from a psychological and mental health perspective. I believe that it is each individual's right and responsibility to examine their own beliefs and values with regard to their own sexuality and to behave accordingly.

16

❤   ❤   ❤

The Exclusive Relationship

Roseanne and Chris had been dating for about three months when one night at dinner she asked, "So, are you still dating other people?"

She held her breath until Chris responded, "Well, no, I'm not. Are you?"

"No, I'm not, either," Roseanne answered. She breathed a sigh of relief, thinking that they had settled the issue of exclusivity.

Roseanne and Chris did have an exclusive relationship at that point. What they didn't have was a clear understanding about what that meant to each of them. To Roseanne, their conversation meant that they were not only monogamous, but had a commitment to each other and to their relationship. To Chris, it meant that he just didn't happen to have anyone else he was going out with at the time Roseanne asked the question, but that he was certainly free to ask out someone new if he wanted.

Two months later, he did exactly that, and when he began being less available to Roseanne, she quickly realized that he was seeing someone else. When she confronted him about their exclusive arrangement, they were both shocked to discover how differently each had interpreted their conversation.

Neither wanted to stop seeing each other at this point, so they decided to continue their relationship with the understanding that they could date other people. They soon discovered that they couldn't manage their feelings of jealousy and remain close to each other. Their relationship deteriorated and they broke up.

Why Be Exclusive?   Roseanne and Chris bumped up against the reality of dating: that if you want a healthy and nurturing relationship, it's almost impossible to be sexually and emotionally intimate with a partner without being monogamous. Human beings by nature seek connection and intimacy, and romantic love offers the opportunity to have both. But getting close to someone requires a great deal of vulnerability, and that means taking a certain amount of risk. That risk is multiplied many times when a relationship isn't exclusive.

In order to be vulnerable and intimate, we need to feel psychologically and emotionally safe. In an exclusive, committed relationship, there is the sense that we are partners: that we are on each other's side, that we are both invested in the romance, and that we are both willing to take the steps to nurture and sustain what we are building together. Furthermore, our energies are with each other and not diverted to other romantic partners. This creates a sort of psychological safety net, and is just what we need in order to be able to open up to our partner, to risk the sharing of innermost feelings.

Some of the purposes for being exclusive include:

• *To create an investment in the relationship.* Romance, like anything else in life, brings rewards to the degree that we make a commitment. When there is a declaration between two people that we are a couple, that our relationship holds a position of high priority in our lives, and that we are committed to creating and maintaining a connection that is healthy and positive for us both, this is powerful glue. This kind of commitment doesn't come all at once or overnight, and having an exclusive relationship sets the stage for it to happen.

• *To create a psychological safety net.* There is nothing riskier in life than an intimate relationship. To make it work, we must open our hearts, be vulnerable, and take a giant leap of faith: that we trust each other to not do harm, to be there when the going gets rough, and to not abandon us.

• *To prevent the spread of sexually transmitted diseases.* This one almost goes without saying in today's world, but needs to be emphasized nevertheless. If you are sexually intimate with your partner, it is vital to your health to do so only within the context of an exclusive relationship.

• *To become a couple.* There is a point in every dating relationship when we choose whether we are going to continue just spending time together or whether we are going to become a couple. As a couple, we have a "relationship," an entity that is greater than our individuality. With a relationship at stake, we now have a greater investment and, therefore, more incentive to make it work.

• *To encourage an emotional bond.* Love relationships have no chance of succeeding without a strong emotional bond. Feelings of love, connection, and intimacy act as a glue that binds partners together, giving them a powerful base from which to resolve issues and differences. But love is a fragile emotion that needs a great deal of reinforcement and nurturing. Without an exclusive relationship, it's difficult to let feelings of love grow.

Avoiding Exclusivity.   Sometimes we resist exclusivity in dating, and there are a couple of reasons for this. First and foremost is the fear of intimacy. Declaring a relationship exclusive demands that we be vulnerable and therefore open to hurt and possible rejection or abandonment.

It has been said that romantic love offers the opportunity for the greatest joy and validation in life; at the same time, it carries with it the highest risk for pain. Few things in life hurt more deeply than being rejected or abandoned by a lover, especially if you've had your heart really open to that person.

For today's single over the age of twenty-five, the chances are that there has been at least one significant love relationship, and possibly several. This means that more than once, you've opened your heart to another person, allowed yourself dreams and hopes of a lifetime together, and then had the relationship fail. Even if you're the one who left, there is still hurt. If you're in your forties or fifties, add in a failed marriage or two, and now let's see how willing you are to open your heart and be vulnerable!

We've all been hurt in love, and it's natural to want to minimize the chances of getting our hearts broken again. I believe it's possible to do that by making wise choices about whom to become involved with and by having lots and lots of straight communication beginning with the very first date. But even then, there's still risk, for the simple reason that no one can predict the future. Life events can intrude into a relationship, individual feelings can change, communication can break down and therefore the relationship itself, and so many other factors, many of which we have little or no control over.

There's no way to avoid taking a risk when we become involved with someone. Once we've made the choice to become intimate, emotionally and/or sexually, with a particular partner, the potential for getting hurt is there. *To try to minimize it by avoiding exclusivity actually sets you up for failure.* Relationships simply cannot develop in a healthy way when there are other partners in the picture. Thus, the fear of intimacy (i.e., fear of being hurt) becomes a self-fulfilling prophecy. *I'll protect myself by not getting too close, but ultimately our relationship will fail because we can't develop it at arm's length; therefore, I end up hurt anyway.*

Time after time, I've counseled individuals who tried to avoid getting hurt by not making a commitment. Ultimately, their partners left in frustration, and they found themselves devastated. Withholding love and avoiding an exclusive relationship and commitment didn't protect them from hurt. It did prevent them from creating a healthy bond with their partners, thus dooming the relationship to failure.

Another reason we resist exclusivity in dating is that we may deny the importance of creating this psychological and emotional safety net. Rationally, we tell ourselves that we should "keep our options open." We tell ourselves that we should have no problem continuing to date around while getting involved with a special person.

These arguments may make sense logically, but in reality they're very difficult to follow through on. It's one thing to tell ourselves that it's really okay for a lover to date someone else, but actually seeing them with that other person is entirely different! Logic breaks down quickly in matters of the heart. The truth is that few people can withstand the emotional threat of another person intruding into a romantic relationship.

Communication, Exclusivity, and Commitment

Because of differing ideas about what exclusivity and commitment mean, the opportunity is ripe for misunderstandings between people who are dating each other. Each may have a different concept of what exclusive means, and certainly the word "commitment" means something different to each person, as we've discussed before. Factor in the differences in the way men and women communicate, and it's easy to see how quickly we can get off track at this point in a relationship!

Consider Rick and Leslie's relationship. On their third date they were kissing passionately and it looked like sex was about to follow, so Leslie stopped and said, "We need to talk." She then informed Rick that she couldn't be intimate with him unless they had an exclusive relationship. He agreed, and they became lovers. The problem is that they agreed on two different things.

To Leslie, exclusive meant that they wouldn't go out with, kiss, or be romantic in any way with another person; that at that point they had a committed relationship. To Rick, exclusive meant that he wouldn't have sex with anyone else, but that he was certainly free to date, kiss, hold hands with, and be romantic with other women. Months later, this misunderstanding caused a huge upset between them when Leslie found out about his other dates. Let's look at some of the distinctions and meanings about these emotionally loaded concepts.

Commitment and Exclusivity.   Often these two words are confused. Sometimes we use them interchangeably, but the truth is that they are actually not the same. To have an *exclusive relationship* basically means that there are no other romantic partners. For most people, this means that we don't go out with, kiss, hold hands with, or do anything romantic with another person. However, because some people view this differently and more loosely, it's important to be specific about what you each mean by exclusive when talking to a dating partner.

To have a *committed relationship* means that we've moved a step farther emotionally; that we view ourselves as a couple, that we place our relationship as a high priority in our lives, and that we value our connection enough to take the steps to nurture and maintain it. We are no longer considering other partners, nor are we just spending time together until something better comes along.

Having a commitment doesn't mean that we have pledged ourselves to each other for life or that our relationship will never end. It does mean that we are both committed to doing everything in our power to create the healthiest connection possible and to maintain that even when it's difficult. It means that we both have a high degree of intention to continue together, even though we realistically don't know what the future will hold.

This is distinguished from a marriage commitment, which does say that we pledge ourselves to each other for life. This is the highest level of commitment attainable in a relationship. It means that we promise each other to stay together no matter what; that we will operate in our relationship as though there is no option for exiting; that we will honor this pledge until one of us dies.

Unfortunately, marriage vows are broken all too often. This is for many reasons, which are too numerous to list here. One reason, however, is that the marriage commitment is not always made at the deep level described above. Instead of truly pledging our lives together forever, we are actually promising to stay together as long as we feel good in the relationship. Or as long as we feel passionately in love. Or as long as we feel our needs are being met. The commitment is contingent upon circumstances and good feelings, and this is not a true marriage commitment. The reality is that, in a long-term relationship such as marriage, feelings of love wax and wane, needs are met on some days and not on others, passion comes and goes, and life events intrude and create problems.

The problem with commitment actually begins much earlier. In dating, we often move into an exclusive relationship without giving thought to the importance of this step. Later, we make a commitment that is weak, failing to fully assume the responsibility for nurturing and maintaining a healthy relationship. When it's time for marriage vows, the level of commitment is lower because we haven't embraced the earlier steps as completely as possible.

Emotional Versus Behavioral Exclusivity. These two concepts are often confused as well. While they seem to be the same, they are actually very distinct. *Behavioral exclusivity* means refraining from any behavior that goes outside the bounds of the relationship: kissing, holding, touching, or having sex with another partner.

Emotional exclusivity is much broader, and includes behavioral exclusivity as well as something more. This means that not only do we refrain from doing sexual or romantic things with another partner, but we refrain from any kind of romanticizing of another, whether verbal, written, or otherwise.

Failing to be emotionally exclusive is playing the game at a lower level of risk, and as we discussed earlier, this will be a barrier to developing the relationship to its full potential.

Drifting Versus Declaring. Consider Kay and Robert. After dating for six months, they both thought their relationship to be exclusive in that neither had any interest in dating anyone else. This couple made a mistake that happens frequently in dating: They *drifted into* an exclusive relationship, with no real communication. By not discussing what each of them considered an exclusive relationship to be, by not declaring themselves in one, they entered this crucial relationship stage with a very low level of intention, thus giving them little basis from which to build toward a real commitment later.

To *declare* an exclusive relationship, however, is entirely different. This means having an actual discussion about what being exclusive means to each of you, agreeing on definitions, then deciding together that that's where you want to be. Now you've entered an exclusive relationship with some intentionality and consciousness. You have set the stage for making a commitment later on.

Pacing and Timing. Often singles ask me, "What is the usual time frame for each of these steps?" The answer, of course, is that there is no particular formula. We each have a different emotional timetable: What's fast to you may be slow to me, and vice versa. The length of time since the last committed relationship or marriage will affect the timing in the current one as well. Someone who's recently divorced will generally want to move more slowly than someone who's been single for years.

First, let's look at an outline of the basic steps in moving a relationship forward to a commitment:

- *First three dates:* The potential relationship is definitely a Maybe at this point. Use it like an interview; be alert for red flags (either resolve them or decide to move on); have the Shopping Conversation (are we looking for the same thing?); look out for the Westbound Train; communicate openly and honestly and look for that in return.
- *Four dates to three months:* The relationship is still a Maybe; continue assessing values (meet your Non-Negotiables). At some point, have your first You and Me conversation, in which you discuss exclusivity and either decide to move on or declare yourselves exclusive, doing this with the intention of moving forward and exploring the relationship for its potential without the threat of other partners. Most couples who are in the market for a serious, committed relationship want to take this step *before* becoming sexual.
- *Three to six months:* The relationship is now a Yes, but is not yet a forever commitment. After exclusivity is established, continue assessing compatibility; have regular You and Me conversations in which you check out whether you are both getting your needs met and feel good

overall about the relationship. At some point, discuss commitment and what that means to each of you; decide whether or not to move into a committed relationship. If you do, do so with the strong intention that the relationship will last, and that you will both make every effort to interact in a healthy way and to maintain your connection.

• *Six months plus:* Of course, the timing of this will vary greatly from one couple to the next, but once you've spent anywhere from a few months to several years in an exclusive relationship, continuing to have regular You and Me conversations, you'll eventually discuss the issue of marriage. At this point, you may both be on the same timetable and it will be a natural process to move into engagement and, later, marriage. Many couples, however, find themselves on two different emotional timetables, with one more anxious to move ahead and get married and the other more reluctant; your process at this point may be more complicated and may even involve getting some counseling if you get stuck.

None of these guidelines are hard and fast, so it's important that you remain flexible and not try to turn this into a set of rules that you try to enforce. Every relationship is different, just as each one is made up of unique individuals. The process of meeting, coupling, growing closer and more committed, and eventually marrying is as unique as your fingerprints. What's important is that you communicate fully each step of the way, regardless of your pace.

A note of caution about moving too fast: Remember that if you marry someone whom you've only known a few weeks or months you're pledging yourself for life with a lot of unknowns. More important, you haven't allowed sufficient time for a solid commitment to develop. The chances are that you're marrying an image or a fantasy, not a real person whom you've taken the time to really know. Therefore, it's generally best to give yourselves at least a full year of dating, preferably two, before making a marriage commitment. This is a strong suggestion, but it doesn't mean that you'll fail if you don't follow it.

Another problematic pace is taking too long for a commitment. Often when a couple dates for years without being able to make a commitment, there's a good reason. There may be a fundamental incompatibility (e.g., one wants children and the other doesn't). One or both may feel deep down that this person just isn't the right partner for them. One or both may have a genuine fear of commitment, even though they're with the right partner. And there are many other reasons. To marry without resolving whatever it is that is blocking the commitment is usually a mistake. After marriage these couples discover that the stumbling block is still there, only now they've made a lifelong commitment, possibly to the wrong partner.

Am I Ready?   One place to begin is to do some self-exploration about whether or not you're ready for an exclusive relationship with your partner. What to consider:

• What is my motive for becoming exclusive with this person? Is it simply so that we can become sexual? Is it because I want to please him or her so I'm not abandoned? Or is it because I see the potential for a great relationship and I want to explore that further with this person?

• Am I clear about my own and my partner's emotional availability? Are we both Northbound Trains?

• Have I resolved any red flags that I've seen?

• Have we had the Shopping Conversation, and are we both looking for the same thing?

• Do our values appear to mesh?

• Do I feel a connection on all three levels with this person (intellectual, emotional, sexual)?

• Based on what I know so far, is this someone who could potentially be my mate for life? Or am I settling for less than what I really want?

You may think of other questions as well to ask yourself at this point. If, when you've done your personal inventory, you come up with a green light, then you're ready to bring up the issue of exclusivity with your partner. If not, *proceed with caution:* You may be setting yourself up for heartache if you go forward without these questions resolved.

The Secondary Relationship

Sometimes couples get together because of needs that they want met (intimacy, companionship, sex), but they are not truly compatible. Or, they may see that there's no potential for falling in love and may not even want that with this person. This is what I call a "Secondary Relationship."

The problems with Secondary Relationships are many, as they have a lot of potential for turning into Settle-for relationships. First, no matter how strongly you may intend to remain emotionally uninvolved, there's simply no way to avoid the dynamics of attachment. One or both of you is going to form a bond or develop expectations, even though you may rationally know that the relationship is going nowhere.

Second, there's a high probability that one of you has a secret emotional agenda, with one partner starting out more attached and hoping the other will "catch up."

Third, even if you both fall in love, you may have tremendous incompatibilities to overcome (which is why you were reluctant to get involved in the first place). At the very least, you will have advanced your relationship without much consciousness or intentionality, and it's very difficult to transform this kind of no-commitment relationship into a committed one later on.

When It Can Work.　　Overall, I don't recommend this kind of relationship because of the high potential for emotional hurt and the low probability of its working. It's much better to find other ways to get your needs met, through platonic friendships and staying busy with activities you enjoy. However, if you must do it, there are ways to at least attempt to manage it. Some pointers:

• *Be totally honest with yourself.* Ask: Is there a potential for falling in love with this person? Write down the reasons for seeing no future with this person, so you can remind yourself later. Ask yourself: Am I just avoiding intimacy, or is this truly the wrong person for me?

• *Be totally honest with your partner.* If you see no future, communicate that to the person you're considering a Secondary Relationship with, including why.

• *Ask for and listen to their thoughts and feelings.* Listen not only to what is said, but to the inflections and nuances of the unspoken. If what you hear and what you feel are not congruent, check out your perception. Stay in the conversation until you feel like you have both spoken the truth as best you know how.

• *Set an end point for your involvement.* Agree that it won't last beyond a certain time (generally, a couple of weeks to a couple of months) and decide in advance on how it will end.

• *Stick to your plan or create another one based on new developments.* If you find your feelings changing, have another You and Me conversation and try to determine how your partner is feeling. If you find it's not working, be willing to end it, even if you haven't reached your agreed-upon ending point.

The You and Me Conversation Revisited

As we've discussed over and over, communication is the key at every step in a dating relationship. If the goal is a healthy connection, then it's necessary to have regular, open discussions about where you are with each other. This means lots and lots of You and Me conversations as the relationship progresses.

Looking at these steps on paper is not the same as doing it in real life, though. As Annie's story illustrates, what we logically intend to do and what we actually do are sometimes very different! In therapy, Annie had resolved to have her first You and Me conversation with her new boyfriend, Frank, sometime in the following week. When their plans to go to the museum turned into drinks first, followed by dinner and more drinks, they ended up at her place and spent the night together. No You and Me conversation.

Annie was still kicking herself when she came to therapy the following week. She still didn't know where she stood with Frank, or even if they had an exclusive relationship. And now they were sexually intimate. What could she do?

The truth is that even the best plans for straight communication can go by the wayside when the chemistry is high. When that happens, I recommend that, rather than beating yourself up emotionally, you be forgiving of yourself, then step back and reassess what it is you want.

Annie wanted to be sure that Frank wasn't seeing anyone else if they were going to continue a sexual involvement, so she resolved to have a conversation with Frank about that as soon as possible (and she followed through on this). She also let him know that she wasn't comfortable with the level of their intimacy at this point, and their next date was spent just cuddling and talking.

Having your first talk *after* you've become intimate isn't ideal and may mean that you'll be hurt more if you discover you're not on the same track. But it doesn't mean that all is lost. Relationships, remember, are a process. They're not like cake recipes where you have to throw the whole thing out if you mess up an ingredient.

When Annie voiced her fear that she would fumble around in her attempts to communicate with Frank and "blow the relationship," I asked her to consider a couple of things. First, if two people are powerfully drawn together (and we've already said lots of attraction is needed and wanted), and they are both available and desire a relationship with each other, then any mistakes you make in communication aren't going to prevent you from going forward. On the other hand, when an attraction is weak or the bonding between two people is fragile, then any kind of mistake can break whatever connection is forming, which is beneficial if it frees you to find someone you'll have a much stronger bond with.

In the long run, the quality and kind of communication in a relationship is the most important factor determining whether your connection is healthy and lasting.

17

♥   ♥   ♥

Breaking Up Is
Hard to Do

Becky, a thirty-four-year-old advertising executive, asked the question that most singles want to know the answer to at one time or another: "How do I end a relationship?" The answer, of course, is simple: Just say it's over.

What Becky and others *really* want to know is much more compli-cated: How do I know that breaking up is the right thing to do? How do I know there's anyone better for me out there? How do I do it without causing anyone any pain? The answers to these questions aren't so simple, and before you can say it's over, these and a host of other issues have to be resolved.

Mind Versus Heart.   For the umpteenth time Jenny was going over the reasons why she should break up with Daryl. "He drinks too much, he'd rather be with his buddies than with me, he forgets birth-days and anniversaries, he makes promises and doesn't keep them, and I can't remember the last time he said he loved me. Besides that, I think he's seeing someone else. I've talked to him about all my con-cerns, but he just says I'm too demanding and that he can't give me what I want. I've asked him to come to counseling, but he refuses. I know I should break up with him. Why can't I just do it?"

Jenny's brain was telling her that this relationship had hit a dead end and that she couldn't get her needs met with this man. But her heart was telling her something entirely different. When I asked what the reasons were for her staying, she said simply, "I love him. I want to be with him, and I don't like thinking about what my life would be without him."

In relationships, like no other area of life, our minds and our hearts don't always agree. Logically, we may know that it's time to move on from this partner, but emotionally, we just can't seem to bring ourselves to do it. We tell our friends what the problems are, and they unanimously chorus, "Just get out!" We tell ourselves to move on, resolving that this time we'll tell him or her it's really over. At the last minute, we excuse ourselves from the confrontation, rationalizing that it's probably not a good time. How does this happen?

In the first few weeks or even months of dating we are in a process of rational evaluation: getting to know each other and trying to decide how much potential there is for a long-term relationship. This is the logical side of love: *Who are you* and *are you right for me?*

Meanwhile, strange processes are occurring in the brain and body over which we have no logical, rational control. Certain chemicals are released by the brain, causing feelings of euphoria, a heightened awareness, dilating pupils, sleeplessness, weight loss, and a host of other responses. Most of us simply call it "falling in love." Others call it insanity.

We may tell ourselves that we're making a rational choice, but if the chemistry is strong enough, we may decide to proceed with the relationship even if there are obvious red flags and clear incompatibility. The heart, it appears, has more power than the mind when it comes to romance.

This phenomenon occurs again when we're considering breaking up. Now that months or even years have passed, there's a strong attachment even if there are clear incompatibilities. Again, we turn the decision over to the mind, asking it why we should leave or stay.

The mind spits back logical answers, all indicating that the answer is *leave*. But the heart intervenes once again, and feelings of attachment win out: We stay, even if it's with a great deal of ambivalence.

It's this tug-of-war between the mind and the heart, between logic and emotion, that makes the decision about breaking up so difficult. So where do we begin to approach this issue? Let's begin with exploring the reasons for why you may want to leave.

Why Leave? Just as there are at least, as the song says, "fifty ways to leave your lover," there are many, many reasons for why you may want to end your relationship. Let's look closely at some typical reasons, as well as possible underlying motives for these reasons.

1. *Partner has too many unacceptable faults.* In the beginning of a romance, when we are first falling in love, we see our partner through rose-colored glasses. They're beautiful, sexy, and almost perfect. We can't believe our good fortune.

Later, when the romantic bliss fades a little, we begin to see their faults. Then, if we're not careful, we begin to store negative information in an invisible file called "what's wrong with my partner." When the file gets full (and usually we've not brought up any of the issues for discussion), we begin feeling the urge to exit from the relationship.

The decision to stay or go at this point may not be about what we think it is. Sometimes, resentments have piled up over time about small but significant issues that haven't been fully addressed. Breaking up may not be the answer. Resolving the resentment first may clear the way for a solution that can be followed through on, whether that's staying or leaving.

2. *Anger and pain.* Sometimes the incidents that occur along the way in a relationship are more dramatic and hurtful. There may be genuine pain and anger that has accumulated over time, and there's a feeling that "you've hurt me too much to continue." In this case, the urge to break up is about getting out of pain, an understandable goal.

The problem is that often after this kind of breakup, once the pain fades, the good feelings that drew you together are recalled once again, and it's tempting to go back. If the old issues are swept under the rug at this point and aren't addressed, you may find yourself in a repetitive dating cycle—interacting in a hurtful way, feeling pain and anger building to an intolerable level, breaking up, cooling off, getting back together, and so on. Rather than impulsively break up in anger, it might be better to get some counseling together to try to change your patterns of interacting to something healthier.

3. *Not enough in love.* Not all romances begin with falling in love. Sometimes individuals pair up in order to get their needs met but really don't ever fall in love. At first it seems okay; the newness of the relationship plus getting some needs met can hold interest for a time. If the attraction isn't particularly strong, however, this may, in reality, be a Settle-for relationship. Eventually, one or both may begin to feel that something's missing and that it has to do with not being really in love.

Sometimes relationships begin with falling in love and then, over time, power struggles and negative incidents act to diminish feelings of love. It's difficult to feel warmly toward someone when you're holding a grudge about something they did two years ago!

When trying to determine whether to break up over the issue of love, ask yourself:

• Was I ever in love with this person? Try to recall your early courtship days and not look back through the filter of anger and resentment. Ask your friends for their take on how you seemed to feel about your partner in the beginning.

• If I was in love at one time, then am I harboring feelings of resentment about things that have happened in our relationship? Could these grudges be obscuring my former, loving feelings about my partner?

If you believe you've made an objective assessment and that no, you were never in love with your partner, and you're dissatisfied with that, breaking up may be the best thing you can do. Love, if it's going to happen, usually happens within the first few weeks and months of a relationship. If it hasn't happened by then, it almost never happens later. Without feelings of romantic love, there's little glue to cement a partnership so that you can weather the inevitable conflict that at some point is bound to occur.

4. *Something's missing.* Sometimes there's just a general, overall sense that there's something missing in the relationship. Usually there's nothing obvious that can easily be seen. You may even think your partner's a wonderful person, but . . . And it's that "but" that has you thinking about breaking up.

Go back to the five factors for healthy relationships. First of all, do you connect in all three of the important ways: intellectual, emotional, sexual? Do your values mesh? Do you both desire the relationship and feel willing to make a commitment?

Again, as with the issue of love, consider whether you had all those things in the beginning of the relationship. Did something change along the way? Or were you always missing one or more of the main ingredients?

Your values may have remained the same, but one of your lives changed in a major way, and new goals were set that no longer mesh well. Maybe you were once very sexually attracted but that changed (sometimes chemistry has a very short life). Whatever changed, you now have the choice of either going forward or trying to recover whatever was lost. If you choose to try to recover what was lost, you may need counseling, either individually or jointly, to accomplish that.

5. *Fear of intimacy.* Sometimes the issues that you think you're breaking up over aren't the real ones. They may be genuine concerns, but they are actually camouflage for something on a deeper level. Fear of intimacy, which is really the fear of getting hurt emotionally, is an example. Consciously the feeling may be one of detachment, anger or resentment, or loss of love, but unconsciously the driving force may be a fear of intimacy.

This fear can manifest itself in many ways, some of which are:

• a pattern in relationships of getting to a certain point of closeness and then suddenly feeling the need to disconnect and break up

- chronic doubt and suspicion about your partner's motives and feelings for you
- cynicism about relationships and love in general
- a pattern of pushing others away through game playing, withheld communication, and emotional dramatics
- keeping partners at an emotional distance by not making yourself fully available
- pattern of choosing partners who aren't quite right for you so that you always have a back door to exit through later
- driving partners away through negligence and mistreatment (e.g., broken promises, infidelity, emotional abuse, etc.)

Obviously, this list could go on and on. The bottom line is that fear of intimacy is a way of attempting to protect ourselves from the pain of possible rejection, abandonment, and other kinds of heartache. "If I can keep from getting too close, then I won't get hurt" is the way our unconscious reasoning goes. So we guard our hearts fiercely, erecting barriers that prevent us from experiencing love and being as fully intimate as we might be.

Of course, these attempts don't really work. As we've already seen, trying to avoid intimacy actually sets in motion the very things we're trying to avoid. By keeping you at arm's length, I am asking you to leave eventually. Even though I tell myself it won't hurt, it always does, even if I deny the pain. By never letting anyone get too close, I am setting myself up to feel the pain of my loneliness and isolation. Ultimately, the fear of intimacy causes more real suffering by far than the legitimate pain of getting close and having things not work out.

If you suspect that this is you, the chances are that you'll need professional guidance in order to make changes. The number one thing you'll need to do is learn to set boundaries in relationships. If I'm not sure I can take care of myself or handle emotional pain, I'll have to keep others from getting too close, avoiding any vulnerability. *When I know I can protect myself in healthy ways, confident that I am the source of my own well-being, I am much freer to move close to others and open my heart to the experience of love.* Remember that we can only love others to the extent that we truly love ourselves (who we are, not just our accomplishments in the world).

There are other deep emotional issues that may not be conscious but keep us from developing love relationships: rage toward a former partner that hasn't been resolved; family issues that are incomplete; damage to self-esteem and the sense of not deserving love; and many others. If you want to end your current relationship and can't pinpoint the reason, but you are filled with the urge to leave, the chances are that it's an emotional issue that's out of reach of your immediate consciousness but that's dictating your feelings and behavior.

6. *Unworkable relationship dynamics.* Sometimes just the way you and your partner interact is painful and dysfunctional. You know it, and you've tried to convey that to your partner. You've tried asking for behavior change, but all you get is resistance.

At this point, you may want to ask your partner to go to counseling with you rather than just breaking up. Ending a painful relationship doesn't always solve the problem. After a time, the pain diminishes, you begin to recall the good times, and you miss your partner. It's tempting to go back and not really deal with the issues that drove you apart.

Perhaps you've already asked your partner to go to counseling with you but all you've gotten is resistance. Sometimes the way you ask may be blocking a positive response. If you imply that *they* are the problem, and that *they* need to get help by going to therapy with you, the chances are that you won't get what you want.

You might try a different approach, something like this: "You know, I've been having some challenges in our relationship, and I'm having a hard time dealing with that. I really need your help so that I can feel good about us again. I'm not sure what the problem is, but I want you to be part of the solution. Will you go with me to counseling to try to find solutions to my unhappiness in this relationship?" However you say it, make the message about yourself, and ask your partner to be part of the solution rather than implying that they are the problem.

If you've made an appeal like this and your partner still doesn't respond, you have some new choices: You may go to counseling yourself to change how you're responding or decide whether to leave; you may leave the relationship; or you may stay and hope for eventual change.

7. *Can't get a commitment.* Maybe you've dated for months and your partner still doesn't act as though you're a couple. Perhaps you've dated for years and your partner won't even discuss marriage or has so much resistance that you just don't see it happening in the natural course of the relationship. All your efforts to resolve this issue with your partner have left you frustrated and empty-handed.

If you've broached the subject of counseling, which may help you resolve this together, and he or she won't go, then you're left with the choice of continuing and hoping your partner will have a change of heart someday or ending it and moving on. This may be a very difficult choice.

Be careful of breaking up in order to get a commitment. Sometimes this works, and sometimes it doesn't. If you do break up for this reason, be fully prepared to go on with your life rather than sitting around wishing and hoping. If you truly intend to move on, this can actually be a wake-up call for your partner, and sometimes a commitment does happen as a result. But if you're just trying to manipulate your partner, the chances are that it will backfire and you'll feel even worse.

8. *This person's just not the partner for me.* Sometimes the feeling is one of caring, respect, and even sexual attraction, but for no particular reason the overwhelming sense is that you just haven't found the right partner yet.

The myth is that you need a good reason to end a relationship when, in fact, you don't. The truth is, that for no reason, or for any reason, certain people just aren't right for you. Leaving behind all the logic, all the lists of what's good and what's not so good, the bottom line in any relationship is very simple: Either you want to spend your life with this person or you don't. This is a gut response, based on intuition and emotion, and it goes beyond logic.

On paper, a person can look like the ideal partner for you: All your Non-Negotiables are met, you connect on all levels, and so on. But if your inner being does not feel that this person is right for you, all the rationality in the world won't make it so. And, if you go forward without the sense that you're with the right person, you'll most likely be frustrated and always feel that something important is missing. You'll be settling for less than what you really want.

To Stay or To Go: Which Is Best?

Now that we've covered many of the typical reasons for wanting to end a relationship, you may still be feeling that tug-of-war between your heart and your head. Ambivalent feelings can keep you stuck for weeks, months, and even years as you try to decide: Should I stay or should I go? Let's look at some things to consider when trying to decide about breaking up.

What Do I Want?   Before you can decide whether to stay or to go, the first thing you need to know is what you're looking for. Just knowing that what you have is unsatisfactory isn't enough. With only a vague sense that something's not right, you're very likely to go out and find someone else with whom you repeat that same experience.

Take some time with this question. Sit down with plenty of paper and a pen, put on your favorite music, and just let your thoughts flow on the subject of what you're looking for in a relationship. Write down whatever you're thinking of, no matter how insignificant it may seem. Don't edit as you write and don't stop to evaluate what you've written so far. When you're finished, go back and put a star by the things that you think are your most important needs, that are realistic and attainable.

What About This Relationship?   Next, ask yourself: Can I get those needs met in this particular relationship? Looking at your own and your partner's emotional capacity to deal with the issues that are important to you, do your best to make a judgment call.

You don't have the ability to predict the future, but you do have a good sense of what's realistically attainable. The most important thing to consider is if you feel strongly that some vital needs of yours just can't be met in this relationship. Then, you have a choice to make about whether or not to approach your partner with this information and ask them to work with you to make the changes necessary so that you can get your needs met.

Fear of Being Alone. The need for intimacy is so powerful that it will keep individuals in bad relationships for months, years, and even a lifetime rather than face the emptiness of being alone. What makes this all the more difficult is that we've all had to face losses in our lives, some more than others, so that many of us are especially sensitized to the pain of loneliness. Add to that the fact that we're not always our own best friend and don't always take the best care of ourselves emotionally, and you've got the ingredients for settling: staying in a mediocre or bad relationship indefinitely.

If fear of being alone is keeping you in an unsatisfactory relationship, you can take steps to help yourself overcome that fear. You may want to review the steps in chapter fourteen about healing your relationship with yourself, and in earlier chapters about creating a network of friendships and support.

- Become your own best friend.
- Reach out to others for friendship and support.
- Learn how to be alone and actually enjoy it.

Fear of Grief. Few things in life bring as much loss as the end of a romantic relationship. It can feel as intense as a divorce or the death of a family member, and the grief may take months or years to deal with. No one wants to choose this kind of pain, and sometimes staying in a dissatisfying relationship seems better than having to deal with the loss.

Typically, this only prolongs and puts off the pain. Time and again, I've counseled individuals who stayed in bad relationships for years, only to have their partners finally end it. The grief and loss was then compounded by feelings of betrayal and abandonment: "I've stayed with you all this time, even though I haven't gotten my needs met, and look how you repay me!"

Remember that if you're dissatisfied with your relationship, ultimately your partner is, too, even though they may be denying it. *There's no such thing as a relationship that works for only one of the people in it.* A relationship is good only if it is a win/win: It works and is satisfying for both partners.

Putting off the pain of grief and loss doesn't make it go away; in fact, it only increases it. The longer you spend with someone, the deeper the investment and the greater the attachment. If you know it's not right and it can't be fixed, the only choice that has any real integrity is to end it. If you can't bring yourself to do what you overwhelmingly feel you should, get help at once. Staying in these dead-end relationships is life-draining and can lead to physical, emotional, and mental illness.

I Don't Want to Hurt Anyone.   We say we don't want to hurt our partner, but in reality it is our own discomfort we're seeking to prevent. There's no way to avoid a certain amount of pain when a relationship ends, even when you're the one who ends it.

Trying to find a way to end a relationship without hurting anyone is like trying to find a way to swim without getting wet. It's not very likely. Even in very short relationships, there's the disappointment of hopes and dreams that won't ever be fulfilled. In longer ones, there are the dynamics of attachment and love, and that means feelings of grief and loss on both sides.

It simply isn't realistic to expect to find a way to end a relationship without feeling or causing any pain. What you can do is minimize the suffering by not delaying.

Right/Wrong Versus Consequences.   One of the myths about breaking up is that there really exists a right or wrong decision, and your job is to by all means find and make the "right" choice. In this point of view, making the right choice means that you will have little or no pain, you'll sail on forward into an ideal future, and everything will turn out okay. This, of course, is your reward for making the right choice.

If you fail and make the wrong choice, however, you'll be miserable and unhappy and unable to change it, and your life will go downhill from there. You'll end up alone or you'll suffer through a disastrous relationship for the rest of your life. This is your punishment for making the wrong choice.

With so much riding on your decision, and with your heart and head playing tug-of-war, how can you possibly choose? After all, you don't know what's in the future, and it's just too risky to make a choice that might be wrong!

You ask your friends for their opinions, gathering other people's advice and hoping someone will tell you what to do. You visit one or more therapists, hoping one of them will give you the right answer. You read every self-help book you can get your hands on, but nowhere can you get the right answer. In this frame of mind, you will most likely avoid making a decision, choosing instead to sit on the fence for as long as possible.

There is another way to look at making decisions like this, however. Instead of considering that there is a right and a wrong choice, you might think about it as being *just a choice, period,* that there is no right or wrong one, and that you won't be either punished or rewarded for either one. The truth is that no matter which one you choose, there will be consequences. That's the only thing you can count on for sure when you make a decision.

The real question is not which choice is right and which is wrong. The question to be asked is: *Which choice provides consequences I am willing to embrace and be responsible for?* If I choose to stay, am I willing to be responsible for that choice, making a commitment to the relationship and doing everything in my power to improve it? If I go, am I willing to be responsible for that choice, releasing blame and doing whatever I need to do to get on with my life?

The answers to these questions won't be found in a book, with a friend or therapist, or in the stars. They will only be found inside you—in your willingness to ask yourself some tough questions and get some tough answers back, and in your willingness to listen to your own heart and intuition. Ultimately, whether you stay together or break up, the real choice is in your ability to be responsible for what you choose and to live your life accordingly.

Deciding to Stay

If the decision you reach is to stay in the current relationship, you've made an important step. If that's all you do, however, the chances are that you'll be right back in the same boat in a few weeks or months: dissatisfied and feeling the urge to leave again.

The concerns you had that made you want to leave are still there. The next step is more difficult than just deciding to stay: making a commitment to improving the relationship. This means:

• taking some responsibility for the problems between you and your partner
• communicating fully to your partner about your concerns, in a non-blaming way
• including your partner in a search for solutions, whether just the two of you do that or whether you see a therapist to help you.

Deciding to Go

One last question to consider if you've decided to end your relationship is this: What is my purpose in leaving? Am I: 1) leaving so that I can get my partner to change? or 2) leaving so that I can take an emotional break? (and try again later) or 3) leaving because I really want it to be over permanently?

Getting Change. Maybe you've talked to your partner, expressed your concerns, and asked for changes. If you've not gotten the response you want, and you've tried more than once to communicate, you may be feeling the urge to break up, hoping they'll finally get the message that you're serious.

If you're leaving to get your partner to change, realize that you may or may not get what you want. Sometimes when a relationship ends, both people focus more on their own inner blocks to being honest and intimate, and when they reunite later they are really capable of a healthier connection. Just as often, they make inner changes and take those to a new relationship. Sometimes they change but you move on and don't want them back later. Many times no changes are made. There's no way to predict the outcome.

Therefore it's important that you treat a breakup like this as though it's permanent, because it just may be. That means allowing yourself to grieve and detach. Let the future take care of itself. In fact, the more you really let go of your partner and take care of yourself, the more likely they are to make real changes. Holding on and not letting your partner go minimizes the breakup and therefore the need for change.

Taking a Break.   Perhaps you've tried really hard to make your relationship work and you're feeling emotionally exhausted. You may be feeling the urge to leave just to give yourself a break from the intensity of being intimate and trying so hard to connect and make changes.

If you're breaking up for this reason, realize that eventually you'll feel some relief, and you will probably want to see your old partner again. The good news is that sometimes a break like this allows both people to shift their perspectives, opening up new possibilities for having a better relationship. The bad news is that breakups like this can sometimes create a rift that can't be overcome later, especially if your partner feels abandoned.

Like anything else in relationships, you assume a certain amount of risk by choosing this path. This is a judgment call, and again, there's no right or wrong choice, only risk and consequences.

It's Really Over.   If you've decided to leave because you know you truly don't want the relationship to continue, your next step is deciding how to convey that to your partner. *This is a crucial point in your life.* Most people break up by either disappearing or by creating so much trouble that they drive the other person away. These ways of breaking up do not allow you to be complete with past relationships so that you drag forward a lot of emotional baggage to the next one.

If you want to be more fully emotionally available in your next relationship, and if you're tired of adding to your emotional luggage, use this opportunity to practice completing a relationship powerfully. This means communicating fully to your partner and allowing them to do the same, if they choose.

What to consider:

• *The depth of the relationship.* If you've only been dating a few weeks and you haven't been sexually intimate, your break-up talk may be very short. If you've been sexually intimate or you've dated for months or years, you may spend a lot of time discussing the breakup with your partner. You may talk with your partner about this more than once or even repeatedly over days or weeks. In long-term relationships, I think of this more as a *process of uncoupling* rather than just a distinct break.

• *What to say.* Again, there's no rule to rigidly follow, but a formula that my clients have followed and that I've used myself goes something like this:

    1.   Arrange a meeting on neutral territory, rather than going to one of your homes. This sets a different context than your usual encounters, conveying the message that something different is about to occur. Also, you're less likely to get romantic, possibly ending up in bed together and not following through.

    2.   Tell your partner that the relationship isn't working for you and that you're not willing to make the necessary changes to have it work, that you want to end it.

    3.   Thank and acknowledge your partner for the time and energy they spent with you. Thank them for anything else you can think of that's important, as long as it's a genuine thanks (don't just make something up). Even in the most empty relationships, there's always something to thank someone for, even if it's only their time.

    4.   Apologize for anything significant that you've done (or failed to do) that you believe may have been hurtful to your partner. Don't do this unless you genuinely mean the apology.

5. Allow them time for a response, including their feelings about the breakup (as long as they're not being abusive). Again, depending on the depth of the relationship, this could take minutes or it could take many hours, and may not be all at one sitting.

6. Don't ask for friendship. Often we add a caveat when we're breaking up that goes something like this: "I'd still like to be your friend." We do this in order to try to minimize the loss, both for ourselves and for our partner. We also mistakenly think that this conveys less rejection to them. In reality, if you're doing the leaving, the chances are that your partner feels deeply hurt that you no longer want to be romantic with them. Asking for friendship at this time may feel like you're taking away the cake and offering crumbs in exchange.

Friendship is something that, if it's meant to be, will naturally occur over time, and only when your ex-partner feels comfortable enough to make the move toward that. It isn't something that should automatically occur at the end of a romance. Sometimes romantic partners never were friends, so creating a friendship may involve some genuine effort that neither of you is willing to invest.

If your partner, as the one being left, offers to remain your friend, you may still want to say something like, "Why don't we just see how we both feel about that in a couple of weeks or in a month or so." This is to give you both a cooling-off and grieving period, after which you can reassess your feelings. Your partner may be offering friendship in order to stay connected to you in the hope of reviving your romance later on. Taking some time off will give you both a chance to consider whether trying to be friends is going to be appropriate for you.

7. Say good-bye and leave. Sometimes this is the most difficult part of breaking up. Often this conversation is the most honest one you've had, and that can generate unexpected feelings of intimacy. It's tempting to want to stay connected and prolong those feelings, but it's not wise to do so unless you genuinely have second thoughts. Sometimes the honesty that happens in a

breakup actually does clear the path for something new to happen. If you both feel that way, it may be appropriate to try again. If not, it's usually best to break contact and move on.

8. Allow yourself to grieve and experience the loss. This is probably the next most difficult step but a necessary one if you are to go forward. You may need one or two good cries, or you may be sad off and on for a long time, depending on the depth of the relationship or the degree of your hopes for the future. You may need counseling at some point if you find yourself getting stuck or if you become too depressed.

Dealing with Resistance. Your partner may have a range of emotions: shock, grief, anger, loss, disbelief, or others. He or she may not want the relationship to end and may resist your attempts to break away. Often this takes the form of asking "Why?"

When your partner asks why you're breaking up, you have a judgment call to make. If you are tempted to provide reasons, ask yourself if you are responding in order to contribute something to this person, or if you are taking the opportunity to act out your anger by criticizing. If you suspect your partner is asking why in order to make promises to change, it's probably pointless to provide reasons for the breakup unless you are really willing to give him or her a chance.

The Exception. If the relationship has been abusive, emotionally or physically, you have no obligation to discuss the breakup or to follow the steps outlined above. Just saying "It's over" is enough, and trying to explain will get you nowhere with an abusive partner. In fact, it will make you vulnerable to false promises of change or other forms of manipulation. *Get professional help if you're in this kind of relationship.*

Deciding Not to Decide

Maybe after reading this entire chapter you still feel powerless to make a choice, and so you decide not to decide. You may think at this point that you've failed, that you *should* just make a choice. Or maybe you've got a rationale for not choosing, such as letting more time go by and seeing what develops.

Actually, deciding not to decide *is* a choice and is just as significant as choosing to go or to stay. By taking this path, you are saying, in effect, that you're not willing or ready to be responsible for making the relationship better or for getting out. Either way, you're not willing to accept the consequences.

There's nothing wrong with this choice. What's important is that you realize that it is a choice, and that there are consequences for it, just as there are for breaking up or staying. What those are for you will vary. One consequence is that the opportunity for any kind of real communication between you and your partner is closed, at least for now.

Another consequence is that you've put off the confrontation that inevitably will occur, whether it's next week, next month, or next decade. The issues that put you on the fence in the first place will still be there, unless they are circumstantial and you're lucky enough that they just happen to go away.

A possible consequence is that your partner, sensing your ambivalence, will eventually choose for you and leave the relationship. Choosing not to choose brings certain risks, and when you take this path you assume the risks and consequences just as when you take any other path in a relationship.

After the Breakup

Even considering a breakup is painful, but nothing compared to actually doing it. When it's mutual or when you're the one doing the leaving, it's tempting to think that because you know it's for the best there will be no pain. The reality is that it always hurts to end a relationship, even when you're the one who wanted it that way.

Unexpectedly, you may find yourself feeling loss and sadness after breaking up. At first, you may think that this means you've made a mistake and should immediately get back together with your partner. This may or may not be true, but it might be wise to just give yourself a few days or even a couple of weeks to grieve, then see how you feel. Once the sadness has diminished, you may find that the same issues that kept you from going forward are still there and are not likely to go away. Or, you may find that you have a whole new appreciation for your partner that you didn't have before, and that you'd like to try again.

There aren't any right or wrong paths to take in deciding which way to go in a relationship. What's important is that you take the time to really assess how you feel and what the facts are before you act rather than just reacting quickly in a knee-jerk fashion. Impulsive breakups usually aren't complete endings; they leave unresolved issues that can inhibit your ability to relate well in the next romance.

18

♥   ♥   ♥

Are You the One for Me?

Robin and Gary met through mutual friends and were strongly attracted to each other. They dated and within a couple of months were in love. Neither was in a hurry for marriage, so they were content to see each other regularly and just enjoy their connection.

After a year had passed, though, Robin began having thoughts about getting married. When she brought the subject up to Gary, he was not quite as enthusiastic as she was. Soon, this became the topic of most of their dates, with Robin arguing in favor of marriage and Gary presenting arguments against it. They went to counseling together, and the therapist helped Gary identify what his fears and concerns were. He quickly moved past them, and four months later they were engaged.

Choosing a Lifetime Partner

Almost all dating relationships eventually run into the question that Gary and Robin wrestled with: Are we going forward into marriage or not? If a couple spends enough time together over a period of months or years, sooner or later one or both of them is going to want to know: Are you "the one" for me? The answer to this question will lead them either down the aisle or down the road without each other.

Resolving this question is different for every dating couple. There are couples like Denise and Lyle, who are so much on the same track that the answer is easy and reached very quickly: Of course we're getting married! This couple dated for only three months before getting engaged, and their wedding was seven months after their first date.

Then there are couples like Michael and Suzanne, who were so far apart that the question could never be resolved. Suzanne wanted marriage very badly, and Michael didn't. Yet they still wanted to be together. This couple dated and lived together off and on for more than ten years before Suzanne finally moved on so that she could find someone who was interested in marriage.

Couples like Dennis and Sharon are not quite in sync but eventually get there. Dennis knew he wanted to marry Sharon from the very beginning of their relationship, but Sharon was reluctant to make the commitment because of her previous divorce. This couple was engaged twice before they made it stick, and they were finally married after five years of dating.

Then there are couples like Keith and Debbie, who don't share a passionate love but who are reluctant to break up and move on. After two years of dating, Debbie was tired of trying to get a commitment from Keith, so she broke up with him and was planning to move to another city. Attached to Debbie and fearful of starting over, although not in love, Keith proposed rather than face the pain of a breakup, but his heart wasn't truly in it. This couple was divorced eight years later over the same issue that almost prevented their wedding: lack of passion. They settled rather than face the truth about their relationship and deal with the difficulty of moving on.

Resolving the question of whether or not to marry is one of the most important processes a couple can go through. How we communicate and deal with the issues involved in this choice determine, to a large degree, the well-being of the future marital connection. If we drift along, never discussing our relationship or our feelings about each other, hoping everything will just magically turn out okay, we won't have developed the emotional muscle or the communication skills needed to adequately deal with the question of marriage. Some couples date and marry in this unconscious way, and then find themselves unskilled in the language of relationships so that they are unable to face and resolve the inevitable problems that arise in marriage.

On the other hand, if we are conscious in the dating process, conscious in courtship, and are willing to discuss feelings and issues (practice the necessary skills), then we strengthen the bond between us and we prepare ourselves for the challenge of modern marriage. Think of it as preparing for a marathon. If you just show up on the day of the race, not having done any kind of physical conditioning, you can expect to finish last or not even at all. If you want to have a shot at winning, though, you'll work out, run regularly, and prepare yourself physically for the race ahead. You'll be committed to being the best possible runner that you can be. While relationships aren't a race, they do require the same level of commitment to practice, skill development, and being the best you can be.

There are a number of issues that need to be considered and resolved in order to make a choice about marriage in a conscious, empowering way. The first is: Why do I want to marry?

The Fantasy Impulse.　　Sometimes the desire to marry is largely about fairy-tale visions of life lived happily ever after. For women it begins with the wedding experience itself: white silk and flowers, diamond rings and chiffon, bridesmaids, showers, and blissful romance. After marriage: love, security, romance, a house in the suburbs, and beautiful babies. For men, it's love, a regular sex partner, someone waiting at the end of the day, a helper, and a mother to their children. The expectations vary from one individual to the next, but with the fantasy connection there's always the sense that getting married will solve most of life's problems and bring ultimate happiness.

Marrying as a fantasy impulse is dangerous. The reality of marriage can never measure up to these visions of perfect bliss. Instead of the romantic suitor she was expecting, she comes home to someone who's tired and grouchy and who immediately retreats behind the newspaper. Rather than coming home to a *Playboy* centerfold who provides a hot meal already on the table, he comes home to someone who's too tired to cook *or* to make love.

Real relationships are about love, caring, and respect between two partners who are committed to being the best they can be for each other. Romance is the spark that ignites the love, which becomes the glue that initially binds them together. But romance eventually fades, to some degree (although it shouldn't die), and other priorities demand our energies: career, bills, children, etc. If love is to be lasting, it needs to be based on meshing values and lifestyles, and a realistic view of the challenge of modern marriage, *not* fairy-tale romance.

Commitment Hunger. Barbara DeAngelis, in her book *Are You the One for Me?* writes about the need to marry *in order to belong to someone* rather than because you've built a solid, healthy relationship and are now ready to make a lifetime commitment.[1] Individuals who are commitment hungry focus far more on whether or not they get the engagement ring than they do on who's giving it to them. Planning for the wedding is much more important than addressing issues in the relationship or learning to communicate effectively with their mate. Concern over whether or not he wants to marry her takes priority over whether or not their values mesh.

Commitment hunger leads to unhealthy relationships. By focusing too much on whether or not you can get this person to marry you, you are stepping over the most important aspects of a romantic relationship: Do we share values? Do we genuinely love each other for who we are? Are we committed to having the best possible relationship with each other? Also, your communication with your partner is going to focus on the commitment you want from him or her rather than on making discoveries about each other and learning how to listen and respond to each other.

[1] Barbara DeAngelis, *Are You the One for Me?* (New York: Dell Publishing, 1992).

You may get the engagement and you may get the wedding, but if you're operating from commitment hunger, chances are you'll find yourself married to someone with whom you don't share values or connect with in a healthy way.

The cure for commitment hunger is the same as the one for love addiction: *knowing and valuing yourself first.* By loving yourself first, you are content to take your time getting to know someone new, letting the relationship take a natural course of growth and discovery. You are much more concerned with finding out if your values mesh and if you connect in all the important ways than you are with getting him or her to make a commitment. You are able to focus on the *process* of relating, how you and your partner communicate and respond to each other, rather than on the *results*—how can I get him to propose by Valentine's Day? By loving yourself first, commitment becomes the natural by-product of a loving, healthy relationship with the right partner.

The Time Is Right.   Sometimes the decision to marry is far more about time of life than it is about being with the right partner. In a Settle-for dating relationship, it's tempting to go ahead and get married because it seems like the right time to marry and there's no one better on the scene. Time of life reasons often look like this:

- All my college buddies are married and I want a life like theirs, with a family.
- I'm thirty-nine years old and it's almost too late to have children.
- I've been divorced for twelve years, and I'm tired of dating and always ending up alone.
- My family keeps asking me why I don't marry the person I'm dating.
- I've reached the top of my career ladder and now I want a relationship.
- Everyone I know is married.
- I want children so I've got to find a spouse as soon as possible.
- I'm in my late forties and I don't want to spend the rest of my life alone.

Internal pressure and the feeling that "now is the time" lead to faulty decision making regarding marriage. One way to check yourself to see if that's what you're doing is to ask yourself questions like:

- If I were ten years younger, and I knew I had ten years to find someone more suitable for me, would I still marry this person?
- When I picture myself already married to this person, what kind of feelings do I get?
- If I knew for certain that all my dreams would be realized (e.g., a great relationship, marriage, children, a loving family life, etc.) no matter what, would I rather marry the person I'm with now or would I rather keep looking?

Marrying someone mainly for reasons like this means making one of the most important decisions of your life from a position of urgency and desperation. The feeling is that if I don't hurry up and do something, my one and only chance at happiness will slip away. Indulging in limited thinking like this leads to limited relationships. How can we have the best possible marriage—both of us free to express ourselves fully, creating a strong and lasting partnership—if one or both of us is here because we ran out of emotional time?

Good decisions about marriage are made from the perspective of an overall contentment with life in general, along with a sense of being able to take plenty of time to search for and choose a right partner. The certainty that there is never just one right relationship, but many possible right ones available (a sense of abundance), provides confidence and, therefore, better decision making. From this perspective, I may like and enjoy my partner, but if I'm not absolutely thrilled at the prospect of going through life with him, I can move on, knowing that there *will* be someone better suited for me.

Avoiding a Breakup. Sometimes the decision to marry is mainly about avoiding a breakup: the subsequent loss and the unpleasant prospect of having to start over and look for a more suitable mate. Moving on can be very difficult, even when a relationship may not feel quite right or there's the sense that something vital is missing. The attachment may be very strong, and months and years of shared history can be very meaningful.

Settle-for dating relationships often lead to this point: It's time to decide about marriage, but one of you isn't really sure you're with "the one." Having drifted along all these months or years, thinking that you can always break up, you are now in the position of having to make a decision because your partner is pressuring you for a commitment. Meanwhile, you've gotten attached to your partner, and you don't exactly have lots of extremely desirable and eligible people beating down your door. Your partner is a good person and really seems to love you and want to please you, and you can't stand the idea of starting over in the dating game. Why not get married?

The reason this rarely works is simple: *Healthy, lasting marriage these days requires a tremendous amount of commitment and love.* When two people equally want it to work, not just a little but a lot, and when they genuinely love and adore each other, there's incentive to do the work that's needed.

When one or both partners are settling for less, when they are attached and maybe even love each other but don't feel thrilled about going through life together, there's much less to sustain a healthy, loving connection. Ultimately, marriages based on settling become very stale and are fertile ground for affairs and divorce.

I have a theory: *Most people would rather get married and divorced than break up a long-term Settle-for dating relationship.* Sound absurd? Let's look at the dynamics.

You've dated enough people to feel frustrated in your quest for the right partner. Then, along comes someone who's right for you in a lot of ways, but not in every way. You like this person, you have things in common, you do have fun together, and there aren't any huge red flags. You continue to date this person, and very soon you've drifted into an exclusive relationship with someone you like a lot but aren't in love with.

Months pass, maybe even years. You share your lives: your families, your friends, your birthdays, the holidays. You travel together, you call each other every day, you're lovers even though there's not much passion. Everyone sees you as "the perfect couple." Your family and friends pressure you to marry, but something keeps holding you back. You're very attached to your partner, but you just feel that *something's missing,* and as soon as you acknowledge that fact, you feel guilty. So you quickly do something loving, trying to persuade yourself as well as your partner that your feelings are genuine.

Finally, your partner tires of waiting for you to commit and issues an ultimatum of some kind: Get on with it or I'm getting on with my life. You consider what it would be like to break up with your partner: the lonely nights, the grief and loss, having to start over and go through all the bad dates before you find someone new, having to tell your friends and family that you let this wonderful person go. You worry about ever finding someone better, and you figure it's your problem since there's obviously nothing wrong with your partner. You envision the years stretching ahead, alone and lonely forever. You make the choice to marry.

After marriage, you experience a honeymoon period in which everything seems okay and you congratulate yourself on making the right choice. Sooner or later, though, the feelings of something just not being right emerge again. You try to suppress them, but they are there anyway. Months pass, years pass, you may even have a child or two together. Then the awareness dawns that this is what you have to look forward to for the rest of your life: an unfulfilling, unsatisfying relationship. There's no way out, just a long, empty road along which you can never truly get your needs met. That prospect now becomes unbearable, much more so than the idea of divorce and starting over. At least then you will have the opportunity to find the right partner. You decide to divorce your spouse.

When I describe this scenario in workshops full of divorced people, I usually see several heads nodding in recognition. In fact, I think this happens quite often, more often than we would like to believe. I believe this explains why marital therapists have a certain percentage of clients for whom counseling does absolutely no good: these are the marriages based on Settle-for relationships. Marital therapy is designed to recover what was lost (love, passion, connection) and enhance what is there. No amount of therapy can bring into existence in a relationship what was never there in the beginning.

Settling is a very poor foundation from which to make one of the most important commitments in life. If you suspect you may be thinking of marrying someone in this way, you may want to seek professional guidance. The consequences to families and children are enormous and devastating when people marry for the wrong reasons.

Choosing a Lifetime Commitment

Getting married for the right reasons is a *fully conscious process*. This means that you've been conscious from your first date: looking for matching values, seeing how well you connect on all levels, and that all-important chemistry. With all the ingredients in place, you've nevertheless taken your time getting to know this person. You've moved the relationship to higher levels of commitment consciously and intentionally, communicating fully with your partner.

At each stage of the relationship, you've had You and Me conversations, each time being willing to let go and move on if you and your partner aren't fully in sync (and you see no prospect of getting there). You've focused far more on the dynamics of your relationship: communicating, responding effectively, giving and receiving genuine, heartfelt love than you have on winning over a desired partner or getting a commitment. You've not compromised your Non-Negotiables nor are you in a Settle-for relationship. You're certain that your partner isn't settling for you, either.

This doesn't mean the road hasn't had some bumps along the way. Tina and Randy's relationship is a good example. When this couple met they both determined very quickly that they had met someone who shared their values and was looking for the same thing: a committed relationship leading to marriage and children. They fell in love and grew to genuinely love each other. But their communication skills weren't the best, and as a result they developed some problems.

The dynamics between them became unhealthy, and Randy finally broke up with Tina in frustration, demanding that they either go to therapy or move on. Once they got some counseling, their communication skills improved dramatically, and their relationship became much healthier. Six months later they were engaged, and they got married later that year. This couple's path wasn't smooth, but they had all the right ingredients. Most important, they were willing to address the dynamics of their relationship first, rather than just blindly going ahead with marriage hoping that everything would miraculously turn out okay.

With these factors in place, you're now prepared to consciously choose a lifetime commitment. Your eyes are open to who your partner is and to the dynamics of the relationship. You're aware of your own shortcomings and you strive to do better. While this doesn't give you a guarantee of happily-ever-after, it does give you a solid foundation on which to build. Your work is just beginning, but you're prepared for it because you've been practicing and acquiring skills; you've been developing the emotional muscle that you'll need for your marriage.

Overcoming Resistance. Maybe you've created a conscious courtship with a right partner. Neither of you is settling. You both clearly desire the relationship and each other. You communicate well, your values mesh, and there's no reason to not go forward, but one of you is hesitant to make the commitment to marriage.

Making a lifetime commitment can be very scary, especially when you have a conscious relationship. With your eyes wide open, you're not living in a fairy-tale romance, sailing happily forward into never-ending bliss. You're two human beings, aware that you're flawed, and you realize that life is constantly in a state of flux. In a conscious relationship, you know that there are no guarantees; life turns on a dime, and you don't know what challenges lie ahead.

This means that you're making a far more significant commitment than the average couple does when they get married. When you're marrying an idealized partner, it's easy to vow to stay together until one of you dies. It's a snap to promise you'll always confront the issues when you've never communicated on a deep enough level to realize what the issues are. Promising forever is no challenge when you're madly in love and your relationship is highly romanticized.

In a conscious relationship, however, you've already peeled away enough layers to realize that you have some challenges. You know that the responsibility for having a successful lifetime relationship lies squarely with yourself and with the commitment between the two of you to create that on a daily basis. This fulfillment isn't going to just drop in your laps.

You're committing to a partner whom you know isn't perfect, knowing that you are not perfect, either. Love being a feeling that waxes and wanes, you realize that you will be called upon at times to behave in a loving way when you don't necessarily feel very loving. The commitment is to give to your partner during times when there's not much in return for you. Your responsibility is to keep the larger picture of your relationship and your commitment in mind rather than indulging in knee-jerk reactions to what's going on in the present.

Marriage is not for everyone. Not everyone is prepared to embrace this level of commitment. For many people, a relationship is only worth having in the good times. As long as I feel romantic, and I feel loving, and I get enough love in return, and you always look this good, I'll stay with you. As long as I get my needs met, then you're the perfect partner for me. For these people, marriage is not a workable option.

Not everyone is willing to assume the risk of marriage: that it may not be all that I dreamed of, that I may not get my needs met, that you may leave. The reality is that if you marry, you risk getting divorced. Even if divorce isn't an option in your way of thinking, that doesn't mean you won't change your mind someday and consider it, or that your partner won't. If you cannot tolerate the risk of your marriage not working out and ending in divorce, then you shouldn't marry.

Lifetime committed relationships require doing the behavior of love: honoring and respecting your partner, endeavoring to meet each other's needs, communicating honestly and openly, creating romantic times together on a regular basis, being intensely loyal to your partner, and placing that relationship above all others, *even when you don't feel like it.*

If you begin your relationship in a genuine state of love, if you practice open and honest communication every step of the way, if you've taken the time to explore the dynamics of your relationship and practice resolving issues over an extended period of time, if you're prepared for the risk, if you haven't settled for less, then you're ready for the next step—a lifetime commitment. Yes, it's scary, and no, there are no guarantees. But maybe this is about as good as it gets: a compatible partner, an open and honest relationship, sufficient love and passion, and values that fit together. This is not the stuff of which Hollywood legends are made, but it's real, it's honest, and it's fulfilling.

Life is a journey, and you get to choose whom to share that journey with. If not this partner, then whom? Because if you don't go forward in this relationship, if you choose to start over, surely someday you will be looking for a partner again.

Love, like anything else worth having in life, involves a choice, and there is great personal power in making it. Whichever way you go with your relationship, the greatest opportunity for your growth is in making the choice responsibly, without regret or blame.

Forward from Here

This book, as promised, is not an answer book. It doesn't really say "Do this and do that and you will get what you want!" It's really more like an exercise book that says "Practice this and practice that and you'll know yourself better, grow personally, and move yourself closer to the right relationship." This book invites you to focus on your journey, your process of discovery and growth, rather than on whether or not you're getting the results you want. And, along the way, I'm betting that you'll get better results.

Smart Book Versus Practiced Person. Now that you're finishing this book, you may feel tempted to put it in your bookshelf next to all those other self-help books you've read over the years. By now, you undoubtedly have lots and lots of "smart books." But you know as well that all the smart books in the world don't make you any more successful in your life.

This book is only as good for you as you're willing to use it: to reread the parts you've already gotten fuzzy about and to practice the skills and take the necessary steps to move your life forward. If you want to be a *practiced person,* keep this book handy, reread it often, and make it your goal to practice a new skill periodically and on a regular basis.

Practice Versus Instant Results.   Remember that getting results, while important and not to be overlooked, isn't the best place to maintain your focus. Results are fleeting and unpredictable, and you ultimately don't have control over them. You may or may not catch someone's eye, get the date, or make a love connection.

You may get impatient from time to time with all this practice. "When am I going to get the results?" you ask. If you're like most human beings and like all my clients, you want the results *now,* not tomorrow or next week or next month.

The kind of result you're really going for, a loving, healthy relationship with the right partner, isn't something you can instantly make happen. The process of expanding your world, practicing communication and relationship-building skills, and going through the three-date interview process with lots of different people takes time. Plus, this journey won't be smooth. You'll undoubtedly encounter lots of challenges along the way and experience setbacks.

The value of practice is that if your focus is on your own growth, you can experience positive results immediately. You step outside your comfort zone, practice moving toward others socially, and meet some new people. You practice being assertive and ask someone for a date. You practice being in touch with your own feelings and speaking honestly and tell someone you're not interested in pursuing a relationship with them. You practice the Shopping Conversation with someone you're interested in.

The results are that you increase your social confidence, you validate yourself by honoring your own feelings, and you strengthen your commitment by screening out Settle-for partners. By practicing these skills you also give your self-esteem a boost. *These results are priceless: they are about becoming a right partner.* They are yours and can never be taken away, and they move you much closer to finding your right partner as well.

Becoming a Right Partner.   Someone once said that all relationships are a mirror and that we can never love or hate something about someone else unless we see that same quality in ourselves. We waste time and emotion when we blame our relationship failures on our partners, thus stepping over the valuable lessons to be learned.

Yes, there are stories we can tell about the wrong they did us. Undoubtedly, our past partners have made mistakes and been less than human. Maybe they've even been downright mean and petty. But, unless there's a perfect person reading this book, the same can be said of all of us.

There's no way to be human and socialize with other humans and always have perfect, loving experiences! It's crazy to expect that, yet we do so when it comes to the dating world. We go to parties expecting everyone else to be friendly and approach us first. We go on dates and expect everyone else to have a sparkling personality and virtually no imperfections.

When do we look at ourselves and begin to ask: What about my flaws? What about my willingness to work on my own end of the bargain? What about my responsibility to move toward other people and *create* positive experiences? What about my own fears of being vulnerable and opening my heart to love?

Before you can *find* a right partner, you will need to *be* a right partner. This means being emotionally available, skilled at communication, having your own life together, being self-caring and self-loving, able to connect in a meaningful way with lots of people, and able to open your heart to love. If you're already all these things, then you should have no trouble drawing in a right partner very soon.

If you're like most people, you fall short in a couple of these categories. This means you have some work to do on yourself before you can scrutinize others too closely. In fact, it's the journey toward being more whole within yourself that often carries more rewards than the search for a partner. And, ultimately, you will attract a right person as you get farther down that road.

On the Field.   The most important commitment you can make to yourself is to get out there and play! Nothing ever changes in our lives unless we're active. As the old saying goes: Do something, anything; get moving! Stop worrying about just exactly what to do, and start doing.

Attend a class, join a singles group, go to an art exhibit, visit a new church, go walking in a park where there are other people, smile at people in your elevator on the way to your office, say hello to someone who looks interesting. In short, it doesn't matter where you begin as long as you do begin.

It's easy to sit on the sidelines, complaining about the lack of a love life or the difficulty of meeting new people. It's no stretch to feel sorry for yourself because you're all alone as you watch rented videos and stuff yourself with ice cream. Having a pessimistic, limited view of your dating possibilities is a cakewalk.

The story of how we got to the moon is that it wasn't in a straight line. The mission was predicated on the assumption that the spaceship would be constantly off course and would need to make thousands of tiny adjustments along the way until it arrived at the goal.

The journey to healthy love relationships is also like this. There's no perfect straight line that we can follow. We simply get going, and we make corrections along the way, constant and never-ending adjustments. In fact, unlike the moon mission, we never really arrive. It is a process that we're engaged in our whole lives, especially after finding the right partner.

Not Ready for a Relationship.   Like many of my clients, you may be reading this book as preparation for the future, realizing that you're not really ready for a romance. Or you may not be sure you really want one.

One of my clients remarked recently, "I'm beginning to realize that not everyone is ready for a relationship. In fact, lots of people I meet are ambivalent." This should come as no surprise, considering the many emotional places we can be in at different times of our lives. Because of past hurts and disappointments, we all have some degree of hesitancy in committing ourselves to the search for a right partner.

You may already be consciously willing to look for a right partner yet find that you get stuck or sabotage yourself. Your own dynamics may be stopping you from moving in the direction you need to and getting what you want.

Singles frequently come to me for dating issues and end up working on other issues such as fear of intimacy, shyness, love addiction, self-esteem problems, and so on. These issues can inhibit or even stop your progress toward finding a right partner. You can be sure that if you're doing all the right things, and you still can't seem to connect with a good partner after months of practicing and taking the right steps, that there's something going on inside you that's keeping you from getting what you want.

You might think that you should have all these kinds of issues completely resolved before you enter the dating scene. I say that it's by being in the game, in action, that you have the greatest opportunity to learn, grow, and resolve your issues.

Thus, I recommend that you use the guidelines in this book to put yourself on the playing field. Then, notice when you get afraid, frustrated, angry, or stop. This is vital information for your growth and continued progress toward healthy relationships, and you can't get this information if you're on the sidelines.

Stay Conscious. The second most important commitment you can make to yourself is to *be conscious* in the dating process: self-knowledgeable and aware, paying attention to your own intuition and gut responses, communicating fully to your partners, and making choices based on important discoveries about yourself, men and women, and relationships.

Being in action and being self-aware is a powerful combination. *You truly can't lose when you're in the dating game, practicing, learning, and growing.* It is a process you can fall in love with: creating a rewarding experience of single life as you move purposefully toward a healthy, loving relationship with the right partner.